Psychoeducational Assessment of Students Who Are Visually Impaired or Blind: Infancy Through High School

Psychoeducational Assessment of Students Who Are Visually Impaired or Blind

Infancy Through High School

SECOND EDITION

Sharon Bradley-Johnson

pro·ed

8700 Shoal Creek Boulevard
Austin, Texas 78757

pro·ed

© 1991, 1994 by PRO-ED, Inc.
8700 Shoal Creek Boulevard
Austin, Texas 78757-6897

Library of Congress Cataloging-in-Publication Data

Bradley-Johnson, Sharon.
     Psychoeducational assessment of students who are visually impaired
or blind : infancy through high school / Sharon Bradley-Johnson. —
2nd ed.
         p.   cm.
     Rev. ed. of: Psychoeducational assessment of visually impaired and
blind students. c1986.
     Includes bibliographical references and index.
     ISBN 0–89079–599–1
     1. Children, Blind.   2. Visually impaired children.
3. Educational tests and measurements.   4. Psychological tests for
children.   I. Bradley-Johnson, Sharon. Psychoeducational
assessment of visually impaired and blind students.   II. Title.
HV1596.2.B72   1994
371.91'1—dc20   93-23211
                                                                      CIP

This book is designed in Century Schoolbook and Frutiger (Frontiera).

Production Manager: Alan Grimes
Production Coordinator: Adrienne Booth
Art Director: Lori Kopp
Reprints Buyer: Alicia Woods
Editor: Tracy Sergo
Editorial Assistant: Claudette Landry

Printed in the United States of America

2   3   4   5   6   7   8   9   10   98   97

Contents

CHAPTER 3

Assessment Issues and Procedures   49

CHAPTER 4

Assessment of Infants and Toddlers   67

Foreword

IN 1986, WHEN I WAS ASKED TO WRITE A FOREWORD TO THE FIRST edition of this book, I was excited about the contents, because the book covered several areas in working with children and adolescents with visual impairment that were not covered elsewhere.

Now in 1993, I write the foreword to this new edition with not only excitement about the added features and updates but also the knowledge of how the book has been used these past few years. While the contents are designed primarily for psychologists working with children and adolescents with visual impairment, other practitioners also have used the book with a great deal of success, by incorporating the information in their practice, sharing information at the college level, and administering the tests within schools and agencies. Teachers have found the book to be an invaluable tool while administering various types of academic tests within the classroom. In my capacity as an advisor, I have felt complete confidence in any reference I have made to this book.

I repeat from the first edition, "This is much more than a guide to assessing the visually impaired. For the evaluator, it gives a thorough evaluation of tools and methods which can be used to determine educational programs for visually impaired students. For the rest of us, it gives an overview of what constitutes a good approach with these same students and their parents. All who interact with the visually impaired could benefit from this book."

Bill J. Duckworth
Research Scientist / Librarian
American Printing House for the Blind

Preface

ASSESSMENT OF STUDENTS WHO ARE NOT MAKING ADEQUATE educational progress is difficult and time consuming. This task is even more challenging when a student has a physical disability. Assessment results need to be educationally relevant and comprehensive and must be obtained from tests and procedures that are reliable, valid, and appropriate for the student being tested. If these conditions are met, then the assessment results should contribute valuable information for developing programs that facilitate academic progress. If assessments are not carried out well, however, using inadequate results can hinder further the progress of students. For professionals whose charge it is to conduct psychoeducational assessments, this is a tremendous responsibility.

Psychoeducational Assessment of Students Who Are Visually Impaired or Blind is written primarily to aid psychologists and educational consultants who are responsible for carrying out such assessments. The material also is useful to other professionals who must read assessment reports, participate in individualized educational planning meetings, and make decisions regarding educational programs for students.

To obtain useful assessment results, an examiner must understand thoroughly the type of information that various tests and assessment procedures can provide as well as comprehend fully the limitations of the information that is obtained. Furthermore, with students who have a physical impairment, examiners must be familiar with procedures that can circumvent a disabling condition, and they must understand how the disability can affect a student's behavior. Such information is necessary to ensure that results accurately reflect a student's aptitude and achievement. If these procedures are not employed, the results will describe only the limiting effect of the physical impairment on performance. In other words, an examiner should use psychoeducational tests for which a student is physically able to make the required responses. This is both a legal and an ethical requirement.

Thus, in order to provide readers with sufficient information to meet the legal requirements and ethical responsibilities involved in assessing students with visual impairments, material is covered in a very detailed fashion. Moreover, the material is practice oriented.

This book is not intended to describe procedures for assessing visual impairment or blindness, because this is the responsibility of professionals in the medical field. Despite the fact that a number of children and adolescents who are visually impaired or blind also have other disabilities, this book does not address the assessment of children and adolescents with multiple disabilities. Because the assessment process for them is very complex, they deserve an entire text specifically devoted to assessments that meet their needs adequately. This book also does not address vocational assessment; assessment of interests, skills, motivation, and personality traits relevant to job training is too extensive to include and would require a separate text for sufficient coverage. However, the information this book provides regarding assessment of aptitude and achievement includes important components of any assessment of vocational potential for students.

Contained in this book are descriptions of: (a) procedures that can be used to obtain information during the process of assessment; (b) issues and background information relevant to assessment of students who are visually impaired or blind; (c) special procedures needed to obtain information on these children and adolescents; and (d) detailed reviews of published, individually administered tests.

There have been many changes since 1986 in the field of education and specifically in the assessment of and intervention with students who are visually impaired or blind. This second edition is meant to reflect those changes. Because of the emphasis on early intervention, it was necessary to write separate chapters on infants and preschoolers for this edition, including information on family assessment. The focus of this book is on obtaining information that can be used to plan instruction. In other words, the focus is on obtaining assessment information directly relevant to classroom instruction and monitoring educational progress. The measures available for assessment have changed considerably, and this information has been updated. A very detailed Information-Organizing

Checklist for Infants and Preschoolers, as well as one for school-age students, has been developed to aid in organizing information obtained from various sources. Additional information has been added to aid in reviewing medical reports, and a discussion of a functional vision assessment now is included. Due to the quantity of information, many tables have been added throughout the book for quick reference. Checklists for each phase of the assessment process are presented, and tables of appropriate measures for each area of assessment also are included.

Specifically, Chapter 1 provides an overview of the assessment process to assist in planning an assessment. Chapter 2 covers background information useful in understanding the needs of these children and adolescents and in interpreting their performance. Chapter 3 addresses procedures used before, during, and after assessment of children and adolescents who are visually impaired or blind, while Chapter 4 covers issues, assessment procedures, and reviews of norm-referenced, criterion-referenced, and curriculum-based tests as well as informal procedures pertaining to infants and toddlers. Chapter 5 addresses the same topics as they apply to the assessment of preschool children, and Chapter 6 covers the same topics as they apply to the assessment of school-age students.

Acknowledgments

THE INFORMATION AND ENCOURAGEMENT I RECEIVED FROM Bill Duckworth is greatly appreciated. His patience with my many questions was particularly helpful. Also, I am grateful for the information supplied by Suzanne Swaffield and to C. Merle Johnson, for his support and computer paper.

Chapter 1

Overview of Assessment

. . . .

WHEN SELECTING MEASURES AND PROCEDURES TO ASSESS THE psychoeducational needs of a student, it is wise to give considerable thought to the purposes for which the information will be used. If this is done, it likely will result in a comprehensive assessment that can be carried out efficiently. Data from assessments can be used to make various types of decisions; however, different decisions require different types of data. Because of the limited time available for assessments and the need for detailed, comprehensive information, the organization of the assessment process is critical. This chapter addresses the various purposes of assessment and the importance of the sequence of the procedures used during the process.

PURPOSES OF ASSESSMENT

There are a number of reasons to conduct an assessment. One reason is to determine which students are at risk for delays in achievement and therefore require more individual attention. Once identified, these students can be referred for more in-depth assessment to determine their specific needs. Because a physical impairment is likely to interfere significantly with a student's educational progress, it is usually unnecessary to screen students with physical impairments to determine that they require special assistance.

Hammill (1987) suggested several other reasons for assessment: (a) to diagnose students' problems, (b) to identify instructional needs, (c) to document progress in special programs, and (d) to provide information for research. These reasons are the focus of this text because they are the primary purposes for assessing students who are visually impaired or blind.

Diagnosis is not a listing of symptoms; rather, it is a theory to explain why the symptoms exist (Hammill, 1987). Typically, a multi-disciplinary team makes a diagnosis based on data collected from a variety of sources. A diagnosis is not helpful in directly remediating problems; however, it can be helpful in determining whether the primary cause of a student's difficulty is a physical impairment or another condition (e.g., mental retardation). If another condition is the primary problem, this information may be useful in planning educational programs.

Decisions regarding eligibility for special education services require norm-referenced interpretation of data. This type of inter-pretation allows comparison of a student's performance with the performance of other students of the same age or grade level. Public Law 101–476 (P.L. 101–476) (Individuals with Disabilities Education Act, 1990) requires norm-referenced information in order to deter-mine eligibility for special education services for those with mental retardation or learning disabilities. Examples of norm-referenced tests include the *Wechsler Intelligence Scale for Children–Third Edi-tion* (Wechsler, 1991) and the *Test of Language Development–Inter-mediate: Second Edition* (Hammill & Newcomer, 1988).

Norm-referenced information serves several other purposes as well. As noted by Mash and Terdal (1988), normative comparisons can be helpful in: (a) identifying what is deficient or excessive per-formance, (b) evaluating adult expectations for children that may be considerably different from existing norms, (c) grouping children into relatively homogeneous groups for remediation, (d) comparing research findings, and (e) evaluating outcomes.

Identification of students' instructional needs is critical. An assessment that does not result in improved academic performance for a student experiencing difficulty serves no useful purpose. The primary goal of psychoeducational assessment is to plan a program that will enable a student to learn more skills. To facilitate academic progress, a student's strengths and areas of difficulty need to be determined. Both areas must be assessed in detail, however, in order to plan effective instruction. For example, a student's general area of difficulty could be reading Braille, but the specific skills that need to be taught might be recognition of the letters *i, j, r,* and the phonograms *–ble, ch,* and *con.* Another example is a student whose general area of strength is addition, but the specific calculation skills that the student has mastered include addition skills through two-column addition with regrouping.

Norm-referenced information can be used to identify general or broad areas of strength and difficulty. Criterion-referenced information, curriculum-based measurement, data from systematic direct observation, and informal assessment procedures, however, are necessary to identify specific instructional needs and design programs that solve educational problems. Examples of criterion-referenced tests include the *Braille Unit Recognition Battery* (Caton, Duckworth, & Rankin, 1985) and the *Revised Brigance Diagnostic Inventory of Early Development* (Brigance, 1991). All of these procedures are discussed further in the following section.

Evaluating progress in instructional programs and providing information for research can require any or all of the types of information previously described. For example, both norm-referenced information and curriculum-based measurement can be used to evaluate a student's progress in a reading program. Frequent monitoring of student progress is essential if high-quality educational programs are to be provided and student achievement is to be enhanced. Norm-referenced information might be used for summative evaluation, whereas curriculum-based measurement could provide information for formative evaluation of programs. If one purpose of a research project is to determine how improved academic performance affects behavior, then norm-referenced information might be used to document improvements in math and reading. In addition, direct observation of behavior could be used to assess the frequency of certain behaviors of interest to the researchers.

THE PROCESS OF ASSESSMENT

Assessment typically proceeds from the collection of general information about a student to the acquisition of data describing specific skills that have been learned, as well as the next skills that are important to teach. The process can be viewed as a funnel, because information gathering proceeds from the general to the specific.

Test administration is only one element of the assessment process. Additional information sources include interviews, review of school and medical records, use of rating scales and checklists, and direct observation. The order in which these sources are used depends on the nature of a student's problem and the schedules of those involved in the assessment. The most efficient order, however, is to employ procedures that yield general information first. These procedures include use of interviews, rating scales and checklists, and review of school and medical records. Based on the compilation of this information, an examiner can formulate hypotheses about the general nature of the problems and plan which specific assessment procedures and measures to use to test these hypotheses. Procedures and measures that would provide more specific information include direct observation and administration of norm- and criterion-referenced tests, as well as use of curriculum-based measurement and informal assessment procedures.

Interviews

The purpose of interviews is to obtain as much information as possible about a student's strengths and problem areas from the perspective of the parent(s), the teacher(s), the student, and relevant others familiar with the student's performance. Information obtained from interviews can be intentionally or unintentionally biased, but despite questionable accuracy, the information obtained from interviews usually is helpful in compiling a comprehensive picture of a student.

An interview with parents can be helpful in understanding a student's level of acceptance of a visual loss as well as the parents' attitudes toward their child and their expectations for him or her. Through the interview process with the parents, examiners usually are able also to discern how willing the parents are to be involved in and assist with a child's educational program.

Professionals other than a student's teacher also can provide useful information, which may differ from that provided by the teacher. These professionals, such as orientation and mobility instructors or speech therapists, interact with the student in settings other than the classroom and in situations with different requirements. For students who are visually impaired or blind, it is particularly important to obtain interview information from several sources because the limitations of a visual disability are likely to vary with the requirements of a particular situation. Thus, information from these various sources can be useful in planning educational programs. For example, the information given by an orientation and mobility instructor who has observed a student's use of right and left orientation in both indoor and outdoor environments, on and off school grounds, may be different from information given by the teacher. The teacher may have observed the student's use of right and left orientation only on school grounds and while the teacher was attending to several other behaviors at the same time.

Obtaining a student's opinion regarding his or her own performance can provide important information for program planning also. For example, if a student's academic performance is poor, yet she or he does not think that this is a serious problem, the examiner and teacher may have to consider motivational problems as well as academic issues if performance is to be improved.

When assessment involves infants or preschoolers, more information usually can be obtained from an interview conducted in the home than in a school or office setting. The home environment allows the examiner an opportunity to observe the interaction of the parent(s) and child in a familiar setting. For a child who is visually impaired or blind, information about the parents' interaction with the child can be helpful in suggesting things parents can do to prevent or reduce delays in development that can occur with these children. These behaviors are listed in the Information-Organizing Checklist for Infants and Preschoolers Who Are Visually Impaired or Blind presented in Figure 1.1.

The Information-Organizing Checklist is designed to help organize information obtained from various sources as well as ensure that necessary information is obtained during interviews and records review. Following Figure 1.1 is a rationale for each of the items. The items are intended to be used as a guide for asking questions and observing during the interview. To enhance the validity of the information obtained, it is preferable to ask questions using an open-ended format rather than one that requires a "yes" or "no" response. For example, rather than asking whether the child has sleeping problems, more valid information is likely to be obtained if the examiner were to ask the parent to describe how well the child sleeps at night.

When the interview is conducted in the home setting, the items in the Observation of the Child and Parental Interaction sections should be answered based on direct observation of the child if possible.

The checklist is designed to provide one form on which information from various sources can be organized. Thus, information for items can be obtained from school and medical records, interviews with parents and daycare or preschool teachers, and observations. Information typically obtained for any type of assessment is included as well as items addressing special concerns for children who are visually impaired or blind.

Infants and Preschoolers

History of Visual Loss

1. *Cause of visual loss*:

    Congenital _____ Acquired _____

    Cause _____

    Child's age at onset _____

    Onset:

          Gradual _____ Sudden _____

2. *Date of last visual exam* _____

    Result _____

    _____

3. *Visual acuity:*

    For right eye _____ (corrected) _____ (uncorrected)

    For left eye _____ (corrected) _____ (uncorrected)

4. *Description of child's field of vision (e.g., peripheral vision or restricted visual field)* _____

    _____

5. *Loss is:* Stable _____ Progressive _____

Other Health Issues

6. *Other disabling conditions* _____

    _____

7. *Other health problems* _____

    _____

8. *Medications child is taking* _____

9. *Date of most recent hearing exam* _____

    Result _____

    _____

Figure 1.1. Information-organizing checklist for infants and preschoolers who are visually impaired or blind.

10. *Date of last orientation and mobility evaluation* _____
   Not applicable because child is too young _____

Home Situation

11. *Family consists of:*
   Two parents _____
   Single parent _____
   Siblings _____
   Other persons living in the home _____
   _____

12. *Does child have:*
   One parent with a severe visual loss _____
   Two parents with a severe visual loss _____
   Siblings with a severe visual loss _____
   Other relatives with a severe visual loss _____
   _____

Daily Care Issues

13. *Does child have sleep problems?*   yes   no
   If so, describe problem and how problem is handled.
   _____
   _____

14. *Does child have toileting problems?*   yes   no   too young
   If so, describe problem and how problem is handled.
   _____
   _____

15. *Does child have feeding problems?*   yes   no
   If so, describe problem and how problem is handled.
   _____
   _____

16. *Does child have food allergies?*   yes   no
   If so, to what foods _____

(continued)

FIGURE 1.1 *Continued*

Observation of Child

17. *Other than making vocal sounds, does the child initiate interaction with the environment (i.e., child is active rather than passive)?*

    yes   no

18. *What type of nonvocal messages does the child use in response to others (e.g., quieting, squirming, turning toward someone)?*

    _____

19. *Does the child seem to be aware of hazards and try to avoid them and/or respond appropriately to "No-no"?*

    yes   no   child is not mobile

20. *Does the child search for lost or dropped objects?*

    yes   no   child too young to do so

21. *Child's favorite playthings* _____

    _____

Interaction with Parents

22. *Does the child receive a considerable amount of physical contact (e.g., being held, cuddled, touched)?*

    yes   no

23. *Do the parents encourage the child to use hands to explore objects?*

    yes   no   child does so spontaneously

24. *Is the child encouraged or prompted to move?*

    yes   no   not necessary as child moves frequently

25. *Do the parents change the infant's position when he or she is lying down (e.g., back, tummy, side)?*

    yes   no   not necessary as child moves frequently

26. *Do the parents name objects and actions for the child frequently?*

    yes   no

27. *Do the parents often use the child's name before saying something to the child?*

    yes   no

---

28. *Does the child seem to be overprotected to the point that it seriously limits interaction with the environment?*

   yes   no

Home Environment

29. *Does the child have a specific place for storing toys?*

   yes   no   child is not mobile

30. *Is the house reasonably uncluttered and organized so that the child can move about without tripping on things or running into objects unnecessarily?*

   yes   no   child is not mobile

Parental Concerns

31. *What are the parents' three primary concerns about their child?*

   _____

   _____

32. *With what aspects of the child's development and care would the parents like some assistance?* _____

   _____

Rationale of information on checklist

The following information addresses the relevance of each checklist item.

1. *Cause of loss and age at onset.* Although *congenital* refers to a condition present at birth, according to Lowenfield (1980), congenital losses of vision also include those losses that occur before 5 years of age because these children retain little visual imagery and memory of color. Such problems with visual memories can make it more difficult to understand some concepts. Thus, because of the implications for education, knowing that a child has a congenital loss could be helpful. Probing questionable responses during testing of these children would be particularly important.

Often if losses occur at a later age, children have more difficulty becoming tactile learners and may have more difficulty adjusting to the loss of vision (Lowenfield, 1980).

Numerous conditions can result in the loss of vision. Examples include retinitis pigmentosa (an inherited condition), cataracts (due to heredity, disease, or accidents), and optic nerve atrophy (damage to some or all of the nerve fibers).

2. *Date of last visual examination.* Visual conditions can change periodically and require changes in type of lens used, size of print for reading, or type of low-vision aid used. Hence, it is important that reports from visual examinations are current. If the latest examination is more than 1 year old, a more current examination should be obtained prior to the psychological assessment. Results from this examination could have implications for selecting testing procedures and measures.

3. *Visual acuity.* This refers to clarity of vision and is measured separately for each eye. If a child wears glasses, acuity may be measured both with and without correction. Normal vision is described as 20/20 when measured in feet or 6/6 in meters. Measurement is carried out using the Snellen Wall Chart. If a child's vision is described as 20/200, this means that the child is able to discriminate letters on the chart at 20 ft that someone with normal vision could discriminate at 200 ft. Acuity may be measured for both near and far (distance) vision also.

4. *Field of vision.* Noting the description of a child's field of vision is important in determining how he or she might employ any usable vision. For example, if a child has only peripheral vision, she or he will have to fixate off center on objects in order to use this vision. If a child has a restricted visual field, but central vision, he or she will need to look directly at an object near the center of fixation.

5. *Stable or progressive loss.* If a child's visual loss can be expected to continue to deteriorate, an instructor or psychologist must plan an educational program that meets a child's changing needs. A progressive loss suggests that support and assistance in adjusting to a progressively worsening condition may be needed.

6. *Other disabling conditions.* If additional impairments are present, further modifications may be necessary during testing to circumvent these problems. This information will need to be considered in educational planning as well.

7. *Other health problems.* This information can be helpful in both testing and program planning because some health problems may negatively affect performance. For example, if a child has allergies, testing should not be carried out on days when allergic reactions occur.

8. *Medications.* If the child takes medications, possible side effects should be noted so that any effect of medication on classroom performance or performance during direct assessment can be evaluated.

9. *Recency of hearing examination.* Hearing examinations need to be current because children who are visually impaired or blind are very dependent on information they hear. If the latest hearing examination is more than 1 year old, another may be needed prior to testing.

10. *Date of last orientation and mobility evaluation.* Training in orientation and mobility is essential to a child's potential independence. This training can begin during the preschool years and should be provided as soon as possible.

11. *Members of family.* This information may be useful in understanding the home environment.

12. *Family members with visual loss.* This information may relate to the degree of acceptance of the child's visual loss and suggests whether the child has been exposed to models with a visual loss.

13. *Sleep problems.* If problems exist in this area, parents may desire some assistance in coping with them. In some cases, helping parents remediate these problems may prevent child abuse (Justice & Justice, 1976).

14. *Toileting problems.* Teaching toileting skills can be quite stressful for parents, and some parents may want help in this area if problems exist.

15. *Feeding problems.* Because a serious visual loss can contribute to a delay in learning some feeding skills, assistance may be needed for some children in this area as

well. Common delays in these skills are addressed in Chapters 2 and 3.

16. *Food allergies.* If food allergies exist, these foods would need to be avoided in a preschool program or when food is used during testing to enhance motivation to participate.

17. *Initiation of interaction.* Children who are visually impaired or blind may become passive because the visual input is not available to entice them to interact with their environment. These children often are delayed in motor skills and self-initiated sensorimotor abilities (Fewell, 1983). Hence, it is worth noting whether a child uses self-initiated motor behaviors, other than vocal responses, to interact with objects in the environment. These behaviors could include such behaviors as reaching for a cookie or bottle, searching for a fallen toy, or kicking or hitting a musical roly-poly toy.

18. *Child's nonvocal messages in response to parents.* When parents talk to their infant who has a severe vision loss, they may be disappointed and even feel rejected because the baby does not make eye contact or orient to their faces. If they do not find it rewarding to interact with their baby, their attempts to communicate will decrease. Thus, parents can benefit from learning what behaviors to look for that indicate that their baby is responding to their attention. The examiner can explain to the parents that lack of eye contact does not mean the baby is not cognizant of their presence. It will be helpful to then make the parents aware of what other behaviors indicate that their baby is responding to them. These behaviors include any rather consistent change in responding following an interaction with the parent. For example: quieting (i.e., a reduction in kicking, waving the arms, squirming), change in facial expression, or change in breathing rate. The parents' positive interaction with their baby is critical for an infant's optimal development.

19. *Awareness of hazards.* Safety is a primary concern. The sooner children learn to protect themselves from danger, the better. Parents cannot always be present when a child needs protection, or parents may not be able to get to a child soon enough to prevent an accident. If a child knows

to stop an activity in response to "No-no," this could prevent an injury.

20. *Search for lost objects.* A child with a severe visual loss has more difficulty learning that a dropped or misplaced toy still exists and can be regained if the child searches for it (i.e., object permanence). Infants who think a dropped or misplaced toy no longer exists can become frustrated or passive. These infants need to be physically prompted to search for and find dropped or misplaced objects.

21. *Favorite playthings.* Knowledge of these objects can be used to enhance motivation to participate during testing and in the classroom.

22. *Amount of physical contact provided.* Children learn a great deal through physical contact, especially children with a visual loss. Physical contact can facilitate development in terms of cognition, socialization, and language and motor skills. Children who are visually impaired or blind need the additional stimulation of being held and caressed by their parents. Children who have learned to find physical contact pleasurable may become less isolated and passive.

    Insufficient stimulation and exercise can impair the physical and mental development of infants. For infants who are small at birth and who are kept for extended periods of time in a nursery, provision of adequate stimulation is particularly a concern (Maurer & Maurer, 1988).

23. *Use of hands to explore objects.* Infants and toddlers who are visually impaired or blind will have to learn a great deal about the environment through the sense of touch. The sooner a baby begins to use touch, the sooner he or she can obtain information via this modality. Very early on, parents can physically prompt their baby to explore objects using touch whenever possible.

24. *Encouragement to move.* Children with a severe visual loss tend to have delays in motor development; hence, they need considerable stimulation to move about so as to prevent these delays. Without the visual stimulation to entice them to interact with their surroundings, they are more

apt to be passive than sighted children. Briefly exercising the baby and physically prompting him or her to move will encourage more activity.

25. *Changing infant's position.* If a visually impaired or blind infant is allowed to remain in one position when lying down (e.g., supine), he or she may become content to remain in that position. Babies who have been hospitalized for lengthy periods may have been kept on their backs. To ensure that a baby uses different muscle systems (especially the upper extremities) and does not become passive, the baby's position will need to be changed (i.e., placed in a side lying position, a sitting position, or in a prone position). If an infant is placed on his or her stomach (prone) and he or she does not have good head control, the infant should be supervised to make sure that he or she does not suffocate.

26. *Naming objects and actions for child.* More exposure to language is necessary for children who are visually impaired or blind because they do not have the visual input of sighted children to aid in concept development. Parents can help by frequently naming objects and describing actions, even for infants.

27. *Use of child's name.* If a child's name is used before something else is said, it will serve two purposes. First, it will help a child learn his or her name, a skill often delayed for children with a severe visual loss. Second, use of the child's name will let the child know that what is about to be said is directed at him or her. This is a beneficial habit for parents to establish.

28. *Overprotection.* As previously noted, safety is a primary concern. Interaction with the environment, however, is important also to facilitate learning and reduce passivity.

29. *Place for storing toys.* If toys are kept in one place, the child will know where to find them independently. Encouraging children to put toys away in the same place teaches them the importance of order and neatness, which will be of great benefit later on as well. A child who is orderly has more control and independence. Parents can begin to teach the importance of organization to children as soon as a child is able to walk.

30. *House well organized.* If a house is reasonably uncluttered and things are kept in the same place for the most part, a child can learn more easily to navigate and to be less fearful and more willing to move about the house.

If rating scales and checklists are to be completed by the preschool teacher and parent, it is helpful to have the forms filled out at the end of the interview so the examiner can be present to answer any questions that a teacher or parent might have while completing the forms. Further, the examiner will have the information in hand prior to directly testing or observing the child. Rating scales and checklists can be used to aid in assessing adaptive behavior, social skills, and classroom behavior. These measures are discussed in Chapters 2 and 3.

For a school-age child or adolescent who is visually impaired or blind, the interview with the teacher is a particularly important facet of assessment. The teacher's perceptions of a student's strengths and difficulties, and what has been tried to remedy the difficulties, must be determined if intervention programs are to be effective. An examiner also needs to determine prior to testing what adaptive devices, special materials, and procedures are used in the classroom that also might be useful during testing. Thus, the teacher interview will be more useful if it is conducted prior to testing a student.

Special concerns need to be addressed in an interview with the teacher and parents of students who are visually impaired or blind. Figure 1.2, Information-Organizing Checklist for School-Age Students Who Are Visually Impaired or Blind, can be used as a guide during the interviews. As with Figure 1.1, this form was designed to facilitate integration of information from various sources (e.g., interviews, school and medical records).

Rationale of information on checklist

1–11. The rationale for these items was addressed previously under the section on importance of items on the Information-Organizing Checklist for Infants and Preschoolers Who Are Visually Impaired or Blind.

12. *Student's friends in neighborhood.* This information is relevant to a student's social development.

13. *Home environment disorganized.* If disorganization of the home interferes with a student's development, this issue may need to be addressed with the parents.

School-Age Students

History of Visual Loss

1. *Cause of visual loss:*

    Congenital _____   Acquired _____

    Cause _____

    Student's age at onset _____

    Onset:

          Gradual _____   Sudden _____

2. *Date of last visual exam* _____

    Result _____

    _____

3. *Visual acuity:*

    For right eye _____ (corrected)   _____ (uncorrected)

    For left eye _____ (corrected)   _____ (uncorrected)

4. *Description of student's field of vision (e.g., peripheral vision or restricted visual field)* _____

    _____

5. *Loss is:*   Stable _____   Progressive _____

Other Health Issues

6. *Other disabling conditions* _____

    _____

7. *Other health problems* _____

    _____

8. *Medications student is taking* _____

9. *Date of most recent hearing exam* _____

    Result _____

    _____

Figure 1.2. Information-organizing checklist for school-age students who are visually impaired or blind.

Home Situation

10. *Family consists of:*

    Two parents _____

    Single parent _____

    Siblings _____

    Other persons living in the home _____

    _____

11. *Does student have:*

    One parent with a severe visual loss _____

    Two parents with a severe visual loss _____

    Siblings with a severe visual loss _____

    Other relatives with a severe visual loss _____

    _____

12. *Does student have friends in the neighborhood?*

    yes _____   no _____

13. *Is home environment so disorganized that it may interfere with the student's mobility or functioning?*

    yes _____   no _____

14. *Can the student travel independently in the neighborhood?*

    yes _____   no _____

    If no, why not _____

15. *Have the parents been actively involved in the educational planning for the student?*

    yes _____   no _____

16. *Are the parents involved outside the home in activities that involve children or adults who are visually impaired or blind?*

    yes _____   no _____

17. *Are adaptive devices used in the home to assist the student?*

    yes _____   no _____

    If yes, list _____

(continued)

FIGURE 1.2 *Continued*

Classroom Situation

18. *Has the student been involved in a preschool program, either classroom or home based?*

    yes _____   no _____

    If yes, age at which child began _____

19. *Present classroom placement:*

    Regular classroom _____

    Special education classroom _____

    Hours per day _____

20. *Does the student participate in classroom activities to about the same degree as other students?*

    yes _____   no _____

21. *Does the student request help when needed?*

    yes _____   no _____

22. *Does the student accept help courteously?*

    yes _____   no _____

23. *Does the student refuse help courteously?*

    yes _____   no _____

24. *Does the student display an appropriate degree of independence?*

    yes _____   no _____

25. *Is the student able to move freely about the classroom?*

    yes _____   no _____

26. *Date of last orientation and mobility evaluation* _____

27. *Is the student currently receiving orientation and mobility instruction?*

    yes _____   no _____

    If no, why not _____

28. *Is the student able to avoid hazards as much as possible?*

    yes _____   no _____

---

29. *Is the student's desk well organized and free of unnecessary materials?*

    yes _____   no _____

30. *Does the student routinely put materials back in appropriate places so that they can be located easily?*

    yes _____   no _____

31. *Does the student require additional time to complete assignments?*

    yes _____   no _____

    If so, about how much _____

32. *Does the student seem to become more fatigued than most students?*

    yes _____   no _____

33. *Does the student listen well to instructions?*

    yes _____   no _____

34. *Can the student handle frustrating tasks without becoming overly upset?*

    yes _____   no _____

35. *Does the student respond appropriately to corrective feedback?*

    yes _____   no _____

36. *Does the student seem to appreciate praise from the teacher?*

    yes _____   no _____

    Examples of effective praise _____

    _____

37. *What type of instructional materials are used?*

    _____ Braille   _____ talking books

    _____ tape recorder   _____ large print (size _____)

    _____ material read   _____ electronic note taker
              to student

    _____ closed-circuit television (CCTV)

    _____ computer output:

              _____ speech   _____ Braille   _____ large print

    other _____

(continued)

FIGURE 1.2 *Continued*

38. *What low-vision aids are used?* _____

_____

39. *What special writing materials are used?*

_____ Braille writer   _____ slate/stylus

_____ typewriter   _____ computer

_____ special paper (raised or bold line)

_____ felt-tip pens

other _____

40. *What special arithmetic aids are used?*

_____ abacus   _____ computer aids

_____ talking calculator   _____ Braille ruler

_____ special paper   _____ special clock

other _____

41. *Type of lighting needed:*

_____ dim   _____ average   _____ intense

Peer Interaction

42. *Does the student have friends in the classroom?*

yes _____   no _____

43. *Is the student teased by peers?*

yes _____   no _____

44. *Does the student interact in a positive way with peers?*

yes _____   no _____

45. *Does the student interact with peers about as often as other students do?*

yes _____   no _____

46. *Does the student participate in clubs or sports?*

yes _____   no _____

If yes, which _____

47. *Teacher concerns about academic performance. (List in order of priority.)*

48. *Teacher concerns about classroom behavior. (List in order of priority.)*

49. *Parent concerns. (List in order of priority.)*

50. *Prior test results.*

14. *Independent travel in neighborhood.* The student's ability to travel independently and safely in the neighborhood can affect the development of social skills and adaptive behavior.

15. *Parents' involvement in student's educational program.* Parents' involvement can enhance a student's achievement considerably. If they have not been involved with the school, attempting to facilitate their participation whenever possible may be helpful to them and to their child.

16. *Parents' involvement with others with a visual loss.* Such involvement can help parents with the adjustment to their child's visual loss and help them understand the condition. Providing them with information on relevant community and statewide agencies or arranging for them to meet others in the community who are visually impaired or blind can be beneficial.

17. *Use of adaptive devices in the home.* If adaptive devices are used, it may be helpful to use them at school and during the assessment as well. When assessing adaptive behavior, if a student can perform a task independently using an adaptive device, this skill should be considered mastered. If no adaptive devices are used, an assessment may be needed to determine whether any of these devices could be employed to enable the student to function more independently.

18. *Student's involvement in preschool program.* Early intervention should facilitate development.

19. *Classroom placement.* This information is relevant to future program planning.

20. *Student's participation in classroom activities.* This may be an important area to target for instruction if problems exist.

21–24. *Student's ability to request, accept, and refuse help and degree of student's independence in classroom.* Students with disabling conditions require more assistance from others. If a student has problems requesting or responding to help, these areas should be targeted for instruction.

25. *Student's ability to move around classroom.* A problem in this area could impact negatively on academic performance and social interaction, making an evaluation by a specialist in orientation and mobility appropriate.

26. *Date of last orientation and mobility evaluation.* The need for different skills in this area can change rather rapidly. Ideally, a student should be evaluated every 6 months to ensure that he or she receives the needed training.

27. *Are orientation and mobility services being received?* For safety, independence, self-confidence, and social development, any student who can benefit from orientation and mobility services should receive them. These skills can make a tremendous difference in a student's ability to function.

28. *Avoidance of hazards.* If a student is not able to avoid hazards satisfactorily, the student may have been overprotected, not taught appropriate safety skills, or both. Training in this area definitely would be appropriate if this is a problem area.

29–30. *Organization.* To function as efficiently as possible, a student who is visually impaired or blind needs to be well organized or time will be wasted in frustrating and unnecessary searches. Such disorganization will impair a student's ability to function independently and should be targeted for instruction.

31–32. *Additional time required to complete assignments and fatigue.* Answers to these two items will be helpful in planning the assessment as well as a student's classroom program. Reading Braille and large print requires much more time and can be more tiring than reading regular-size print. Employing any usable vision a student has can result in fatigue as well. An examiner should discontinue testing when a student appears to be tiring.

33. *Student's listening skills.* Students who are visually impaired or blind must rely heavily on auditory input to function. If a student has not learned to listen well, this skill should be an area for instruction.

34. *Ability to deal appropriately with frustration.* Limited visual input can make many tasks quite frustrating. Students who are visually impaired or blind may require special instruction on how to cope with frustration.

35. *Student's response to corrective feedback.* Students who are visually impaired or blind are likely to require more corrective feedback on some tasks than their sighted peers. A student may need to learn how to cope with this additional input.

36. *Response to teacher praise.* Because praise from the teacher is often the only reward available in many classrooms for good work, students who do not enjoy teacher praise will be at a disadvantage. Hence, an appreciation of teacher praise may need to be learned. Statements that have served as effective praise can be used for good work during the assessment to enhance and maintain a student's willingness to participate.

37–41. *Special materials and equipment used in classroom.* An examiner needs to know what types of special materials and equipment are employed in the classroom so that these materials can be used during the assessment. It will be important to have this information prior to the assessment so that any preparation of needed materials can be done. Depending on the type of visual loss, special lighting conditions may be required to facilitate use of any functional vision a student has. For example, high illumination is needed for myopia and optic atrophy, while dim light is needed for aniridia and albinism. Use of a desk light with a rheostat is helpful in controlling the amount of light provided.

42–46. *Quality and quantity of peer interaction.* If problems exist in these areas, they should be targeted for instruction. Problems with social skills should be assessed in depth using the social skills scales described in Chapter 6. Participation in clubs and attendance at sports events should be encouraged in order to prevent isolation.

47–49. *Concerns of teachers and parents.* These issues need to be addressed in the assessment and are of primary concern.

50. *Prior test results.* In order to assess a student's progress over time, a comparison of current and prior test results is needed.

During the interview with the teacher, it is helpful to obtain samples of a student's work, especially in areas of difficulty. From an examination of work samples, the examiner often can determine error patterns. It may be possible to design a remedial program to correct such error patterns.

As was noted for younger children, if teachers or parents will be asked to complete rating scales or checklists, it is wise to have the forms completed at the end of the interviews.

One rating scale designed specifically for students who are visually impaired or blind is the *Pupil Behavior Rating Scale* (Swallow, Mangold, & Mangold, 1978). The scale is completed by teachers and consists of 24 items dealing with auditory comprehension and listening, spoken language, orientation, behavior, and motor skills. Each item has five choices that range from superior performance to extremely poor performance. Though the obtained information is general, the results suggest areas that may need to be investigated further by systematic direct observation or testing.

Review of Records

School records

School records should be reviewed prior to direct observation and testing for two reasons: (a) to obtain information useful in planning how to conduct observations and testing, and (b) to avoid repeating assessment procedures that have been used recently. During this review, the examiner should take organized, comprehensive, yet concise notes so that he or she will not need to return to the files to obtain information needed for the report. The following information is important to note:

- dates and results of tests for hearing, speech, and medical problems
- dates and results of prior assessments
- names and dates of schools previously attended
- relevant family information, such as the person with whom the student lives

- dates and notes regarding prior school contacts with the family

Medical records

A review of medical records, especially those pertaining to a student's visual loss, is important. Ophthalmologists or optometrists can make recommendations for medical intervention, prescriptions, and restrictions on use of the eyes, if necessary. A number of items at the beginning of the Information-Organizing Checklist address these issues.

The eye report can provide a considerable amount of information that is helpful in understanding a student's visual loss. The following abbreviations may be useful in interpreting eye reports:

O.D. *ocular dexter (right eye)*

O.S. *ocular sinister (left eye)*

O.U. *oculi unitas (both eyes)*

P.P. *near point*

P.R. *far point*

V.A. *visual acuity*

V.F. *visual field*

W.N.L. *within normal limits*

S., S.S., S.C. *without correction*

C., C.C. *with correction*

L.P. *light perception*

N.L.P. *no light perception; totally blind*

N.V. *near vision*

C.F. *count fingers; suggests student is able to see physician's fingers to count them*

H.M. *hand movements; suggests student is able to see movement of physician's hands (Neither C.F. nor H.M. is an accurate measure of visual acuity.)*

The eye report will provide information on visual acuity, measured separately for each eye with and without correction. A comparison of visual acuity with and without correction describes the degree of improvement in vision that can be expected with glasses. Usually this information is provided for distance vision and for near vision. Near vision is particularly important for schoolwork.

When appropriate, the report also will provide information on the student's field of vision. Typically, a sketch will be used to describe where vision is restricted and the extent of restriction. Such information may be helpful in determining areas of functional vision and the direction of gaze that can be employed to most effectively use functional vision. Students with a considerable loss of their visual field will need to learn to peruse the environment in order to obtain the visual information they need. They also will need to learn to use nonvisual cues to obtain information on people or objects that are in areas of the field where their vision is not functional.

The eye report can provide information on cause of the visual loss, age at onset, visual aids that are needed, special lighting requirements, and whether any restrictions on physical activity are required.

Information in an eye report should be interpreted with some degree of caution by educators because recommendations based on clinical tests may not generalize to performance in the classroom environment. Anxiety and the unfamiliar environment of the clinic may affect visual performance. Hence, a functional vision assessment is needed as well.

Functional vision assessment

"A functional vision assessment offers an organized plan for observing how the students use their vision to perform routine tasks" (Levack, 1991, p. 36). Routine tasks can encompass many activities, including play activities for young children and infants, and school assignments and completion of daily living activities for older students. This type of assessment is carried out by either a teacher or a consultant certified in working with students who are visually impaired or blind. For school-age students, this assessment is likely to include a learning media assessment to determine the most appropriate media for a student to use to receive information and the most efficient media for reading and writing. A student may use more than one medium. Information in the functional vision report will be particularly relevant to arranging an optimal environment and using appropriate procedures and materials when conducting a psychoeducational assessment. For example, the report will contain recommendations regarding appropriate lighting, appropriate viewing distance for materials, print size needed, seating arrangements, and other modifications that facilitate use of functional vision. Levack (1991) suggested various categories of adaptations that might be made in a functional vision assessment, several of which are listed as examples (see Table 1.1).

The report from a functional vision assessment should contain a considerable amount of information useful in planning a psychoeducational assessment and in planning a student's educational program. Obviously, it is important to consult with the teacher or the consultant for students who are visually impaired or blind before testing and when developing recommendations based on test results.

Obtaining information from school and medical records and the functional vision assessment prior to direct testing is particularly important. Unfortunately, however, not all states require a functional vision assessment.

TABLE 1.1. *Possible Adaptations in a Functional Vision Assessment*

	For a young child	*For a school-age student*
COLOR AND CONTRAST	Use a bright yellow ball with bold black stripe (rather than solid color).	Use dark pens or markers with width and color based on student's needs and preferences.
ILLUMINATION	Use penlights or flashlights to get child's attention.	Use reading stand to increase light on materials and eliminate shadows. Use a lighted pen.
SPACE AND ARRANGEMENT	Reduce number of choices of toys child has to look at when playing.	Arrange math problems so that there is white space around each of them.
SIZE AND DISTANCE	Bring toys close to eyes to magnify and enhance vision.	Use enlarged print of appropriate size for student's needs.

Observation

Systematic direct observation of a student's performance is an integral part of any educational assessment for a student who is visually impaired or blind. Observation in the classroom environment is needed to plan a realistic educational program. "Classroom observation is the most neglected yet the most useful form of performance assessment that is available" (Brackett, 1981, p. 60).

Observation of a student in the home setting can be helpful but may yield different information from that obtained in the classroom. Because the home situation is more familiar to a student, and the parents' expectations for a student may differ from those of school personnel, it is worthwhile to observe the student in the home. For example, the willingness and ability of a student who is visually impaired or blind to independently travel throughout the home may be quite different from his or her willingness and ability to travel around the classroom. Comparing information from observations in both settings can help determine how the classroom or home environment can be changed to facilitate a student's independence.

Observation in the classroom prior to direct testing allows an examiner to become familiar with a student's needs and behaviors.

Observation is especially important for examiners who have limited experience in assessing students who are visually impaired or blind because it will help them to know what to expect during testing. This information should strengthen an examiner's confidence and help him or her to relax during testing so that more attention can be paid to the student.

The accuracy of data obtained from systematic behavior observation depends on the training and experience of the examiner. The more systematic the method of data collection, the more reliable the data are apt to be. Several resources describe procedures for the systematic observation of behavior (e.g., Alessi & Kaye, 1983; Gelfand & Hartman, 1984). A videotape that provides examiners with practice and feedback accompanies the Alessi and Kaye text. These sources also contain descriptions of procedures for determining the reliability of the data, which is necessary for accurate interpretation of results.

Testing

Once interviews with the parents, teacher, and student have been completed; school and medical records reviewed; and systematic direct observation carried out, an examiner should be prepared to conduct direct testing, if it is necessary. On occasion, completion of interviews, records review, and observation provides sufficient information about a student's strengths and problem areas to plan an educational program to fix the problems without direct testing. Compiling the information on the Information-Organizing Checklist should help to organize the information for meaningful interpretation and ensure that sufficient background information is obtained to plan direct testing that will be useful, comprehensive, and efficient.

It is clear from the information presented thus far that a multidisciplinary approach to assessment is critical for children who are visually impaired or blind. Information, consultation, and recommendations are needed from various sources including parents, teachers, consultants for students who are visually impaired and blind, physicians, orientation and mobility specialists, and even the students themselves in order to plan an appropriate psychoeducational assessment. If such input is obtained and organized as described above, even examiners with little or no experience with these students should be able to obtain valid information from direct testing. The next step in the assessment process is to select appropriate tests and procedures, if further information is necessary.

Norm-referenced information is necessary to determine eligibility for special education services. The Ethical Principles of Psychologists (American Psychological Association, 1981) require that a test be accompanied by a manual that describes the development, rationale, reliability, and validity of the test, as well as complete information about the normative sample characteristics. In addition, the Individuals with Disabilities Education Act (1990) states that tests must be valid for their employed purpose. Thus, the use of technically adequate measures is necessary. The following criteria were used to evaluate the technical adequacy of the norm-referenced tests presented in the chapters that follow.

Standardization

Demographic data should be provided to demonstrate that the sample is similar to the U.S. Census data in terms of gender, race, ethnicity, socioeconomic level, geographic distribution, and urban/rural residence. Approximately 100 subjects should be included at each age or grade level (Salvia & Ysseldyke, 1991). This information allows the examiner to determine whether the normative group is an appropriate comparison group for the child to be tested.

For tests with norms for students who are visually impaired or blind, additional demographic data are needed to describe the sample because this is such a heterogeneous population and many variables related to loss of vision have a considerable effect on performance. Ideally, the normative sample of students who are visually impaired or blind should be described in terms of age at onset of the loss, type of loss, etiology, degree of loss, and presence of other disabilities.

Reliability

Internal consistency and test-retest reliability data should be presented for each age or grade level, because collapsing data across levels can obscure low values, particularly at the extreme ages or grade levels of a test. Correlations of .85 or higher are considered adequate for decision making (Aiken, 1991; Guilford, 1978). Retest intervals should be moderate in order to minimize the effects of learning, but not so short as to be of no use. Salvia and Ysseldyke (1991) note that a 2-week interval traditionally is used. Information on standard error of measurement should be provided by age or grade level also.

Validity

Construct validity data are required to show that the test scores conform to theory and research underlying the construct. Construct validity is particularly important for intelligence tests. Content validity information is necessary to demonstrate that the test items measure the area to be assessed and that they do so in an appropriate and comprehensive manner. Content validity is particularly important for measures of achievement. Criterion-related validity data should be presented to describe the extent to which the scores are related to other acceptable measures.

Test selection

Occasionally, an examiner may need to use tests or parts of tests that do not meet the minimum criteria for technical adequacy. When this is necessary, results must be interpreted with great caution, and information from as many sources as possible should be used in decision making. Unfortunately, the choices for tests for students who are visually impaired or blind are fewer than for students with normal vision. With fewer test choices, it will sometimes be necessary to administer tests with less-than-adequate technical adequacy.

Whether to use test norms for sighted students or students who are visually impaired or blind is a question for which there is no simple answer. In making this decision, the examiner must consider the purpose for testing and the background of the student. If the purpose is to compare a student's current level of performance with that of sighted peers, and if the student is able to understand the instructions and make the required responses, then norms for sighted students might be considered. In using these norms, however, one assumes that the acculturation of the student has been similar to that of sighted students in the norm sample, which is not likely to be the case. For example, a student may have been overprotected because of a visual loss and thus have had somewhat limited experience interacting with the environment. If a student attended a residential school for students who are blind or visually impaired, his or her educational experience differs from that of the norm group. Furthermore, if adaptations are necessary to circumvent the student's visual loss, the standardized administration procedures are altered, and the comparison with the norms may not be appropriate. If, however, data are available on use of a test with students who are blind or visually impaired to show that the means and standard deviations are the same as for sighted students, then using the sighted norms may present no problem. If the purpose is to use the information for planning an educational program, then adaptations and practice items could assist in determining strengths and difficulties.

Tests standardized on students who are blind or visually impaired are not without problems either. Only a limited number of such tests are available, and many have problems with different aspects of technical adequacy. The requirements for responding to items, however, are more appropriate, and the normative sample may be more appropriate. The population of students who are blind or visually impaired is very heterogeneous. Age at onset of visual loss, type of loss, and amount of usable vision are examples of factors that cause considerable individual variation within this population. Hence, it is important that a relatively large and representative sample of students who are blind and those who are visually impaired participate in the standardization of these tests to avoid bias in the norms.

Because there are problems in interpreting results for students who are blind or visually impaired on tests standardized either on sighted students or on students with a severe visual loss, conclusions regarding educational programming and special education placement need to be based on data from other sources of information as well as on standardized tests. To determine the validity of results from standardized tests for a particular student, an examiner should compare the norm-referenced results with information obtained from interviews with several people who know the student well, data from review of school records, criterion-referenced test results, curriculum-based measurement results, and data from systematic direct classroom observation. Furthermore, an assessment that considers areas such as cognitive performance, academic performance, and adaptive behavior is required in order to draw valid conclusions about a student's abilities. Periodic reevaluation helps determine the validity of test results, provides data on changes in a student's performance, and describes progress over time.

When possible, an examiner should obtain data from tests standardized on both sighted students and students who are visually impaired or blind. These results, combined with data from other sources, should provide a good information base from which to draw conclusions.

If data from norm-referenced tests, interviews, review of records, or observation suggest that a student is having difficulty with specific academic areas, further testing with criterion-referenced tests, curriculum-based measurement, or both is likely to be needed.

Results from criterion-referenced tests are not used to compare a student's performance with the performance of others. Instead, performance is assessed in terms of whether a student is able to perform a certain task to a preset level of mastery (i.e., a student passes or fails an item depending on whether she or he reaches a criterion). For example, a mastery level for a skill might require that a student correctly recognizes three out of three times the short vowel sound for *u* in consonant-vowel-consonant words. Items on criterion-referenced tests are based on a detailed task analysis of skills. These tests assess more skills than do norm-referenced tests, and each skill is usually tested three or four times to ensure reliable results. This specificity is critical for planning instructional programs.

Criterion-referenced tests have an advantage over norm-referenced tests with a student who is blind or visually impaired because various objects and materials can be used during testing. Use of adapted materials (e.g., Braille materials, larger toys) can help determine what a student is capable of doing. Furthermore, because the tests are not standardized, flexible administration procedures can be employed. This flexibility can help to determine the most appropriate procedures for teaching a skill to a particular student.

For published criterion-referenced tests for infants and preschoolers, age levels are assigned to items. These age levels typically are based on literature reviews. Because the tests are not standardized, the age levels cannot be interpreted as norm-referenced scores. The age levels only suggest the age at which children typically demonstrate the skills. When using these age levels it is important to consider that rates of development are highly individual during infancy, and environmental and cultural differences are factors that can influence the development of skills in young children. Generally, the development of skills for students who are blind or visually impaired follows the same pattern as that of sighted children but sometimes at a slower rate. Thus, consideration needs to be given to those skills that usually require more time to learn for children who are blind or visually impaired. These skills are discussed in detail in Chapter 4.

With curriculum-based measurement, the materials used for instruction are those used for assessment. The primary purpose of curriculum-based measurement is to determine how well an individual student is progressing within a particular curriculum. This information indicates whether changes might be needed in the curriculum used in the classroom, in the teaching procedures, or in both. Unfortunately, little research is available on the use of curriculum-based measurement with students who are blind or visually impaired. Nonetheless, the procedures may be useful for frequently monitoring progress in academic areas. These procedures and their technical adequacy are discussed in Chapter 6.

An examiner also should try to determine the types of strategies a student uses to solve problems (Hammill, 1987). If a teacher is aware that a student is using an incorrect or inefficient strategy, then it is relatively easy to provide the student with one that is more effective (Hammill, 1987). For many problems, more than one strategy will enable a student to arrive at a correct answer. Examples of such individual-referenced interpretations follow. Each of these strategies makes the student's performance inefficient.

> Kate uses her fingers to count when completing addition problems for sums greater than 10. (Hence, Kate needs to learn these math facts.)

> When encountering high-frequency words (i.e., words that occur frequently in print), Riley slowly sounds them out. (Hence, Riley would benefit from increasing his sight vocabulary so that he recognizes these words instantly as he reads.)

Various procedures including interviews, rating scales and checklists, review of records, observation, and direct testing are needed to move from general information to the specification of the exact nature of a student's academic problems. To carry out a comprehensive assessment of a student who is visually impaired or blind, an examiner is likely to need all of these sources.

LIMITATIONS OF ASSESSMENT

Educational assessment of students who are visually impaired or blind is a time-consuming process when it is done well. Despite the time requirements, interviews with teachers, parents, and students are rich sources of information, and systematic observation of a student's performance in the classroom is extremely important. Despite the inherent limitations in current assessment instruments, an examiner usually can obtain a considerable amount of norm-referenced information and detailed information required for instructional planning. It is well worth the time required to obtain this information, which will enable professionals to make accurate decisions regarding educational programs for students who are visually impaired or blind. Detailed, comprehensive information also is necessary to plan effective educational programs that can make a difference for these students.

The instruments described in the following chapters provide a considerable amount of useful information. A major problem in assessing students who are visually impaired or blind, however, is that nearly all tests designed for this population of students fail to meet minimum standards for technical adequacy. Although many tests developed for sighted students are technically adequate, these tests may not be appropriate for students who are visually impaired or blind. Authors of new tests developed for these students can make a major contribution to the field if the tests are well standardized and have good reliability (especially in terms of test-retest data) and validity (particularly construct validity for intelligence tests and content validity for achievement tests).

More research is necessary in the area of assessment of students who are visually impaired or blind. Specifically, new tests are needed that have norms for sighted students, students who are blind, and students who are visually impaired. The tests and procedures that have the greatest potential for assisting in the education of these students, however, are systematic direct observation, criterion-referenced tests, and curriculum-based measurement procedures. Any progress in these areas will be particularly important in advancing the delivery of educational services to students who are visually impaired or blind.

Chapter 2

Issues in Understanding Children Who Are Visually Impaired or Blind

IN ORDER TO OBTAIN VALID TEST RESULTS, ACCURATELY INTER-pret children's performance, and provide useful information for educational planning, examiners must understand a number of issues about visual impairment and blindness. These issues, discussed in this chapter, include: definitions of visual loss, incidence, etiology, types of loss, age effects for onset of vision loss, effects of additional disabilities, sensory functioning, medication considerations, orientation and mobility skills, behaviors affecting social interaction, language development, and issues in working with families.

DEFINITIONS

The term *blind* frequently is applied to those with a complete loss of sight. Few people are totally blind; rather, most are able to perceive light and/or details to some degree. More than 75% of persons who are blind in the United States have some usable vision (American Foundation for the Blind, undated).

To be classified as "legally blind" (making one eligible for some benefits from the government), however, one must have visual acuity of 20/200 or less in the better eye with correction or have a restricted visual field with a diameter of no more than 20˚. The legal definition of blindness is of little use in educational planning because students whose corrected vision is 20/200 in the better eye often are able to use visual material in the classroom (Scholl, 1985). Scholl (1985) suggested that "the term 'blind' is appropriately applied to pupils who must use senses other than vision in their educational process" (p. 205). That is how the term will be used in this text. These students require use of tactile input, auditory input, or both. To function well in the classroom, they may use Braille, recorded material, or readers as well as technology such as voice or Braille output computers and talking calculators.

Visually impaired or *visually handicapped* refers to students with a visual loss who require more than glasses to function adequately in the classroom. These students have some degree of vision that can be used in the educational process. These terms include students described as having "low vision" who can see materials if they are held close to their eyes. These students may be able to use large type or even regular print but need low-vision equipment such as magnifiers. Some of these students may even require tactile and auditory material for instruction.

INCIDENCE

Blindness occurs most frequently in the elderly population. Though approximately 500,000 people in the United States can be classified as legally blind, the majority are over 65 years of age.

Under the Individuals with Disabilities Education Act (1990) (IDEA), students who are blind and those who are visually impaired are both categorized as "visually impaired." In the 1990–91 school year, 17,783 students classified as visually impaired were served under IDEA, Part B (U.S. Department of Education, 1992). These students made up 0.4% of the students eligible for special education services between the ages of 6 and 21. For the 1989–90 school year, 84.1% of students classified as visually impaired were placed in regular schools, 4.5% were placed in a separate school, and 10.9% were placed in residential facilities. These percentages do not include students with multiple impairments.

Of children considered legally blind or severely visually impaired, 80 to 90% have low vision (Corn & Coatney, 1984; National Advisory Eye Council, 1981; O'Donnell & Livingston, 1991). Thus, few children or adolescents are without any sight; most are able to perceive light and/or details to some degree.

ETIOLOGY

There are many types of visual loss and, hence, numerous etiologies. Conditions present at birth are referred to as congenital and those appearing after birth as adventitious or acquired. Congenital losses can have genetic origins or result from prenatal damage. Frequently, however, the cause is unclear (Finkelstein, 1989). Most visual losses in the school-age population are congenital (Scholl, 1985). Acquired losses can be a result of disease or accidents.

TYPES OF LOSS

According to Hatfield (1975), the most frequent eye problems for school-age students are retrolental fibroplasia, congenital cataracts, optic nerve atrophy, and albinism.

Retrolental fibroplasia was previously thought to be due to the exposure of newborns (especially premature infants) to excessive oxygen while in incubators, but now etiology is unclear (Finkelstein, 1989). This condition involves an abnormal number of blood vessels in the eye and may result in scar tissue, bleeding, and a possible detachment of the retina. The result can be total loss of sight.

Congenital cataracts occur when the lens of the eye is clouded, blocking light from passing through. Cataracts are one of the most frequent causes of blindness in the United States (Finkelstein, 1989). Considerable progress has been made in surgical techniques for removing the affected lens. Surgery, combined with corrective glasses or contact lenses, can improve vision.

Optic nerve atrophy typically occurs when pressure on the optic nerve cuts off the blood supply. The pressure can result from conditions such as a tumor or hydrocephalus. Optic nerve atrophy can be due to hereditary factors or possibly prenatal damage. The resulting loss of vision is irreversible.

Albinism, a lack of pigment in part or all of the body, is a result of hereditary factors. Typically, vision is poor, eyes are severely oversensitive to light, and nystagmus is present (an abnormal movement of the muscles resulting in constant jerking of the eyes). Though no cure exists, special lenses can enhance vision and reduce the amount of light entering the eye.

There are many other conditions that result in loss of vision. For more information on the conditions described above and other eye problems, consultation with a student's medical specialist and teacher or consultant certified to work with students with a visual loss should be helpful. A multidisciplinary approach is essential when working with these children and adolescents.

AGE AT ONSET

All other things being equal, the younger the age at onset of a visual loss, the greater the negative impact on development. Loss of vision before age 5 has the most serious effect on educational progress (Salvia & Ysseldyke, 1991). If a child has had vision for the first 5 years of life, she or he will have visual memories that can aid in learning. Those children who do not have visual memories because of an early visual loss must learn concepts based on input obtained from senses other than vision. For example, a child who is congenitally blind would have to learn concepts through tactile and auditory modalities, making instruction difficult. A child who has lost vision after age 5 may be able to remember having seen objects and colors, for example, and not require detailed instruction. Thus, age at onset of visual loss has implications for a child's educational program.

In addition, a significant loss of vision before age 5 may result in delays in the development of motor skills. Without adequate vision, infants and toddlers may become sedentary and, therefore, not use fine and gross motor movements enough to develop these skills at a level comparable to their sighted peers. Encouraging frequent movement for these children would be an important part of their educational programs.

ADDITIONAL DISABLING CONDITIONS

Knowledge of the etiology of a child's visual loss can alert an examiner to the possible presence of additional disabling conditions. For example, a child with a visual loss due to maternal rubella also may have a hearing loss or cardiac problems. Those whose visual loss is a result of Rh incompatibility also may have cerebral palsy and/or a hearing loss. Examiners should be aware of diagnostic categories that may involve multiple impairments so that they can make arrangements to ensure that these other disabilities do not interfere with performance during the assessment. For example, in the cases described above examiners should make certain these students have had a comprehensive hearing examination prior to the psychoeducational assessment.

Kirchner (1983) reported that approximately 30 to 50% of children who are blind or visually impaired have one or more additional disabilities. Thus, children with a serious visual loss tend to have substantially more disabilities than their sighted peers. The presence of additional impairments compounds assessment problems faced by examiners of these children. If additional disabilities are present that might negatively affect performance, consideration of methods to circumvent these problems as well as the visual loss during the assessment will be necessary.

The lack of information regarding psychoeducational assessment of children who are visually impaired or blind with additional disabilities highlights the need to follow basic guidelines for assessment. Gathering as much relevant data as possible about the student prior to testing is critical in assuring that abilities rather than disabilities are assessed. Because appropriate standardized assessment instruments may not be available, observation, interviews, criterion-referenced tests, and curriculum-based measurement gain importance. Decisions must be based on such multiple sources of information.

SENSORY FUNCTIONING

For students who are visually impaired, optical aids and a particular size of print may be recommended. Eye conditions change periodically and require changes in such recommendations. Hence, when observing a student in the classroom and during testing, the examiner should note how well the aids and print size a student is using appear to work. If, after consultation with the teacher, there appears to be a problem, a referral for another eye examination or functional vision assessment would be appropriate.

Because children who are visually impaired or blind must rely heavily on auditory input, periodic hearing assessments are critical.

Some hearing problems occur on an intermittent basis, and these difficulties can be missed on a screening test. Thus, periodic comprehensive hearing examinations provide good insurance against a missed diagnosis of hearing problems that might further interfere with development of children who are visually impaired or blind.

Students who are visually impaired or blind are not more sensitive than sighted students in terms of their ability to discriminate using hearing, taste, touch, and smell. Instead, they attend better when receiving information via these senses and thus are better able to interpret this information.

MEDICATION EFFECTS

Medication may affect behavior. For example, alertness, willingness to perform, and activity level may be enhanced or depressed. As much information as possible should be obtained from teachers and parents regarding how the medication seems to affect a student's performance. It may be necessary to discuss the effects of the medication with the physician also. If possible, the examiner can observe performance just before the medication is taken and again about an hour later to determine whether any behaviors change. If changes are evident, testing should be scheduled for a time when medication effects are least likely to interfere with performance.

ORIENTATION AND MOBILITY

Evaluation and training by a specialist in orientation and mobility is an essential aspect of an educational program for a student who is visually impaired or blind. Such training can begin as early as the preschool years. An orientation and mobility instructor has had specialized training in teaching these students how to travel effectively and safely within the environment. Examples of skills taught include: (a) appropriately seeking help from the public to request assistance with orientation or mobility when needed, (b) finding and using a pay telephone, (c) using public transportation systems, (d) safely and independently traveling within the school and home environments, and (e) using appropriate gait and stride when walking. Unfortunately, these services are not required in all states.

Considering the impairment, the ability of a student who is blind or visually impaired to move about the environment may seem quite good to someone not trained in orientation and mobility. A specialist, however, may be able to make suggestions that could increase considerably a student's level of independent functioning.

Assessment and training in orientation and mobility is another example illustrating the need for a multidisciplinary approach to assessment and remediation for these students.

BEHAVIORS AFFECTING SOCIAL INTERACTION

Sighted students learn many social skills by observing their peers and the adults in their environment. Students with a severe visual loss do not have this opportunity. Therefore, a number of social skills, especially those involving nonverbal communication, may need to be taught intentionally to these students.

When talking with someone, a sighted person will turn his or her face toward the speaker. For students who are severely visually impaired or blind, this usually must be taught. Orienting to the speaker may not be an easy task, especially in a group of people where several speakers are talking simultaneously. If, during an assessment, a student who is severely visually impaired or blind turns away when the examiner is speaking, she or he is not necessarily trying to avoid the situation or the examiner. The student may not yet have learned to orient to the speaker. If this is the case, the examiner should note the behavior and include it in the Individualized Educational Plan (IEP) as a skill to be taught. If a student does not learn this skill it could make social interactions with others unnecessarily difficult.

Examiners who have had limited experience with persons who are visually impaired or blind may find it difficult to interpret the emotions of some of these students. Some students may never have seen others' use of gestures. Gestures are learned from observing others modeling this type of nonverbal communication. Hence, caution is needed in interpreting the emotional reactions of students who are visually impaired or blind. The students may be experiencing feelings appropriate to a situation but may not have learned to express these feelings through the usual forms of nonverbal communication.

Certain mannerisms or forms of self-stimulation by these children or adolescents may seem bizarre. It is not appropriate to refer to these behaviors as "blindisms." Everyone, whether sighted or not, when bored or under stress, will on occasion engage in some level of self-stimulation. For example, think of people sitting in cars while traffic is tied up. It is common to observe different types of self-stimulation such as picking at fingernails, foot tapping, lip biting, and even rocking. It is not unusual for students who are visually impaired or blind to engage in self-stimulation, particularly when they are bored or stressed. The type of self-stimulation, however, may not be as acceptable, may be at a more intense level, or may be at a higher frequency than for sighted persons.

One type of self-stimulation used often, especially by young children who are visually impaired or blind, is eye pressing or poking. As Scott, Jan, and Freeman (1985) noted, the behavior can begin around 12 months of age with frequent rubbing of the eyes and, by about 18 months, can progress to a well-established habit in which the child presses the thumbs against the eyes. If continued, this can result in deeply depressed eyes that are discolored with dark circles. The behavior makes a child look strange to others and is a difficult habit to eliminate (Scott et al., 1985). Brambring and Troster (1992) reported that eye poking and body rocking were the most frequent forms of self-stimulation observed in a group of blind children ranging in age from 5 months to 72 months.

Other types of self-stimulation that children who are visually impaired or blind might engage in are light gazing, head rolling, body rocking, and finger waving or flicking. Some of these behaviors are transitory, but eye poking and body rocking tend to be quite stable (Brambring & Troster, 1992). One reason eye poking may be particularly difficult to eliminate is that manipulation of the eyeball can result in visual stimulation if the neural connection between the retina and the cortex is functioning (Jan et al., 1983). These self-stimulatory behaviors make a child appear unusual to others, interfere with learning, and, in severe cases (e.g., head banging and eye poking), can cause physical harm.

If eye poking or rocking is observed, it should be targeted for remediation. The types of situations in which self-stimulation is likely to occur should be identified, and educators may need to teach a child other more appropriate ways to handle stress or boredom in order to eliminate the behaviors. Ross and Koenig (1991) significantly decreased head rocking in an 11-year-old child who was blind using a physical prompt. Brambring and Troster (1992) reported that the more frequently self-stimulation occurs, the more likely it is to remain stable. They also suggested that when these behaviors occur in children over 4½ years of age they are particularly stable even if they occur at a low frequency. Thus, the earlier the intervention, the better.

LANGUAGE DEVELOPMENT

The development of concepts is more difficult for a child who is visually impaired or blind than for a sighted child, particularly if the loss of vision occurred before age 5. Without visual memories, these children will have to learn many concepts through auditory, tactile, and olfactory senses only. Learning concepts without the benefit of vision can result in a child acquiring only a limited understanding of certain concepts.

Higgins (1973) investigated how children who were blind used (a) words that can be experienced and (b) abstract words. Based on this work, Higgins suggested that a child who is blind may use a word in what seems to be a meaningful way, but that does not guarantee consistent logical use of the word in other contexts. In other words, a child who is blind may have an incomplete understanding of the word, making it relatively useless for application in other situations.

The extent of differences in concept development between sighted children and children who are visually impaired or blind requires considerably more research. For example, though many studies have suggested that differences exist, Anderson and Olson (1981) found no significant differences in the verbal descriptions of common objects between sighted children and children who were congenitally blind.

Hence, conclusions regarding results of verbal tests must be made with caution. Sometimes a child who is visually impaired or blind may receive a great deal of reinforcement for rote memory of information. This can contribute to the development of prolonged echolalia, both immediate and delayed. To avoid overestimating a child's level of performance, it is important to probe questionable responses and to observe a child's verbal behavior in a variety of contexts. Results of tests based on verbal items should be interpreted only in light of observation of a child's performance on other tasks in the classroom and at home.

FAMILIES

The assessment of the strengths and needs of families with infants and preschoolers who are visually impaired or blind is discussed in detail in Chapters 4 and 5. The information that follows applies to families with children of any age.

Assessment of a child who is visually impaired or blind necessitates involving the child's parents in the process. This may require helping them cope with their child's disability, especially if they are new parents. They are likely to be very concerned, even frightened, about the responsibility of raising a child who is visually impaired or blind. This prospect is particularly difficult if they have not had much contact with people who are visually impaired or blind. Their concern is realistic because they will have to face some stressful times as parents.

Professionals can help parents by discussing with them the shock, grief, anger, and resentment parents feel when first informed that their child has a disability. Talking about these feelings and acknowledging that many parents of children with disabilities feel this way can help. The fact that most children who are visually impaired or blind grow up to be happy, productive adults needs to be emphasized. It may be useful to invite other family members (e.g., siblings and grandparents) to participate in the discussions if they will be involved with the child and can provide support to the parents. Arranging for the family to talk to adults who are visually impaired or blind about their experiences or arranging for the family to meet other parents in the area who have children who are visually impaired or blind is beneficial. The parents also should receive a list of parent groups and local and state agencies concerned with children who are visually impaired or blind.

Another way to assist parents is to ensure that they recognize they are an important part of the educational planning process. Helping parents understand their child's abilities and to set realistic goals for current and future educational programs is very important. The message that they are competent to help make decisions regarding their child's education must be conveyed and may help them cope with their child's visual problems by fostering a sense of control over the family's situation.

To involve the parents in the planning process, avoid educational and psychological jargon in reports and when discussing test results. Jargon interferes with communication and can cause a parent to feel incompetent in understanding the material and alienated from the process. The use of common English should increase parents' satisfaction in working with school personnel.

Professionals can help by giving parents some suggestions for activities related to a child's current educational program that can be carried out at home. Activities should be clearly explained, require minimal time to carry out, and take into consideration the family's strengths and limitations. Self-help skills, play activities, and lan-

guage are areas in which family members can be particularly helpful in teaching their child.

Commenting on things parents have done already to help their
child can strengthen their feelings of competence. Commenting on
activities such as having taken their child to the physician, having
made an accurate observation of a child's skills, having taught a
child to feed himself or herself, or having taken the time to come to
the school to discuss results of an assessment are noteworthy. As
Cruickshank (1980) noted some time ago, the parents' attitude and
the support they provide are critical to the child's adjustment.

Chapter 3

Assessment Issues
and Procedures

. . . .

THE FIRST SECTION OF THIS CHAPTER ADDRESSES THE REQUIRE-
ments for assessing students who are visually impaired or blind as
mandated by Public Law 94–142 (P.L. 94–142) (1975) (renamed P.L.
101–476, Individuals with Disabilities Education Act, 1990) and presents general issues relevant to selecting tests and procedures to
ensure valid results. The remainder of the chapter addresses specific issues requiring consideration before, during, and after direct
testing of a student; each of these sections is followed by a checklist
to aid in applying the information at the appropriate time.

PUBLIC LAW 101–476 AND
REQUIREMENTS FOR ASSESSMENT

Implementation of P.L. 94–142 and its current version, P.L. 101–476,
has had an impact on the way children with disabilities are identified, as evidenced by the law's regulations pertaining to assessment.
Mandated requirements for the assessment are that

  (a) tests and other evaluative materials
     (1) are provided and administered in the child's native language
         or other mode of communication, unless it is clearly not feas-
         ible to do so;

(2) have been validated for the specific purpose for which they are used; and

(3) are administered by trained personnel in conformance with the instructions provided by their producers;

(b) tests and other evaluation materials include those tailored to assess specific areas of educational need and not merely those which are designed to provide a single general intelligence quotient;

(c) tests are selected and administered so as best to ensure that when a test is administered to a child with impaired sensory, manual, or speaking skills, the test results accurately reflect the child's aptitude or achievement level or whatever other factors the test purports to measure, rather than reflecting the child's impaired sensory, manual or speaking skills (except where those skills are the factors which the test purports to measure);

(d) no single procedure is used as the sole criterion for determining an appropriate educational program for a child;

(e) the evaluation is made by a multidisciplinary team or group of persons, including at least one teacher or other specialist with knowledge in the area of suspected disability; and

(f) the child is assessed in all areas related to the suspected disability, including, where appropriate, health, vision, hearing, social and emotional status, general intelligence, academic performance, communicative status, and motor abilities. (*Federal Register,* 1977, pp. 42496–42497).

These regulations specify important issues for testing and planning educational programs for students who are visually impaired or blind. First, because visual impairment and blindness sometimes are associated with additional disabilities, initial assessments need to include a variety of instruments and procedures to identify related disabilities, assess educational need, and plan appropriate programs. Second, selected measures must assess abilities rather than disabilities due to impaired vision. Hence, instruments must circumvent visual requirements for which a child does not have the enabling vision skills, and instruments must be administered by a trained examiner according to test instructions and procedures.

These federal mandates have defined the procedures for providing educational services to children with disabilities, most noticeably through the requirement that an Individual Educational Program (IEP) be developed for each student with a disability. A requisite to the IEP is that disabilities, skills, and skill deficits have been identified through assessment. Given the assessment requirements of the law as they pertain to students who are visually impaired or blind, examiners should be aware of: (a) the characteristics of students who are visually impaired or blind as described in Chapter 2, (b) the fundamental issues involved in the assessment of these students as discussed in this chapter, (c) the available assessment instruments and their technical adequacy, and (d) methods to enhance the relevance of assessment results in planning educational programs. These latter two areas are addressed in Chapters 4, 5, and 6.

A detailed discussion of assessment issues specified by P.L. 99–457 (Education of the Handicapped Act Amendments, 1986) as they apply to infants and preschoolers is presented in Chapters 4 and 5.

ISSUES TO CONSIDER BEFORE TESTING

It is not unusual for an examiner who has had little or no experience with persons who are visually impaired or blind to feel uncertain and anxious at the prospect of testing such a student. As Scholl and Schnur (1975) suggested, the best advice is to respond to the student as a person and to use common sense. They pointed out that if an examiner is uncertain of how to handle a situation, asking the student is likely to provide the answer. Also, it never hurts to ask a student if she or he needs help with something.

The following considerations and procedures, if employed before testing, will aid in obtaining valid results and in making the process go smoothly for both the student and the examiner.

Timed Tests

Time limits on tests are likely to penalize students who are visually impaired or blind. Reading Braille and large print takes about 2 to 2½ times longer to read than regular type; the time varies depending on the medium, the material, and a student's visual problem. Even if a student who is visually impaired reads using regular-size print, he or she is more likely to experience eye fatigue than a sighted student. Also, when they primarily use the tactile sense, students with significant visual impairments require more time to locate and interpret manipulable objects. Hence, when selecting tests, avoid any that are timed if possible.

Restriction of IQ Definition

In an effort to use measures that do not assess disabilities, examiners of students who are visually impaired or blind may choose to administer only selected portions of an instrument (e.g., only the verbal portion of the *Wechsler Intelligence Scale for Children–Third Edition*). Authors of cognitive scales generally include a variety of tasks on a scale in order to assess a wide range of cognitive skills. Even using a variety of tasks, however, may not tap a sufficiently large number of cognitive skills to provide a comprehensive sample of skills. For example, Guilford and Hoepfner (1971) indicated that the Wechsler scales tap only 11 of the 120 structure-of-the-intellect abilities, and these 11 abilities are assessed only in a superficial manner. Eliminating some portions of a scale further restricts the range of completeness of assessed skills and subsequently reduces the number of skills represented by the overall score. Thus, the examiner must use extreme caution when reporting and interpreting scores based on the administration of only a portion of a test. This is not to suggest that portions of intelligence tests should not be used, but rather that test scores must be interpreted according to the skills that are measured. Because cognitive assessment of students who are visually impaired or blind often involves giving only part of a scale, the resulting standard or scale score represents a restricted measure of the overall test score and should be interpreted accordingly. Even some measures (e.g., the *Blind Learning Aptitude Test,* Newland, 1971) that do not require the elimination of any portions if given to students who are visually impaired or blind do not assess a variety of skills and should be recognized as producing an overall score based on the assessment of a limited sample of cognitive skills.

Low-Vision Equipment and Technology

Examiners of students who are visually impaired or blind need to be familiar with any low-vision aids a student uses in the classroom because these aids should be used during testing also. The examiner can become familiar with this equipment by consulting the teacher and observing the student in the classroom to be certain that the equipment is used correctly during the assessment.

Students who are visually impaired or blind can employ a variety of tools. For students with low vision, optical devices might be used for magnification or distance viewing. These devices may be

Figure 3.1. Book stands free hands and lessen fatigue.

mounted on a stand or on the student's glasses, worn on a headband, or held in the hand. Magnifiers are either hand held or mounted on a stand, which eliminates fatigue from holding the device and frees the hands for other activities. Monocular or binocular telescopes for viewing at a distance can be either hand held or mounted on glasses. Microscopes are lenses that can be mounted on glasses to magnify for near vision.

Closed circuit television (CCTV), a nonoptical device, magnifies text electronically and displays it on a television monitor. Some of these devices are portable and use a hand-held device for scanning written material.

The use of book stands lessens the fatigue resulting from bending over and holding material close to the eyes (see Figure 3.1). These stands also free the hands to hold a magnifier, if needed, and in some cases may help to eliminate shadows on the written material.

With the appropriate software, computers may be used with large print and with or without speech output. Scanners called optical character recognition systems can be used to input information into a computer and provide output in large print.

Equipment for Students With Little or No Functional Vision

These students may use computer systems of several types, with optical character recognition system scanners that can input written material and provide output in speech or Braille.

If the student does not use a computer for writing, she or he may use a Braille writer or a manual slate and stylus (see Figure 3.2).

Other tools include signature guides, which are metal guides that, when placed on paper, allow a student to write his or her signature in a straight line. Some students also may use an abacus for math calculations. Use of this device should be allowed during math testing for these students. Students who use talking calculators for math, however, should not be allowed to use them during an assessment because this would preclude assessing a student's ability to do calculations.

Braille rulers, clocks, or watches also may be needed when assessing measurement skills (see Figure 3.3).

Special Materials

Some students who are visually impaired will require large print in order to read. The appropriate size for print should be indicated in the functional vision report or the eye report. Some material can be enlarged by photocopying as long as a sufficient contrast is maintained between the dark print and the white paper. Meet with the student's teacher or consultant on this issue. A number of testing materials are available through the American Printing House for the Blind (APH) in large print.

For writing, some students who are visually impaired may need bold-line paper or raised-line paper. Students who lost their vision after learning to write may be able to write using raised-line paper, which is available from APH also.

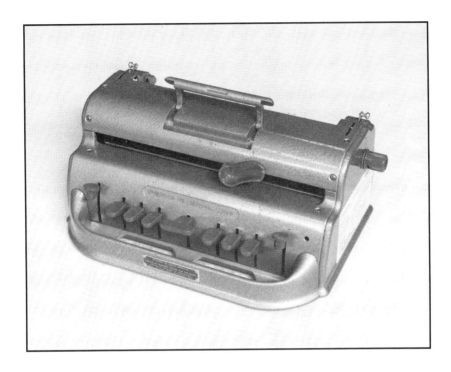

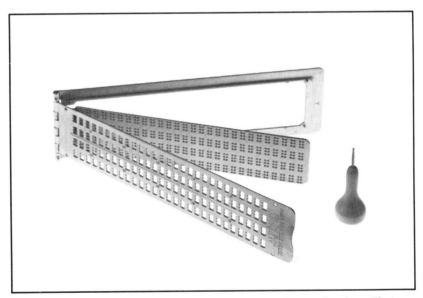

Figure 3.2. Top: Brailler (Braille writer). Bottom: slate and stylus. (Photos courtesy of American Printing House for the Blind).

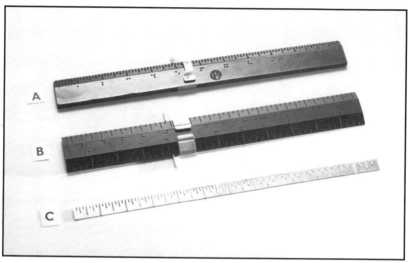

Figure 3.3. Braille rulers. (Photo courtesy of American Printing House for the Blind).

Glare on any materials will interfere with a student's use of functional vision. Hence, plastic or shiny pages should be eliminated. The use of a yellow plastic laminate over written material can increase contrast of print and, thus, produce a sharper copy, but it may result in glare and reduce perception of color. Whether or not the laminate is helpful for a particular student will have to be decided on an individual basis, but it is worth a try.

If manipulable objects are to be used during testing, present them on a tray, which keeps the objects where a student can easily locate them and reduces the need to search for fallen objects. Sides of the tray, such as the Work/Play tray available from APH, should be about 2 inches or less for easy access (see Figure 3.4).

Familiarity With Testing Instruments

Examiners need to be very familiar with the tests they will be using. If they are not, administration and scoring errors are likely, and the examiner may miss important observations of a student's performance while he or she searches through the manual for directions. Examiners who are unfamiliar with a particular test should administer it to sighted children first. This will demonstrate how sighted children perform on the test and give the examiner needed practice.

Figure 3.4. Work/Play trays. (Photo courtesy of American Printing House for the Blind).

Establishing Rapport

The assessment process for a student who is visually impaired or blind will require considerably more time than that required for a sighted student. Plan the schedule accordingly and try not to rush the process. A rushed examiner will have difficulty establishing good rapport and may miss important observations.

When accompanying a student who is blind or severely visually impaired to a room for testing, offer your arm to hold. If the student would like you to lead the way, she or he will take hold of your upper arm or elbow. Keep your arm close to your body. With young children, hold their hand or let them hold your wrist. Lead the way to the room, and *never* push a student. If you come to stairways or curbs, say so, and indicate whether it is a step up or down.

When talking to a student, first use his or her name so that the student knows to whom you are speaking. Speak using a normal voice level. The fact that a student has a visual problem does not mean that she or he has a hearing impairment also. Even if the student did have a hearing problem, speaking loudly would only distort the information.

It is not necessary to avoid using terms such as *see* or *look.* People who are blind readily use these words in their speech, and conversation will be awkward if an examiner tries to avoid using these terms.

On arrival at the room in which testing will take place, a student will need time to become oriented by exploring the room and feeling objects in the room. An examiner can physically guide or verbally encourage a student to do this. The examiner can help by describing the room, including the arrangement of furniture and the objects in the room. If a student chooses to explore the room independently, doors must be completely open or closed; a student could be injured by walking into a half-opened door. The same information that a sighted student obtains about the testing situation through sight will need to be conveyed to a student who is visually impaired or blind through auditory or tactile means.

The student will need to locate a chair and sit down to begin the testing. An examiner can help with this task either by placing the student's hand on the back of a chair and allowing the student to seat himself or herself or by positioning the student so that the side of his or her leg contacts the front of the chair. If the latter method is used, the examiner should indicate verbally that the student's leg is touching the chair in which he or she is to sit.

Adequate rapport is necessary prior to any testing. For some students this may require an extra session or two in which the only purpose is for the examiner and student to get to know one another and to establish easy communication. The purpose of the testing should be clearly explained to help reduce stress. If students who are visually impaired are tense, it can negatively affect their ability to employ their usable vision (e.g., as with nystagmus). A tense examiner is likely to miss observing relevant behaviors and have difficulty administering the tests.

The Testing Room

An important consideration is the room chosen for testing. (A boiler room or closet is *not* appropriate!) Not only should the room be free of glare, but it needs to be relatively free of background noise and reverberation.

Maximize the use of any usable vision that a student has by considering the following issues:

- Select a room without patterned wallpaper and without numerous items on the wall, such as mirrors and pictures.

- Seat the student so that he or she is not facing a window.

- Arrange the room so that testing materials are placed conveniently for the examiner but so that only materials currently in use are visually available to the student.

- Eliminate any flickering light. It can interfere with vision and may cause unnecessary fatigue.

- Some students will need light of rather high intensity whereas others will need low-intensity illumination. A light with a rheostat works well in adjusting light. The light source should come from the side of the more efficient eye.

Because students who are visually impaired or blind rely heavily on auditory input, extraneous noise must be minimized. The following factors should be considered:

- If possible, select a carpeted room with curtains or draperies. Acoustical tiles in the ceiling also help to provide an environment conducive to testing.

- Keep doors and windows closed.

- Avoid rooms with noisy air conditioners and heating ducts. Fluorescent lights that hum or buzz also may be distracting.

- Use of a "Quiet please. Testing in progress" sign can help to provide a quiet environment.

Checklist of Considerations Prior to Assessment

Figure 3.5 is a checklist of factors to be addressed prior to testing a student. If, at the scheduled time, preparations for assessment are not complete, or for some reason the student is not able to perform well, testing should be postponed (Boyle, 1977).

Considerations Prior to Assessment

☐ Complete the Information-Organizing Checklist for Infants and Preschoolers Who Are Visually Impaired or Blind or the Information-Organizing Checklist for School-Age Students Who Are Visually Impaired or Blind using information from interviews and school records.

☐ Carry out systematic direct classroom observation.

☐ Select appropriate assessment instruments, considering the test selection issues presented in this chapter and the reviews presented in the following chapters.

☐ Discuss the appropriateness of the selected assessment measures and procedures with the student's teacher and/or a consultant for students who are visually impaired or blind if there are any concerns.

☐ Practice administering and scoring any unfamiliar tests.

☐ Become familiar with any low-vision aids or other equipment the student uses in the classroom.

☐ Select a room that will maximize the student's use of hearing and any usable vision.

☐ Make sure that vision and hearing reports are up-to-date before testing.

☐ Arrange to have any special equipment and materials available for use during testing (e.g., large-print material, raised-line paper).

☐ On the day of testing, check with the student's teacher to ensure that the student does not have a problem with a cold, allergies, or other factors that might interfere with performance.

☐ Encourage student to explore testing room prior to testing.

☐ Answer any questions the student has and explain the purpose of the testing.

☐ Take a sufficient amount of time to establish rapport and easy two-way communication.

© PRO-ED, Inc. 1994

Figure 3.5. Checklist of considerations prior to assessment.
PRO-ED grants permission to duplicate this figure for teaching or clinical purposes only.

ISSUES TO CONSIDER DURING TESTING

The direct assessment of a child or adolescent who is visually impaired or blind is complex and time consuming. Use of several procedures during test administration will enhance the validity of results and aid in obtaining comprehensive information for eligibility decisions and planning educational programs. A discussion of these issues follows.

Description of Examiner Activity

Test taking can be anxiety provoking, especially for a student who is visually impaired or blind and who cannot see all that is taking place. To help reduce this anxiety and enable the student to understand what is occurring, the examiner should describe what she or he is doing. For example, an examiner can explain that she or he is putting materials away or taking them out, or can describe the fact that she or he is recording answers given by the student. With such descriptions, the student will not have to guess what is taking place during down times in sessions.

Use of Materials During Testing

Students who are blind and some students who are visually impaired cannot see objects or materials that are handed to them. Thus, it is helpful if an examiner explains that she or he will be handing the student something and then touches the student's hand with the object or places the student's hand on the material to identify its location. This procedure should prevent startling the student.

If materials or objects fall on the floor during testing, allow the student to pick them up, providing verbal rather than physical guidance. Verbal directions must be specific. For example, "To your left" is a functional direction, whereas "Put it here" or "That way" is meaningless to a student who is visually impaired or blind.

Communicating Directions

Additional examples or practice items may be needed to help a student who is visually impaired or blind understand the requirements of some tasks. Many tests have sample items. If it is apparent that a student does not understand a task after communication of directions and sample items, additional sample items may be necessary. It is critical, however, to avoid providing too many items and contributing to a practice effect (i.e., an inflated score resulting from practicing a particular type of task). To help a student understand task requirements, an examiner may wish to compare a new task with a previously completed task, ask the student to indicate what he or she is being asked to do, or use failed initial items or items skipped at an earlier age level as teaching items.

Praise for Effort

Because students who are visually impaired or blind are unable to see smiles and facial cues well, if at all, the examiner needs to convey approval of a student's performance through what is said and the tone of voice used. This often requires a conscious effort by an examiner. Physical contact, such as a pat on the shoulder, also can enhance a student's motivation to perform well as long as it does not startle the student.

Fatigue

Fatigue can interfere substantially with the performance of students who are visually impaired or blind. Eye strain and fatigue due to employing usable vision are likely to occur. Students who use Braille are apt to become fatigued from the effort and time it takes to read using this medium. Stress and fatigue can negatively affect a student's ability to use vision (e.g., in cases involving strabismus and nystagmus). There are many eye problems for which students are likely to suffer eye fatigue rather quickly. These include albinism, aniridia, and conjunctivitis. Testing should be discontinued when fatigue becomes evident. To ensure that fatigue does not depress performance, the examiner may need to administer each test over the course of several short sessions.

Students' Behavior

During testing, examiners may have different expectations for the behavior of a student with disabilities than for a student without

Considerations During Assessment

☐ Be sure the student is wearing glasses and uses visual aids if needed.

☐ Reduce stress for the student by describing your activity (e.g., recording responses or getting materials).

☐ Use specific rather than general directions (e.g., "To your left").

☐ Prior to handing the student something, indicate that you are going to do so before having the material or object touch the student's hand.

☐ Ensure the student's understanding of test directions by using a moderate number of practice items, comparing with prior tasks, or asking the student to explain the directions.

☐ Encourage the student to ask questions when uncertain.

☐ Praise the student for effort frequently and use an upbeat tone of voice.

☐ Be sensitive to fatigue by

_____ scheduling several short sessions,

_____ taking frequent breaks as needed, and

_____ discontinuing testing if fatigue is evident.

☐ Use behavior management procedures to maintain appropriate behavior and optimize test performance.

© PRO-ED, Inc. 1994

Figure 3.6. Checklist of considerations during assessment.
PRO-ED grants permission to duplicate this figure for teaching or clinical purposes only.

disabilities and thus be less willing to discipline a student who is disabled. Examiners should strive to maintain discipline throughout testing of a student who is visually impaired or blind, regardless of the presence of an impairment, because a child's inappropriate behavior can hinder test performance and result in an underestimate of abilities.

Checklist of Considerations During Assessment

Issues that are useful to consider while carrying out an assessment of a student who is visually impaired or blind are noted in Figure 3.6.

ISSUES TO CONSIDER AFTER TESTING

Once testing is complete, consideration of several factors can enhance the validity and usefulness of the information. These factors are addressed below, followed by a checklist to help in applying the information.

Notes on the Session

Because there are many things to keep in mind during the assessment of students who are visually impaired or blind, examiners should document difficulties encountered during testing, as well as any other factors that may qualify a student's performance. These notes should be made immediately after testing, or as soon thereafter as possible, when recall of the events is best.

Summarizing Procedures

Just as the examiner explained to the student the purpose of testing, he or she should inform the student when assessment is completed or when it will resume for another session. In either instance, an examiner can reduce anxiety by thanking a student for participating and by providing information about what will happen next.

The teacher should be consulted upon completion of testing to discuss the general findings, to plan any additional testing, and to confer regarding possible recommendations. This consultation should enhance the relevance of the final report.

Some caregivers tend to be overprotective of a child with an impairment and so may be anxious about their child's performance. They may fear that the child's visual loss impaired his or her performance and that results will, therefore, underestimate the child's abilities. It can help to communicate with the caregivers, informing them when the assessment is complete and providing some positive comments about a student's efforts. This contact also would provide caregivers an opportunity to ask any questions they have.

Reporting Results

It is more accurate to report test results using the standard error of measurement and to give results in terms of a range of performance than to report a single score from a test. This is particularly important when students with disabilities are assessed, because many of the tests used lack sufficient technical adequacy and because many other factors may affect test performance. Allen, White, and Karchmer (1983) noted that when student progress is slow, the use of the standard error of measurement is particularly important in describing results. Hence, use of the standard error of measurement is strongly recommended when reporting results of norm-referenced tests for these students.

When scores of questionable validity are obtained, some examiners report the scores with a qualification as to why the scores are questionable. Performance ranges (e.g., Below-Average Range) can be substituted for the scores along with appropriate qualification to help avoid misinterpretation.

Another consideration for reporting test scores is the age of the test used. Because it is sometimes necessary to administer out-of-date tests (i.e., older than 15 years) to visually impaired or blind students, inflated test scores may be obtained. Flynn (1984) found that, on the average, intelligence test scores tend to increase 0.3 of a point per year. Hence, a test that is 20 years old may yield a score that is inflated by as much as 6 points. An assumption of this point inflation should be made with caution, however, because it has not been found to occur in all types of tests.

If discrepancies occur between tests given to a student, the differences must be resolved in order to make appropriate decisions about a student's needs. Usually, the examiner can resolve a discrepancy by using the standard error of measurement, considering the age of tests used, and considering other differences in test characteristics. One test characteristic that might account for differences in results is a variation of technical adequacy, with the more technically adequate test being more likely to be accurate. Other test characteristics that may affect results include differences between the skills tested and in the type of responses required. Item-by-item comparisons may help resolve discrepancies.

Considerations After Assessment

☐ Record any difficulties that occurred during testing.

☐ Communicate the status of the assessment to the student and to his or her caregivers.

☐ Consult with the student's teacher regarding results, interpretations, and recommendations.

☐ Use assessment information to make recommendations for educational programs, placement, teaching procedures, and behavior-management strategies.

☐ Use the standard error of measurement to report norm-referenced test results.

☐ Use ranges of performance rather than test scores if test scores must be qualified.

☐ Resolve differences in results from different tests considering age of tests, differences in technical adequacy, test construction, and task requirements.

☐ Follow up on recommendations to evaluate their effectiveness.

☐ Objectively monitor the student's progress.

© PRO-ED, Inc. 1994

Figure 3.7. Checklist of considerations after assessment.
PRO-ED grants permission to duplicate this figure for teaching or clinical purposes only.

Follow-Up

To create a successful educational program, follow-up on recommendations resulting from the assessment must occur. An objective evaluation of a student's progress will indicate when modifications are needed in his or her educational program and when periodic reassessment may be needed. The use of systematic direct observation for behavior problems and curriculum-based measurement for achievement enables frequent monitoring of progress in these areas.

Checklist of Considerations After Assessment

Figure 3.7 provides an overview of issues to consider once testing is completed.

Chapter 4

Assessment of Infants and Toddlers

THIS CHAPTER DESCRIBES HOW THE ASSESSMENT OF INFANTS and toddlers differs from the assessment of older children. A discussion of the process of assessing young children who are visually impaired or blind follows, and background information on each area to consider for an assessment is presented, along with alternative measures. Areas addressed are: social skills, play, language, cognitive development, motor development, and adaptive behavior. The last two sections of the chapter contain detailed reviews of norm- and criterion-referenced tests, curriculum-based measures, and informal assessment methods.

DIFFERENCES FROM ASSESSING OLDER CHILDREN AND ADOLESCENTS

For this text, the terms "infants" and "toddlers" will include children from birth through age 2. The assessment of these young children differs from the assessment of older children and adolescents in several respects. In comparison, assessment of such young children is a new area, and therefore less is known about the process. The differences and the relatively limited amount of information available make assessment of infants and toddlers difficult, especially when the process is complicated by a serious visual loss.

One difference in the assessment process is the limited expressive and receptive language skills of these children and their inability to follow examiners' instructions. Hence, a considerable amount of information must be obtained from interviews and observation of an infant's or toddler's behavior during testing (Short, Simeonsson, & Huntington, 1990). An examiner must understand the development of young children well enough to know what behaviors to observe, in order to avoid missing a child's demonstration of skills. A good understanding of normal development and development of young children who are visually impaired and blind is needed. Becoming an efficient observer requires extensive experience with infants.

There are more areas to consider for assessment and intervention when working with infants and toddlers than when assessing older children. For example, in addition to considering social development, language, and cognitive development, the examiner must make note of areas such as play, motor skills, and parent-infant interaction. This makes the assessment time consuming, and infants and toddlers rarely are patient for extended periods of direct testing, further complicating the process.

In the assessment of older children, the skills tested are typically those that the children are taught directly, including math, written language, and reading. Most of the skills tested with infants and toddlers are those typically learned incidentally or as a result of maturation (e.g., walking, babbling). Therefore, if delays are found, it may be necessary to develop programs to teach these skills directly or to increase the child's rate of development.

During the period from birth through age 2, growth is especially rapid. In addition, the measures currently available for the assessment of young children often have problems with technical adequacy, especially those for children with severe visual losses. Thus, in order to obtain a valid picture of the development of such a young child, periodic reassessment is required. Conclusions about the development of an infant or toddler should be based on the trends of a child's development over time. The use of trends in development over time is particularly important when an infant or toddler is visually impaired or blind.

Finally, the assessment of young children requires the parents' involvement in the assessment process and in carrying out intervention plans. To involve the parents in a meaningful way during assessment, the examiner must be sensitive to the needs of the parents and infant and demonstrate good interpersonal skills. Making the parents active partners in the assessment provides an opportunity for the examiner to model appropriate interaction with the child and to demonstrate appropriate teaching methods. This involvement also may stimulate parents to ask questions and to provide valuable information that otherwise may not be available. Using common English, rather than scientific jargon, should help to make the parents comfortable and facilitate their involvement.

Despite the difficulties in testing infants and toddlers, the process is as interesting and enjoyable as it is challenging.

FAMILY ASSESSMENT

The passage of Public Law 99–457 (P.L. 99–457) (Education of the Handicapped Act Amendments, 1986) established a grant program for states to encourage the provision of services to infants and toddlers from birth to 36 months of age. Those who are eligible include children with documented delays in their development. In addition, states may choose to provide services to children in this age group who are at risk for substantial delay, such as children born to teenage mothers.

In addition to requiring an Individualized Educational Plan (IEP) for each child served, P.L. 99–457 requires the development of an Individualized Family Service Plan (IFSP) when services are provided to infants and toddlers. Parents and other family members should be actively involved with the multidisciplinary team in developing the IFSP. This plan should focus on the family's strengths, include the family's goals, and be reviewed every 6 months. Family assessment is a critical component in the provision of services to infants and toddlers with disabilities. For further discussion of the requirements of P.L. 99–457, see Short, Simeonsson, and Huntington (1990).

A number of the current measures for assessing family functioning are designed to tap constructs that at this time are of little use in intervention, such as parental stress. Some measures assess areas beyond those in which school personnel would intervene, such as marital conflict. And some measures have little if any data on their technical adequacy. Hence, the focus of the following discussion will be on measures that should provide information relevant to intervention, that have some demonstrated technical adequacy when possible, and that address areas of concern to school personnel.

Research on how to effectively carry out family assessment and intervention is only beginning to accumulate. The process can be very detailed and complicated, depending on the approach used. For a thorough and well-written description of the family assessment process, see *Family Assessment in Early Intervention* (Bailey & Simeonsson, 1988). Much of the following material is based on the work of Bailey & Simeonsson (1988).

Though family assessment could focus on many areas, three appear to be particularly relevant for families with infants and toddlers who are visually impaired or blind: family needs, critical events, and family resources. Other areas related to family functioning, including the home environment and parent-infant interaction, will be addressed in other areas of this chapter.

Bailey & Simeonsson (1988) warned examiners who are assessing family needs to avoid judging what a family "really" needs. Instead, they emphasized the importance of being responsive to each family's unique needs. A measure that can aid in an objective assessment of this area is the Family Needs Survey (Bailey & Simeonsson, 1988). This 35-item questionnaire completed by parents covers six categories of need: (a) information on a child's disability (such as the need for additional information on the child's condition or on techniques for teaching the child), (b) support from others (such as the need to talk with other parents of children who are visually impaired or blind), (c) help explaining the child's disability (such as how to explain the child's condition to his or her siblings), (d) help obtaining services (such as getting baby-sitters), (e) financial assistance (such as help paying for sitters or day care), and (f) help with family functioning (such as help planning recreational activities). A 3-point scale is used, with a 3 indicating that help definitely is needed. After the parents complete the survey, they are given paper and pencil and asked to list their "5 greatest needs as a family" (p. 109). This information can help set priorities and identify any needs that the scale might have missed. Finally, the examiner should discuss with the parents any needs that seem evident from this information. No technical data are available at this time on the survey, but items on the scale were based on the authors' work on a 5-year research project involving families with young children who have disabilities. The purpose of the project was to develop and field-test a model for assessing family needs.

Though all families experience some critical events that are disruptive and stressful, families of children with disabilities must deal with more such events. Bailey and Simeonsson (1988) described critical events that can be particularly difficult for families of children with disabilities. These events include: (a) coping with the initial diagnosis, (b) not reaching developmental milestones when peers without disabilities would, (c) obtaining services, (d) transitions from one program to another, (e) medical crises, and (f) normal life events. They suggested that families can cope better with these events if they anticipate them and receive needed support. A Critical Events Checklist, designed to be completed by an examiner while discussing the events listed with the parents, was developed by Bailey et al. (1986). The checklist consists of eight items: four nondevelopmental events (e.g., diagnosis, medical events) and four developmental events (e.g., child reaching age at which most children begin walking). Follow-up should be provided for events of concern. The authors warned examiners not to assume a problem if parents do not perceive one and to be careful not to create a problem by drawing attention to issues on the checklist. They also noted that situations change, making frequent monitoring to anticipate critical events necessary. Though no information on the technical adequacy of this scale is available, Bailey and Simeonsson (1988) cite numerous studies acknowledging these events as problems for families whose children are disabled.

In order to enhance the parents' confidence in their ability to address their child's needs, the examiner should consider the strengths of the family. P.L. 99–457 requires that family strengths be included in the IFSP; strengths can include resources within as well as outside the family. Dunst and Leet (1987) developed the *Family Resource Scale,* a 30-item scale to be completed by the parents. It tests seven factors ranging from basic nutrition to opportunities for growth. The factors are: (a) food and shelter, (b) financial resources, (c) time for the family, (d) extra family support, (e) child care, (f) specialized child resources, and (g) luxuries. A 5-point scale is used for each item, with a 1 indicating that a need is not at all adequately met and a 5 indicating that a need is almost always adequately met. Data on technical adequacy indicate a correlation of .92 for internal consistency and .95 for split-half reliability. Test-retest reliability, however, is only .52. Some data on validity are available with a measure of personal well-being ($r = .57$) and a measure of commitment to intervention ($r = .63$).

Information obtained when completing the Information-Organizing Checklist for Infants and Preschoolers Who Are Visually Impaired or Blind (see Figure 1.1) will address a number of family-functioning issues as they pertain specifically to young children who are visually impaired or blind. Items 13–16 of the checklist address daily care issues, 22–28 interaction with parents, 29–30 home environment, and 31–32 parental concerns.

THE ASSESSMENT PROCESS FOR YOUNG CHILDREN

Typically, a complete assessment of an infant or toddler who is visually impaired or blind requires several sessions. One reason for scheduling several sessions is to allow sufficient time to obtain comprehensive information on the various areas that will need to be assessed. These areas include social and play skills and development of language, cognition, motor, and adaptive skills. As noted above, assessment of family functioning will need to be carried out as well.

Another reason for spreading the assessment over several sessions is that covering all of the areas noted above is time consuming, and young children are likely to become fatigued and frustrated with too much interaction and stimulation, leading to a deterioration in performance.

Several sessions also tend to result in a more representative sample of behavior than would be obtained in a single session. Observing the child and family members on at least two different days provides a larger data base from which to draw conclusions.

During the first assessment session, the parents should complete as much of the Information-Organizing Checklist for Infants and Preschoolers Who Are Visually Impaired or Blind as possible. Conducting this interview in the home environment can help the parents and child to feel comfortable during their first encounter with the examiner, and a home visit allows an examiner the opportunity to observe the environment and the interaction of family members when in the home. If the interview is conducted outside of the home, an examiner must rely solely on the parents for accurate reporting of this information.

Once as much of the Information-Organizing Checklist has been completed as possible, the examiner should give the parents any surveys (e.g., the Family Needs Survey), rating scales, or checklists that they will need to complete. If the parents complete these scales while the examiner is present, they will be able to ask questions about the scales and any items with which they might need assistance. The examiner then can leave with the completed scales rather than waiting for the materials to be returned at a later date.

Prior to direct testing of a child who is visually impaired or blind, the examiner should review medical records to ensure that examinations for vision and hearing are up-to-date. A review of the functional vision report should provide considerable information relevant to planning the psychoeducational assessment (e.g., amount of lighting needed, whether to present light-colored toys on a dark background).

In order to avoid underestimating the ability of a young child with a serious visual loss and to help parents cope with missed developmental milestones, developmental progress for these children must be put into perspective. Frequently, infants and toddlers who are visually impaired or blind display delays in several areas, including social skills, play skills, language development, cognitive development, motor skills, and adaptive behavior. These delays are addressed in detail under the corresponding subheadings that follow. Typically, however, the delays are not large, usually amounting only to several months. If parents are made aware that certain skills such as walking may be delayed, they should not be as upset if their child does not walk at the age sighted children do as they would if they had not been prepared for this possibility. The general sequence of skill development for children with little or no vision is similar to that of sighted children. Ferrell et al. (1990), however, presented some preliminary data on infants with visual impairments suggesting that the sequence also may differ somewhat for these children.

With effective programming these delays can be lessened or avoided. By the time these children reach school age, they usually have caught up with their sighted peers in most areas. Social skills are likely to continue to be delayed, however, as well as some language skills. Whether these delays occur and to what extent varies with the individual child and his or her experiences.

Whenever norm-referenced tests standardized on sighted children are used with children who are visually impaired or blind, results should be interpreted in light of the fact that certain skills often require more time to develop for these children. Comparison with the norms for sighted children must be made only with qualifications, because experiences may differ considerably for children who are visually impaired or blind. The information that follows regarding possible delays should be considered when interpreting results from tests standardized on sighted infants and toddlers.

During direct testing of a child who has a severe visual loss, an examiner must be vigilant. Careful observation of a child's responses and methods of nonverbal communication is essential. The examiner must be sensitive to a child's signals, or important information will be lost. It is important to note a child's methods of nonverbal communication so that these can be discussed with the parents, in case they are unaware of these responses.

The pace and length of a testing session should be determined by an infant's or toddler's tolerance level. Rush yourself in order to obtain a child's best performance, but never rush a young child.

Using toys in which a child has shown an interest will enhance participation and help to keep a child engaged. Some trials with different objects may be necessary to determine which toys and objects are of the most interest.

During testing, the examiner must be particularly careful to avoid startling an infant or toddler who is visually impaired or blind. Many of these children will not be able to see a toy or person approaching them. Thus, when picking up a child or presenting an object, do so slowly and cautiously, and address the child by name before picking him or her up.

AREAS FOR ASSESSMENT

Detailed descriptions of the tests mentioned below are presented in either the Norm-Referenced Tests section or the Criterion-Referenced Tests, Curriculum-Based, and Informal Measures section that follows this section.

Social Skills

Bagnato and Neisworth (1991) suggested that play and social skills may be more important and relevant when assessing young children than the typical focus on cognition. Likewise, Rogers and Puchalski (1984) noted that teaching developmental skills should be delayed until "rewarding, reciprocal interactions for both mother and baby during play (and feeding!) are well established" (p. 56). Therefore, a discussion of social skills appears first in this section to emphasize the importance of this area for assessment and intervention for infants and toddlers.

Unfortunately, skills related to social competence are delayed for many children with visual impairments (Skellenger, Hill, & Hill, 1992). Raver and Drash (1988) also noted that it is not uncommon for children with a severe visual loss to require improvement in some social skills.

Social skills are first taught during infancy, and difficulties in this area are evident for many infants and toddlers who are visually impaired or blind. Before a child is able to communicate verbally, much of the interaction between infants with sight and their care-givers is through nonverbal behaviors that involve sight, such as facial expressions and eye contact (Field, 1982). Thus, a severe visual loss can negatively affect the quality of the interaction between an infant and caregiver (Fraiberg, 1974, 1977). Both infants and toddlers who are visually impaired or blind and their parents have been found to be deficient in the use of these nonverbal behaviors (Kekelis & Andersen, 1984; Preisler, 1988).

Rogers and Puchalski (1984) compared infants and toddlers who were visually impaired or blind (4 to 25 months old) to sighted infants and toddlers. The infants who were visually impaired or blind were less responsive to their mothers, in several ways were less reinforc-ing to their mothers, made fewer bids for attention, showed more negative affect, and displayed more negative vocalizations. Mothers of these infants were not as positive vocally and looked at their babies' faces less, which may have caused them to miss some of their infants' cues. Bailey and Simeonsson (1988) noted that these infants exhibited irregular smiling and smiled in response to auditory cues only. Preisler (1988) observed that parents were prone to misin-terpret nonverbal attempts at communication by 10- to 12-month-old infants with visual impairments. Thus, it is clear that severe visual losses interfere with the ability of these infants and toddlers to enjoy interacting with others. Such a situation requires special assistance in order to prevent, lessen, or eliminate these problems in interaction.

Assessment of social skills of infants and toddlers who are visu-ally impaired or blind requires systematic observation of the parents and the child. Assessment of the parent-child interaction is one com-ponent of a comprehensive family assessment (Bailey & Simeons-son, 1988). Some observation can occur during direct assessment of a child. For parents and infants or toddlers for whom there is concern, further observation may be necessary in the natural environment or clinic setting. Videotaping of a free play situation between the par-ents and child can be useful for assessment and intervention, and a tape can be coded using some method of systematic direct observa-tion, such as that described by Alessi and Kaye (1983). Then the tape might be used for teaching the parents to read their child's signals better and to use more effective patterns of interaction.

A norm-referenced measure of social skills for young children is the Personal-Social domain on the *Battelle Developmental Inventory* (Newborg, Stock, Wnek, Guidubaldi, & Svinicki, 1984). Though the

TABLE 4.1. *Measures for Instructional Planning for Social Skills for Infants and Toddlers Who Are Visually Impaired or Blind*

Tests	Sections	Type of Assessment	Adaptations
Bayley Scales of Infant Development (Bayley, 1969)	Infant Behavior Record	Informal rating scale	Only 1 item requires vision
Revised Brigance Diagnostic Inventory of Early Development (Brigance, 1991)	General Social & Emotional Development	Criterion-referenced	8 of the 36 items require some vision
Carolina Curriculum for Infants and Toddlers With Special Needs (Johnson-Martin Jens, Attermeier, & Hacker, 1991)	Self-Direction; Social Skills	Curriculum-based	Adaptations suggested in manual
Informal Assessment of Developmental Skills (Swallow, Mangold, & Mangold, 1978)	Social–Emotional	Informal checklist	None required
Oregon Project for Visually Impaired and Blind Preschool Children (Anderson, Boigon, & Davis, 1986)	Socialization	Curriculum-based	None required

test was standardized on sighted children, few of the items require vision. Besides being norm-referenced, the test may provide some general information for planning remedial programs.

Several measures listed in Table 4.1 can provide the detailed information needed for instructional planning. Information from these measures is particularly useful when combined with information obtained from systematic direct observation.

Play

Children learn to interact with the environment through play. Piaget (1952) described the importance of play to cognitive development. Play has an important role in the development of language and social skills as well.

With little or no visual stimulation, a child is unlikely to interact with the environment as a sighted child would. In the extreme case, if a child with little or no vision is not encouraged to explore the environment and to play, he or she will become passive and uninterested in his or her surroundings. If this child fails to actively explore the environment, motor, language, cognitive, and social skills may be negatively affected. Therefore, it is particularly important to observe the play behavior of an infant or toddler who is visually impaired or blind.

Children who have a severe visual loss may be delayed in the development of fine motor skills, resulting in a delay of play that requires fine motor skills as well.

Toys that are relatively large, such as giant texture beads and large peg boards available from the American Printing House for the Blind, are easy for a child with a serious visual loss to locate and use. Toys that provide auditory stimulation also are easier for these children to locate. Response-contingent toys help a child to learn that she or he is capable of affecting the environment. In other words, toys that move, make a noise, or provide tactile stimulation as a result of a child's action are appropriate. Some children with little or no vision are frightened by fuzzy or furry toys (Scott, Jan, & Freeman, 1985), but toys that provide other types of tactile input are suitable, including textured pegs and large textured blocks also available from the American Printing House for the Blind (see Figure 4.1).

These infants and toddlers should have access to a variety of toys that are appropriate for their developmental level (Skellenger et al., 1992). Use of the scales Schemes for Relating Objects or Construction of Objects in Space from the *Ordinal Scales of Psychological Development* (Uzgiris & Hunt, 1989), along with the Dunst (1980) supplementary manual, will help to determine what behaviors an infant or toddler uses with toys. Knowing what skills the child has learned and which should be taught next aids in selecting toys appropriate for a child's stage of development.

Figure 4.1. Large textured pegs. (Photo courtesy of American Printing House for the Blind).

When planning intervention programs for play, the examiner should ensure that infants and toddlers who are visually impaired or blind thoroughly explore toys to obtain tactile and kinesthetic input. It may be necessary to prompt some children to turn objects around and to explore them through touch. In other words, exploring objects may need to be targeted for instruction if these behaviors are not evident during testing.

Toddlers who are walking should have a specific place to store their toys. Children with a severe visual loss must learn the importance of organization early. Once they are walking, they should be given physical and verbal guidance to get their toys from the storage place and to return them to that place once they are finished playing with them. This is the beginning of teaching a child organization skills. Having a specific place for toys also encourages independence because it allows a child to locate his or her toys with minimal or no assistance.

Measures that can be used to obtain information for planning instruction of play skills are listed in Table 4.2.

TABLE 4.2. *Measures for Instructional Planning for Play for Infants and Toddlers Who Are Visually Impaired or Blind*

Tests	Sections	Type of Assessment	Adaptations
Bayley Scales of Infant Development (Bayley, 1969)	Infant Behavior Record	Informal rating scale	Only 1 item requires vision
Revised Brigance Diagnostic Inventory of Early Development (Brigance, 1991)	Play Skills; Work-Related Behavior	Criterion-referenced	7 of the 35 items require vision
Carolina Curriculum for Infants and Toddlers With Special Needs (Johnson-Martin et al., 1991)	Functional Use of Objects	Curriculum-based	Adaptations suggested in manual
Ordinal Scales of Psychological Development (Uzgiris & Hunt, 1989)	Schemes for Objects; Construction of Objects in Space	Domain-referenced	1 item requires vision; 11 items require vision, 8 could be adapted

Language Development

Though the language development of children who are visually impaired or blind is similar to that of sighted children, there are some differences, particularly in the rate of development of certain skills.

Scott et al. (1985) noted that children who are visually impaired or blind learn to recognize their names at about 12 months of age; sighted children typically acquire this skill between 7 and 9 months. Though these children babble at about the same age as sighted children, some may be delayed in speaking their first words, and a delay in labeling objects may be noted also (Fewell, 1983).

Scott et al. (1985) suggested that children who are visually impaired or blind should learn position concepts early. Thus, assessment of a toddler's knowledge of these concepts is beneficial. It may take a child with a severe visual loss longer to learn concepts such as *up* and *down*. Furthermore, these children must rely heavily on these concepts, more so than sighted children, to function effectively. Hence, they must learn these concepts as early as possible.

The use of personal pronouns such as *I* and *you* also may take longer to develop (Ferrell et al., 1990; Fewell, 1983; Fraiberg, 1977). Additional modeling and instruction may be needed to assist in the use of pronouns.

A norm-referenced measure that provides a score to describe language development is the *Battelle Developmental Inventory* (Newborg et al., 1984). There are 17 items in the Communication section for children from birth to 36 months old. Five of these items require some vision.

There are several options for obtaining information relevant to planning instruction in prespeech as well as speech and language skills. These measures are noted in Table 4.3. For prespeech skills the *Ordinal Scales of Psychological Development* (Uzgiris & Hunt, 1989) Vocal Imitation section would provide the most comprehensive information.

Cognitive

Presently no norm-referenced test of cognitive development has been standardized on children under age 6 who have little or no vision. Furthermore, the norm-referenced tests standardized on sighted children from birth to 36 months old require vision on a number of items, and it is not possible to adapt all of these items to circumvent limited vision or lack of vision. Because of these problems, it is impossible at this time to obtain a valid IQ score for infants or toddlers with little or no vision.

The best alternative for testing these children seems to be to estimate a child's abilities by using age-referenced items that do not require vision from tests standardized on a sighted population, or to use items that can be adequately adapted to circumvent visual requirements and still measure the same skills. Results can be described as an age range for items that a child was able to demonstrate. This type of estimate can help identify a child's current needs. An example of such a description follows.

TABLE 4.3. *Measures for Instructional Planning for Language for Infants and Toddlers Who Are Visually Impaired or Blind*

Tests	Sections	Type of Assessment	Adaptations
Revised Brigance Diagnostic Inventory of Early Development (Brigance, 1991)	Speech & Language	Criterion-referenced	*APH Tactile Supplement* (Duckworth & Stratton, 1992)
Carolina Curriculum for Infants and Toddlers With Special Needs (Johnson-Martin et al., 1991)	Language	Curriculum-based	None required
Informal Assessment of Developmental Skills (Swallow et al., 1978)	Language	Informal checklist	None required
Ordinal Scales of Psychological Development Uzgiris & Hunt, 1989)	Vocal Imitation	Domain-referenced	None required
Oregon Project for Visually Impaired and Blind Preschool Children (Anderson et al., 1986)	Language	Curriculum-based	None required

Elizabeth was able to complete nearly all of the cognitive tasks that did not require vision typically performed by children age 14 months and younger. Several items were adapted so that visual responses were not required, and feedback from sounds and touch was maximized. Adaptations included use of a larger set of pegs and pegboard that enabled Elizabeth to locate items and insert the pegs. Also, blocks with bells in them were used when she was asked to put blocks in a cup.

Tests that have sections assessing cognitive development with age-referenced items include the *Bayley Scales of Infant Develop-*

ment (Bayley, 1969) for children age 2 to 30+ months, the *Battelle Developmental Inventory* (Newborg et al., 1984) for birth through age 8, and the *Cognitive Abilities Scale* (Bradley-Johnson, 1987) for children age 24 to 48 months. All of these tests were standardized on sighted children; hence, many items on each scale require vision. Adaptations could be made to circumvent visual limitations for some items on these tests.

Because of the problems in using age-referenced items when overall scores cannot be determined, the results require very cautious interpretation. Results should be described along with information on other areas of development obtained from other tests and in light of observational and interview data.

Currently it is unclear what skills should be taught to infants and toddlers to enhance their cognitive development. Thus, though there are measures that provide results that could be used for developing programs to intervene in the cognitive area, the educational importance of each item on these scales should be evaluated for each child before instruction is planned. All of the scales listed in Table 4.4 contain a number of items of questionable relevance for later development.

Motor Skills

Both fine and gross motor development may be delayed for infants and toddlers who are visually impaired or blind. There can, however, be a great deal of individual variability in motor skill development, as there is for sighted children. A child's experiences can play a major role in either facilitating or inhibiting the development of motor skills. It seems that delays in development for children who are visually impaired or blind may not be a result of loss of vision alone, but a result of lack of experience in gross motor interaction with the environment as well (Schneekloth, 1989). If an infant has been hospitalized for a period of time and kept on his or her back, the baby's muscle tone is likely to be poor. Such a limited opportunity to practice moving can result in a serious delay in skill development.

Because a child with little or no vision is not enticed through visual stimulation from the environment, she or he may become passive compared to sighted peers. If a caregiver stimulates a child with sound-producing toys and physically prompts the child to move, few if any delays may be evident. Provision of orientation and mobility services to infants who are visually impaired has begun recently (Joffee, 1988; Hill, Dodson-Burk, & Smith, 1989). Such services can help to foster interaction with and exploration of the environment.

TABLE 4.4. *Measures for Instructional Planning for Cognitive Development for Infants and Toddlers Who Are Visually Impaired or Blind*

Tests	Sections	Type of Assessment	Adaptations
Revised Brigance Diagnostic Inventory of Early Development (Brigance, 1991)	General Knowledge & Comprehension	Criterion-referenced	*APH Tactile Supplement* (Duckworth & Stratton, 1992)
Carolina Curriculum for Infants and Toddlers With Special Needs (Johnson-Martin et al., 1991)	Cognitive	Curriculum-based	Adaptations suggested in manual
Informal Assessment of Developmental Skills (Swallow et al., 1978)	Cognitive	Informal checklist	None required
Ordinal Scales of Psychological Development (Uzgiris & Hunt, 1989)	All scales	Domain-referenced	5 of the 7 scales require vision; adaptations not given in manual
Oregon Project for Visually Impaired and Blind Preschool Children (Anderson et al., 1986)	Cognitive	Domain-referenced	None required

Some parents of children with disabilities become so concerned with their child's safety that they are overly protective and thereby severely limit their child's movement and interaction with the environment. Protecting a child from harm is critical, but a child who is visually impaired or blind needs as much contact with the environment as possible to avoid delays in development. Exploring the environment will facilitate cognitive, motor, and social development, independence, and curiosity. Thus, a safe, interesting environment where a child is encouraged to explore is very important for infants and toddlers who are visually impaired or blind.

When carrying out an assessment of motor development, an examiner should consider that it is not unusual for a child who is visually impaired or blind to take longer to develop some motor skills. This does not mean that all children with serious visual problems will be delayed in these areas. A visual impairment or blindness, however, does make it more difficult to learn the following skills.

Skills typically learned by sighted babies between birth and about age 1 that may require more time for a child with little or no vision to learn are:

- turning to sound

- reaching for toys that make sounds

- searching for a dropped toy (Most sighted babies exhibit this skill from 5 to 10 months of age, while infants who are visually impaired exhibit the skill at about 12 months of age, Ferrell et al., 1990.)

- lifting head and chest when on stomach

- holding head erect

- turning over

Anderson et al. (1986) suggested that the following skills may be delayed from birth to age 1 also:

- sitting self-supported and moving in and out of sitting position

- pulling to standing position

- crawling

Skills typically learned by sighted babies between approximately 1 and 2 years of age that may require more time to learn are:

- walking (Most blind children walk by about 20 months of age, Scott et al., 1985.)

- turning book pages
- using pull toys
- rolling and catching a large ball (Anderson et al., 1986)

Whenever norm-referenced tests standardized on sighted children are used with children who are visually impaired or blind, results should be interpreted in light of the fact that certain motor skills often require more time to develop for these children. The comparison with the norms for sighted children must be made only with qualifications, because the experiences for developing motor skills are different for children who are visually impaired or blind.

One gross motor behavior used between the ages of 18 and 30 months by some children who are visually impaired may seem to be unusual unless the reason for it is understood (Scott et al., 1985). Often children with visual impairments hold things several inches from their eyes in order to see them better, and this behavior can be tiring on the arms. Because the child's hip joints at this age are about at the midpoint of the body, some children may discover that it is possible to bend over and make a tripod by putting their head on the floor. This position, with forearms placed on the floor, is comfortable for the children and enables them to examine objects in their hands for rather lengthy periods of time. When the child's legs grow longer and the children can no longer be comfortable in this position, this behavior will disappear.

Two norm-referenced measures for assessing motor skills are the Motor Scale from the *Bayley Scales of Infant Development* (Bayley, 1969) and the Motor domain of the *Battelle Developmental Inventory* (Newborg et al., 1984). Both scales were standardized on a sighted population, but adaptations could be made for many of the items requiring vision.

Information for instructional planning can be obtained from several sources listed in Table 4.5.

Adaptive Behavior

There are several self-help skills that may require more time for some children to learn because of visual impairments or blindness:

- Often these children have difficulty learning to chew solid foods. Factors that contribute to the delay in learning to chew include the lack of visual enticement from the food and the difficulty seeing others chewing their food.

TABLE 4.5. *Measures for Instructional Planning for Motor Development for Infants and Toddlers Who Are Visually Impaired or Blind*

Tests	Sections	Type of Assessment	Adaptations
Revised Brigance Diagnostic Inventory of Early Development (Brigance, 1991)	Preambulatory Skills; Gross Motor Skills; Fine Motor Skills	Criterion-referenced	*APH Tactile Supplement* (Duckworth & Stratton, 1992)
Carolina Curriculum for Infants and Toddlers With Special Needs (Johnson-Martin et al., 1991)	Fine Motor Skills; Gross Motor Skills	Curriculum-based	None required
Informal Assessment of Developmental Skills (Swallow et al., 1978)	Psychomotor	Informal checklist	None required
Oregon Project for Visually Impaired and Blind Preschool Children (Anderson et al., 1986)	Fine Motor; Gross Motor	Curriculum-based	None required

- Learning to handle a spoon may take longer than for sighted children. Scooping can be particularly difficult.

- Children who are visually impaired or blind are more likely to throw a cup than to put it back on the table.

- Delays in fine motor skills can result in delays in self-help skills that require fine motor abilities.

TABLE 4.6. *Measures for Instructional Planning for Adaptive Behavior for Infants and Toddlers Who Are Visually Impaired or Blind*

Tests	Sections	Types of Assessment	Adaptations
Revised Brigance Diagnostic Inventory of Early Development (Brigance, 1991)	Self-Help Skills	Criterion-referenced	None required
Carolina Curriculum for Infants and Toddlers with Special Needs (Johnson-Martin et al., 1991)	Self-Help Skills	Curriculum-based	Adaptations suggested in manual
Informal Assessment of Developmental Skills (Swallow et al., 1978)	Self-Help Skills	Informal checklist	None required
Oregon Project for Visually Impaired and Blind Preschool Children (Anderson et al., 1986)	Self-Help Skills	Curriculum-based	None required

When assessing self-help skills, the examiner should note the degree to which the parents encourage and prompt a child to learn these skills. Bauman (1973) noted that in trying to be helpful to children who are visually impaired or blind, adults may interfere with, and even prevent, the usual learning experiences. Parents who are overly helpful will need to learn to allow their child to develop self-help skills in order to avoid an unnecessary delay in the child's development.

The Adaptive domain of the *Battelle Developmental Inventory* provides norm-referenced results for adaptive skills.

Table 4.6 lists four options for obtaining information for instructional planning in this area.

NORM-REFERENCED TESTS

Norm-referenced tests were reviewed if they were (a) designed to be individually administered, (b) published within the last 15 years (so that the content and norms were reasonably current), and (c) able to circumvent a visual loss (to ensure that results reflect a child's skills rather than a visual loss). One exception to these criteria was the *Bayley Scales of Infant Development*. This test was published more than 15 years ago and has numerous items that require vision, but it was included because the test options for assessing cognitive development are so limited that this test must be given consideration. The *Bayley Scales* currently is undergoing revision, with a new version to be available soon.

Many infants and toddlers with visual impairments can be tested with instruments designed for sighted children. In some cases, magnification or enlargement of test materials, special lighting, and other adaptations may be required.

The tests were reviewed in detail using the criteria presented in Chapter 1 to evaluate their technical adequacy. Descriptions of administration procedures, responses required, materials used, and scoring procedures are presented.

. . . .

• Battelle Developmental Inventory

> *Authors:*   Jean Newborg, John R. Stock, Linda Wnek,
> John Guidubaldi, & John Svinicki

> *Publisher:*   DLM/Teaching Resources
> One DLM Park
> Allen, TX 75002

> *Copyright:*   1984

GENERAL DESCRIPTION

The *Battelle Developmental Inventory* (BDI) is designed for children from birth through age 8. The purposes of the inventory are to provide data to aid in making decisions regarding diagnosis and eligibility for special education services, and to plan instructional programs.

The inventory consists of five domains: Cognitive, C
munication, Motor, Adaptive, and Personal-Social. E
domain is divided into several subdomains. Information ɪor
scoring can be obtained by directly testing a child, through
interviews, and through observation in the natural setting.
The manual suggests that "examiners should use the procedures that will yield the best data" (p. 8). Scores are given
for the total test, each domain, and each subdomain. Scores
are in the form of percentiles, standard scores (Z, t, deviation
quotients, and normal curve equivalents), and age equivalents. The BDI also has a Screening Test.

The Screening Test takes from 10 to 30 minutes to administer. The BDI requires 1 hour or less for children under 3 or
over 5 years old, and 1½ to 2 hours for children between age 3
and 5.

Each item is scored either 2 (full credit), 1 (attempted or
an emerging skill), or 0 (fail). This is a useful scoring system
for planning educational activities because items scored as
emerging would be appropriate to target first for instruction.

Materials for the BDI include an examiner's manual, six
test books, and an envelope of visual materials. Toys and
other materials needed are those "commonly found in preschool and primary level programs" (p. 2) and must be obtained
by the examiner prior to testing along with supplementary
materials for children who are visually impaired or blind.
Lists of these materials are presented in the manual. An
examiner would have to gather the materials in advance of
testing, especially for older children, because of the time
needed to make or obtain them. For example, on the Cognitive
domain, two items require Braille cards, one a raised figure,
and one a Braille clock. On the Motor domain, 10 raised figures are needed, and a beeper ball is required for several
items.

Both general adaptation procedures and specific adaptations for certain items are suggested for children with disabilities. The purpose of the adaptations is "to provide a means by
which specific barriers to assessing a given behavior, posed by
given handicapping conditions, can be overcome without
changing the behavior that is being assessed" (p. 15). Unfortunately, this is not the case for children who are severely
visually impaired or blind. For these children, each domain
contains items for certain age levels that must be scored 0
because of a child's visual loss. Some of these items are scored

0 because the adaptation indicates that it is "for instructional use only," whereas other items have no adaptations and require vision. Most of these items appear on the Cognitive domain, making it almost impossible to obtain a valid score at any age level for this type of child. If enough of these items were scored 0 and a test score determined, the score likely would underestimate a child's performance. In the other domains there are from one to four of these items. Hence, valid scores might be obtained on this test for children who are visually impaired but not for children with no useful vision on all domains. However, the BDI still could provide useful information for instructional planning for children with little or no vision or for describing a range of performance based on the age levels of items passed.

DESCRIPTIONS OF THE SCREENING TEST AND DOMAINS

Screening test.

The 96-item Screening Test contains two items per age level from each of the five domains. The Screening Test helps determine whether to give the entire BDI. If a child scores one standard deviation or more below the mean, the entire BDI should be given. Because of the limited number of items per age level, the Screening Test will not be of much use, especially for a child with little or no vision. It would be risky to make a decision on a child's abilities based on such a small sample of behavior. A better approach may be to skip the Screening Test and go directly to the BDI domains.

Cognitive domain.

This domain taps abilities "conceptual in nature" (p. 6) and consists of four subdomains: Perceptual Discrimination (e.g., feeling and exploring objects, matching words), Memory (e.g., following an auditory stimulus, repeating digits), Reasoning and Academic Skills (e.g., uncovering a hidden toy, simple math problems), Conceptual Development (e.g., identifying objects by use, sorting by shape and color). There are 56 items on the domain, but the number of items per age level varies from 3 to 12, with the majority of levels having fewer than 7 items. Thus, the number of items provides a very limited sample of a child's skills, especially if a child has no useful vision. Following is a list of the number of items that must be scored 0 for a child with no useful vision:

Age level (months)	Number of items scored 0
0–5	2 of 6
6–11	0 of 3
12–23	0 of 3
24–35	3 of 5
36–47	0 of 4
48–59	0 of 8
60–71	1 of 12
72–83	3 of 8
84–95	1 of 7

Depending on his or her age, a score determined from this domain for a child with little or no vision likely would be an underestimate of the child's ability. Scores for the four sub-domains within the Cognitive domain would be based on so few items that they would be meaningless. Even scores for children with at least some useful vision would have to be interpreted cautiously because of the limited number of items involved. The number of items administered is further limited by the basal and ceiling rules.

Communication.

This domain assesses both the receptive and expressive aspects of language and is made up of 59 items. The Receptive subdomain tests discrimination (e.g., discriminates nonsense and real words) and meaning (e.g., follows two-part commands). The Expressive subdomain covers sounds (e.g., produces one or more vowel sounds), grammar rules (e.g., uses plural ending with *s* or *z* sound), and meaning-usage (e.g., uses 10 or more words). The number of items per age level ranges from 4 to 10, with the majority having fewer than 7 items. Only 3 items in this domain would be scored 0 because of lack of vision: 1 of 7 items at the 4- to 5-year level, and 2 of 10 items at the 5- to 6-year level. Considering the basal and ceiling rules and the limited number of items, scores from this domain may be questionable as well.

Motor.

This domain assesses use of large and small muscles and is made up of five subdomains: Muscle Control (e.g., holds head up for at least 5 seconds when on stomach), Body Coordination (e.g., turns a somersault), Locomotion (e.g., runs a distance of 10 ft. without falling), Fine Muscle (e.g., folds a sheet of paper), and Perceptual Motor (e.g., reaches for and touches an object). The domain consists of 82 items, with a range of 6 to 11 items per age level. The majority of levels have more than 7 items. Thus, the domain score will sample quite a few behaviors, even with the basals and ceilings applied. Whether the subdomains sampled enough behaviors to yield a score that can be interpreted will have to be examined for each child tested. Only 3 items must be scored 0 if a child has little or no vision: 1 of 9 items at the 5- to 6-year level, 1 of 7 at the 6- to 7-year level, and 1 of 6 at the 7- to 8-year level.

Adaptive.

Five subdomains make up the 59-item Adaptive domain. Subdomains are: Attention (e.g., visually attends to an object for 5 seconds or more), Eating (e.g., anticipates feeding), Dressing (e.g, puts on shoes without assistance), Personal Responsibility (e.g, demonstrates caution and avoids common dangers), and Toileting (e.g., sleeps through the night without wetting the bed). The number of items per age level ranges from 3 to 10, with the majority having fewer than 7 items. Again, with the basal and ceiling rules, the small number of items per age level, and the five subdomains, the subdomain scores probably will be based on too few items to be valid. Further, at the 0- to 5-month level, 2 of the 5 items are scored 0 if a child has no usable vision. At the 6- to 11-month level, 2 of the 7 items are scored 0.

Personal-social.

This 85-item domain assesses abilities related to "meaningful social interactions" (p. 5). There are six subdomains: Adult Interaction (e.g., explores adult facial features), Expression of Feelings/Affect (e.g., enjoys playing with other children), Self-Concept (e.g., identifies self in mirror), Peer Interaction (e.g., shares property with others), Coping (e.g., complies with adult directives), and Social Role (e.g., dramatizes in play). The number of items per age level ranges from 4 to 15, with the majority having more than 7 items. Depending on a child's age, the domain score might be based on a sufficient sample of behaviors, but the subdomains probably will not. Only 1 item on this domain receives a 0 if a child has no vision, and this is at the 6- to 11-month level. This domain seems worthwhile to administer, especially for children who are visually impaired or blind.

TECHNICAL ADEQUACY

Standardization.

Data were collected from December of 1982 until March of 1983. The sample corresponds closely to the 1981 U.S. census data in terms of geographic distribution, gender, and race. According to more recent census data, however, the percentages of black children (8.9%) and those of Spanish origin (6.4%) are too low. In terms of geographic distribution, about 75% were urban and 25% rural. No data are presented on the socioeconomic status of the parents except that it is stated in the manual that test sites that had a wide range of socioeconomic levels were selected. The number of subjects per age level for 24 months through 95 months approximates 100 (range 90 to 102). For birth to 23 months there were only 49 to 54 subjects per level, which is considerably below 100. Thus, the sample appears to be representative in terms of geographic distribution, gender, and urban/rural residency, but data on race and ethnicity do not appear to be representative according to recent census data. Data are needed on socioeconomic status, and more subjects are needed for age levels below 24 months.

Reliability.

Test-retest data are given by age level for 183 children (about 18 per age level) with a 4-week interval. Correlation ranges for the domains were: Cognitive .84–.98, Communication .76–.96, Motor .88–.99, Adaptive .84–.99, and Personal-Social .92–.99. Range for the BDI total was .90–.99. Data are provided for subdomains also.

Interrater reliability is presented by age level for subdomains, domains, and totals. The range for the total score was .93–.99. Domain ranges were: Cognitive .86–1.0, Communication .85–.98, Motor .91–.99, Adaptive .93–.99, and Personal-Social .86–.99.

Standard errors of measurement are given by age level for subdomains, domains, and total test.

Validity.

Items were selected based on review of existing tests and then evaluated by numerous experts in each area. The instrument was pilot tested several times, the last time with 500 children from birth to age 8. Item difficulty and item-total score correlations were used for assigning age levels and sequencing the items. These procedures suggest good content validity, and the test does seem to sample a range of important behaviors. The problem is the lack of sufficient items per age level, resulting in a limited sample of skills.

In terms of construct validity, factor analysis indicated that the subdomains intercorrelate quite well. The domains tend to be more accurate for children over 2 years old. The intercorrelation of BDI component scores is quite high. Age comparisons indicate that scores tend to increase with age.

In terms of diagnostic validity, a study was carried out with clinical (160 children with different disabilities) and non-clinical samples. All domain and total scores indicated significant differences between the two groups.

For criterion-related validity, comparisons were made with the *Vineland Social Maturity Scale* (Doll, 1965) ($n = 37$), the *Developmental Activities Screening Inventory* (DASI) (DuBose & Langley, 1977) ($n = 36$), the *Stanford-Binet Intelligence Scale* (Terman & Merrill, 1960) ($n = 23$), the *Wechsler Intelligence Scale for Children–Revised* (WISC–R) (Wechsler, 1974) ($n = 10$ for Verbal and Performance, 13 for Full Scale), and the *Peabody Picture Vocabulary Test* (PPVT) (Dunn & Dunn, 1981) ($n = 15$). The BDI correlated most highly with the *Vineland* and the DASI. This was true even for the Cognitive domain. Although acceptable correlations were obtained with the *Binet,* WISC–R, and PPVT (though all of these studies used only a small number of subjects), the BDI seems to measure skills that are more similar to tests assessing adaptive behaviors and motor skills than to intelligence tests.

CONCLUSIONS

Standardization of the BDI appears representative except that no socioeconomic data were given, an insufficient number of children were included below 24 months of age, and racial and ethnic groups were underrepresented according to current census data. Excellent data were obtained on reliability. Additional validity information is needed on the test's ability to discriminate between specific diagnostic groups, predictive ability, and criterion-related validity with larger samples. Because of the small number of items, most subdomain and some domain scores would be meaningless, especially for children with little or no vision.

This inventory has the advantage of describing how many of the items can be adapted for children with little or no vision, though not all items can be adapted. The age-referenced item groups could be used to help describe a range of performance for children with little or no vision. Some general information could be obtained for instructional planning, but criterion-referenced information would be needed for program planning also. A particular strength of the test is the Personal-Social domain.

. . . .

• Bayley Scales of Infant Development

Author: Nancy Bayley

Publisher: The Psychological Corporation
555 Academic Court
San Antonio, TX 78204

Copyright: 1969

GENERAL DESCRIPTION

The *Bayley Scales of Infant Development* was designed for children age 2 to 30 months. Normal or above-average children of 24 months or older may not achieve a ceiling on this test. The purpose of the *Bayley Scales* is to provide norm-referenced scores to describe a child's current level of performance in terms of mental and motor development. The *Bayley Scales* consists of three parts: the Mental Scale, the Motor Scale, and the Infant Behavior Record. The Infant Behavior Record is an informal measure rather than a standardized test; thus it is reviewed in the Criterion-Referenced Tests, Curriculum-Based, and Informal Measures section of this chapter.

Scores for the Mental and Motor scales are standard scores in the form of deviation quotients with a mean of 100 and a standard deviation of 16. Each item is scored *pass, fail,* or *other. Other* includes omissions, refusals, and parent report. Only *pass* items are considered in scoring.

Administration time for both scales is from 45 to 75 minutes. Tests are to be given with the mother or a mother substitute present.

Materials include a test manual, record books for each of the three sections, and numerous toys contained in the kit. Also needed for testing, but not included in the kit, are sheets of 8½- by 11-in. paper and some facial tissues for the Mental Scale, and a set of stairs and a walking board for the Motor Scale. Examiners must exercise caution to ensure a child's safety when using some of the test materials. The rattle that usually comes with the kit is of a size considered dangerous by the Consumer Product Safety Commission because it is small enough to become lodged in a child's throat. The cubes, beads, and doll head (for "Mending broken doll") also are small enough to fit in a child's mouth, and a child could choke on them.

No adaptations are given in the manual for using the *Bayley Scales* with children who are visually impaired or blind. Many items do require vision.

DESCRIPTION OF THE SCALES

Mental scale.

This scale consists of 163 items. A wide variety of skills are tapped, but sensory and motor abilities primarily are emphasized. According to the manual, the following skills are tested: sensory perception, object constancy, memory, learning, problem solving, vocalizations, early verbal communication, formation of generalizations, and classification. There are too few items in each of the areas to be able to draw conclusions for planning specific educational programs. The results can be used only to describe a child's current overall level of performance.

Motor scale.

A wide variety of gross and fine motor skills are assessed. Of the 81 items on this scale, 14 require vision.

TECHNICAL ASPECTS

Standardization.

A total of 1,262 subjects participated, with 83 to 95 children per age level. Subjects were selected to correspond to the 1960 census data in terms of gender, race, educational attainment of the head of household, and urban/rural residence. Children in rural areas were underrepresented, and a geographically representative sample was not obtained, as indicated in the following information where the data are compared to the 1960 and 1990 census data:

	Bayley	**1960**	**1990**
	Percentage	*Percentage*	*Percentage*
Northeast	28	23	19
Northcentral	18	30	24
South	17	32	36
West	37	16	21

There were too few children from the Northcentral and South regions and too many children from the West.

Reliability.

No test-retest data are reported in the manual on the current version of the test. On an earlier version of the *Bayley Scales,* a 1-week retest was carried out for twenty-eight 8-month-old babies. Agreement obtained was 76% on the Mental Scale and 75% on the Motor Scale. The 1-week interval was too short to be of much use, and the percentages were too low for data used in eligibility decisions. Furthermore, data are needed for each age level, not just for babies 8 months old.

Interrater reliability for ninety 8-month-olds was calculated using percent agreement. For the Mental Scale an 89% agreement was found, and a 93% agreement was obtained for the Motor Scale.

Standard errors of measurement are provided for both the Mental and Motor scales by age level.

Split-half reliabilities range from .81 to .93 for the Mental Scale and from .68 to .92 for the Motor Scale.

Validity.

The examiner must be cautious when interpreting results from the Mental Scale because it is questionable whether some of the items are measuring mental abilities related to later intelligence (e.g., reaches for a second cube, places pegs in 30 rather than 40 seconds, drops six beads in a box). This may be one factor that accounts for the poor predictive validity of the Mental Scale. Fagan (1982) pointed out that studies correlating the *Bayley Scales* (given during the first year) and the *Binet* (given at about age 3) show average correlations of about .18 for high-risk and clinic samples. He suggested that the sensory and motor skills assessed may be unrelated to later intelligence.

One concurrent validity study is cited in the manual for the Mental Scale with the *Stanford-Binet* (Terman & Merrill, 1960) for 120 children. Correlations ranged from .47 to .64.

CONCLUSIONS

Given the problems with the standardization, reliability, and validity, and because of the lack of adaptations on the Mental Scale for children with little or no vision, the *Bayley Scales* is not a useful test for children who have severe vision problems. Presently there are so few options for assessing cognitive development for infants and toddlers that some information from the test probably will have to be used. Such information must be evaluated in light of the limitations of the test and in conjunction with information from testing other areas of development with other measures. No valid score will be possible for children with little or no vision on the Mental Scale, though it may be possible to obtain a valid score for many children who are less visually impaired. Because the items are age-referenced, the age levels of items on which a child with little or no vision was successful could be used to describe a performance range for the child. Most items on the Motor Scale could be used with children who are visually impaired or blind. A new version of the *Bayley Scales* will be available soon.

. . . .

• Cognitive Abilities Scale

Author: Sharon Bradley-Johnson

Publisher: PRO-ED
8700 Shoal Creek Boulevard
Austin, TX 78757-6897

Copyright: 1987

GENERAL DESCRIPTION

The *Cognitive Abilities Scale* (CAS) is designed for children 2 and 3 years old to assess their cognitive development using educationally important tasks.

The CAS consists of five subtests: Language, Reading, Mathematics, Handwriting, and Enabling Behaviors (assessing imitation and memory skills). There are some items on each of the subtests that require vision. Hence, no overall score or subtest score could be obtained for a child with little or no usable vision. There are 45 items that do not require vision, and test items are age referenced. The age-referenced information could be helpful in describing a child's performance.

For children who do not have a severe visual loss, a Cognitive Quotient (mean = 100, standard deviation = 15) is used to describe overall cognitive development. A Nonvocal Cognitive Quotient can be used to describe overall cognitive development for children who cannot talk, will not talk, or whose speech cannot be understood. Standard scores (mean = 10, standard deviation = 3) or percentiles can be used to describe subtest performance for children whose language is understandable.

Administration time for the entire test varies from 30 to 45 minutes. The time varies as a function of a child's skills and the sections used, and the CAS is administered individually.

Materials consist of an examiner's manual, a record form, a child's book and a set of 31 toys. For children with vision, the set of picture cards is needed also.

DESCRIPTION OF THE SUBTESTS

Language.

This 30-item subtest has 14 items that could be used with children who have little or no vision. Nine of these items tap the understanding of position words such as *in* and *up*. Five items assess expressive syntax including use of regular plurals and apostrophes indicating possession. The sections assessing understanding and use of nouns and pronouns require vision.

Reading.

There are 16 items on this subtest, and all but 2 require vision. One item that does not require vision involves asking the child to remember one idea from a story he or she is told; the other requires turning pages of a book one at a time. Other skills assessed include book-handling skills, response to books, and knowledge of letters.

Mathematics.

This is a 22-item subtest, with 15 items that do not require vision. These items tap various skills including an understanding of concepts applied to objects such as "big" and "little," rote counting, and three of the steps for meaningful counting.

Handwriting.

Skills assessed on this subtest include writing posture, pencil grip, copying, and imitation of figures related to writing letters. Vision is required for all six items on this subtest.

Enabling.

The 14 items on this subtest assess auditory memory and willingness to imitate verbally and physically. All items could be used with children with little or no vision. For the items involving physical imitation, physical guidance would be needed to demonstrate the movement.

TECHNICAL ADEQUACY

Standardization.

The standardization sample of 2- and 3-year-olds included 536 children, with 91 to 170 children per 6-month age interval. The children's demographic characteristics corresponded closely to the 1985 census data in terms of parents' occupational levels, race, geographic distribution, ethnicity, gender, and urban/rural residence. No data are available on children who are visually impaired or blind, nor have any studies been carried out with this population using the CAS.

Reliability.

Test-retest reliability was evaluated in two studies using a 2-week retest interval. Stability coefficients by age level for the Cognitive Quotient were .90 or higher. Correlations for subtests ranged from .69 to .98.

Internal consistency coefficients ranged from .75 to .94 for the subtests. For the Cognitive Quotient, the correlations were .90 or higher.

Standard errors of measurement are given by age level.

Validity.

Item selection was based on item analysis. Also, a rationale for the educational importance of each item is presented in the manual.

Some of the items on the CAS are of the type typically found on intelligence tests; whereas others are of the type typically found on achievement tests. Thus, it is difficult to characterize the test as either an intelligence or achievement test. The expectation was that results from the CAS would be related to results of both types of tests, and correlations indicated that this was the case. When compared to the *Kaufman Assessment Battery for Children* (KABC) (Kaufman & Kaufman, 1983) Mental Composite and Achievement sections, the *Stanford-Binet Intelligence Scale,* Form L–M (Terman & Merrill, 1972), the *Test of Early Reading Ability* (Reid, Hresko, & Hammill, 1981b), and the *Test of Early Language Development* (Reid, Hresko, & Hammill, 1981a), correlations ranged from .59 to .84.

Long-term predictive validity over approximately a 5-year period was examined with both intelligence and achievement tests for 2- and 3-year-olds (Clemmer, Klifman, & Bradley-Johnson, 1992). A correlation of .50 (.66 corrected) was obtained with the *Stanford-Binet Intelligence Scale–Fourth Edition* (Thorndike, Hagen, & Sattler, 1986) and .52 (.63 corrected) for the *Wechsler Intelligence Scale for Children–Revised* (Wechsler, 1974). For achievement tests correlations were: .37 (.52 corrected) with the *Test of Early Reading Ability–Second Edi-*

tion (Reid, Hresko, & Hammill, 1989), .43 (.59 corrected) with the *Test of Early Mathematical Ability* (Ginsburg & Baroody, 1983), .42 (.52 corrected) with the *Kaufman Test of Educational Achievement* (KTEA) (Kaufman & Kaufman, 1985) Reading, and .50 (.61 corrected) with the KTEA Mathematics.

Data are provided to show that CAS scores increase with age and discriminate between children with and without mental retardation. Moderate correlations were found for all subtests with the Cognitive Quotient.

CONCLUSIONS

No data are available on the use of the CAS with children who are visually impaired or blind. Given the limited number of appropriate instruments available for this population, however, it may be necessary to use items from this scale with these children because the items are age referenced. Caution should be exercised in interpreting results when this is done, given the lack of data on children who are visually impaired or blind. The CAS has been shown to be well-standardized, reliable, and valid for sighted children. Its results seem to hold up even over a 5-year period. An overall score could be obtained for some children who are visually impaired but not for children who are blind or who have little usable vision.

. . . .

CRITERION-REFERENCED TESTS, CURRICULUM-BASED, AND INFORMAL MEASURES

One criterion used to select measures for review was that the measures were comprehensive enough to provide the detailed information necessary for instructional planning. Checklists were not considered because of the cursory nature of the information they provide. A second criterion for selection was that the instruments did not require vision, or provided adaptations, for most of the items.

The test reviews that follow include an evaluation of the technical adequacy of the measures and descriptions of materials and administration procedures.

. . . .

• Bayley Scales of Infant Development: Infant Behavior Record

Author: Nancy Bayley

Publisher: The Psychological Corporation
555 Academic Court
San Antonio, TX 78204

Copyright: 1969

GENERAL DESCRIPTION

The Infant Behavior Record (IBR) is part of the *Bayley Scales of Infant Development* but is not a part of the standardized test. Instead, this is a type of rating scale in which ratings for each item can be compared to a table indicating the percent of children in an age group who received the same rating. The purpose of the IBR is to assess a child's "characteristic behavior patterns" (p. 99).

The only materials needed are the manual and record book. The IBR is to be completed by an examiner immediately after the administration of the *Bayley Scales*. The IBR could be used after completing testing with other measures as well. Thus, ratings are based on observation of a child's performance during testing. No adaptations are needed for children who are visually impaired or blind. One item requires rating a child's interest in sight-looking. This item could be left out of the ratings if needed.

DESCRIPTION OF ITEMS

There are 30 items on the IBR. The first 15 assess categories of behavior such as cooperativeness, fearfulness, activity, and general emotional tone. Most items are rated on a scale of 1 to 9, two have scales of 1 to 5, and two are scored yes or no. In addition, for eight of these items there are checklists for other related behaviors that were noted. Nine items deal with a child's degree of interest in sensory areas such as listening to sounds, body motion, and mouthing or sucking a pacifier. Three items tap the degree of energy and coordination displayed; one item requires the examiner to rate the adequacy of the test as an indication of a child's characteristics; one requires noting any deviant behavior observed; and the last is a general evaluation of a child as normal or exceptional.

TECHNICAL ADEQUACY

Field test or standardization.

Frequencies in the table are based on data for 40 to 94 cases per age level. More than half of the age levels had fewer than 55 subjects. Most of the children were those who participated in the standardization of the *Bayley Scales*.

In the manual, various "suggestive" findings of work with the IBR are discussed. The findings show that certain items seem to be related to cognitive performance, and some items may discriminate between groups of "suspect" infants and normal infants. However, too little information is presented on the studies to draw any conclusions.

Reliability and validity.

No reliability or validity information is presented for the IBR.

CONCLUSIONS

The ratings on the IBR are based on subjective impressions of the examiner and should be interpreted as such. The IBR could be used as one source of informal information to describe some of a child's social and play behaviors. Behaviors observed that could affect learning (in either a positive or negative way) would be useful to note for instructional planning. The IBR prompts an examiner to consider many important behaviors that might otherwise be overlooked; herein lies its strength.

. . . .

• Revised Brigance Diagnostic Inventory of Early Development

Author: Albert Brigance

Publisher: Curriculum Associates
5 Esquire Road
North Billerica, MA 01862-2589

Copyright: 1991

• APH Tactile Supplement

Authors: Bill J. Duckworth & Josephine M. Stratton

Publisher: American Printing House for the Blind
1839 Frankfort Avenue
P.O. Box 6085
Louisville, KY 40296

Copyright: 1992

GENERAL DESCRIPTION

This inventory is designed for children from birth through age 6. Its purpose is to provide criterion-referenced information for instructional planning.

Eleven sections make up the test: Preambulatory Motor Skills and Behaviors, Gross Motor Skills and Behaviors, Fine Motor Skills and Behaviors, Self-Help Skills, Speech and Language Skills, General Knowledge and Comprehension, Social and Emotional Development, Readiness, Basic Reading Skills, Manuscript Writing, and Basic Math.

The administration time can vary from 15 minutes to 2 hours depending on how much of the inventory is used. Administration procedures are described clearly and concisely in the manual.

Materials consist of the manual and a record book. Quite a few easily obtained toys and materials are needed, and an optional materials kit is available. For examiners who choose to use their own materials, arrangements will need to be made to ensure that the items needed are available before testing begins. The author gives permission for duplication of pages needed for testing.

No adaptations are suggested for children who are visually impaired or blind; however, the American Printing House (APH) for the Blind has prepared a tactile supplement for this inventory. The *APH Tactile Supplement for the Brigance Diagnostic Inventory of Early Development* (Duckworth & Stratton, 1992) is to be used in conjunction with the print edition from Curriculum Associates. The *APH Tactile Supplement* provides alternative procedures and tactile materials for items that involve visual stimuli. Additional directions and suggestions are provided where necessary. For example, alternative methods are suggested for eliciting behaviors from children with little or no vision. Materials for the *APH Tactile Supplement* include an examiner's manual, a flip-book of tactile stimuli, and tabs to be placed on pages in the *Brigance* manual (see Figure 4.2).

DESCRIPTION AND EVALUATION OF SUBTESTS

Preambulatory Motor Skills and Behaviors.

This subtest consists of 14 skills tested in supine, 10 in prone, 10 when sitting, and 12 when standing. This comprehensive section has pictorial sequences that are particularly useful for educating parents about what behaviors to teach next and why. The *APH Tactile Supplement* provides alternate methods of eliciting behaviors as well as cautions regarding differences that can occur in development of these skills for infants and toddlers who are blind. For example, it is noted that children with visual impairments frequently dislike being in the prone position and therefore may have had limited experience in this position. This situation may result in delayed development of skills requiring the prone position, such as crawling.

Gross Motor Skills.

Skills tested include standing, walking, stairs and climbing, running, jumping, hopping, kicking, using a balance beam, catching, and rolling and throwing. The *APH Tactile Supplement* is needed for this section when assessing children with little or no vision.

Fine Motor Skills and Behaviors.

Skills tested include general eye/finger/hand manipulative skills, block tower building, prehandwriting, drawing a person, copying forms, and cutting with scissors. A number of these items require vision. Hence, for children with little or no vision, the *APH Tactile Supplement* should be consulted.

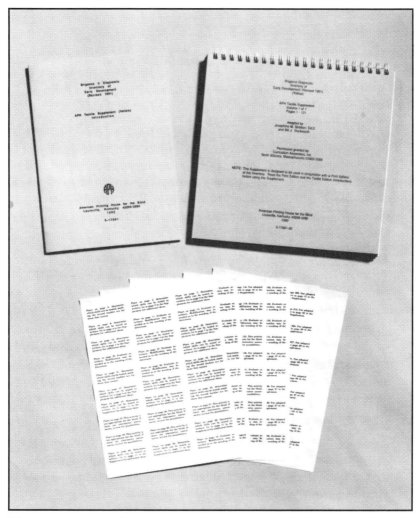

Figure 4.2. Materials for the *APH Tactile Supplement*. (Photo courtesy of American Printing House for the Blind).

Self-Help Skills.

This section includes 37 items that assess feeding/eating skills (from forming a tight seal around nipple when sucking to using a knife for cutting), 50 that tap skills for dressing and undressing (from cooperating in undressing to dressing independently), 20 that address toileting, and 30 that assess bathing and grooming skills. The *APH Tactile Supplement* is not needed for this section.

Speech and Language Skills.

There are 39 items that assess prespeech skills, including receptive language, gestures, and vocalizations. The General Speech and Language section contains 45 receptive and expressive items ranging from saying at least three words to answering "when" questions. In addition, length of sentences; ability to give personal data, follow verbal directions, and understand and use vocabulary; and memory for number strings and sentences of varying lengths are assessed. In order to plan an effective instructional program for children who are not yet talking, the information from this section should be combined with the information from the Vocal Imitation section of the *Ordinal Scales of Psychological Development* (Uzgiris & Hunt, 1989). The *APH Tactile Supplement* should be consulted for many subtests for this section.

General Knowledge and Comprehension.

This section has been expanded to include many subtests that were classified under other sections in the previous version of this scale. The first 19 items address a child's response to and experience with books. Receptive and expressive knowledge of body parts, colors, and shapes are covered with 106 items. Knowledge of quantitative and directional/positional concepts is assessed with 26 items. Sixteen items cover the ability to recognize various classes of objects. Fourteen items assess knowledge of what to do in different situations; 13 deal with use of objects; 12 cover understanding of the function of community helpers; and 12 assess knowledge of where to go for services. The *APH Tactile Supplement* should be used with this section for children with little or no vision.

Social and Emotional Development.

Three subsections comprise this section. General Social and Emotional Development consists of 65 items ranging from looking attentively at a human face to having a best friend of the same sex. There are 35 items on the Play Skills and Behaviors section, ranging from getting excited when a toy is presented to playing cooperatively with others for at least 20 minutes. There are 22 items on the Work-Related Skills and

Behaviors section ranging from holding arms out to be picked up to remaining at a task when "school" distractions are occurring. The *APH Tactile Supplement* is not required for this section.

Readiness.

Two sections tap visual discrimination of symbols, while one assesses recitation of the alphabet. Two sections cover matching, pointing to, and naming uppercase and lowercase letters. The *APH Tactile Supplement* is needed for children with little or no vision during use of this section.

Basic Reading Skills.

Auditory discrimination is a listening, not a reading, skill; therefore, this subtest is misplaced under reading. There is a subtest to determine word-recognition grade placement and oral-reading grade level. This is not a norm-referenced test, so results from these sections cannot be interpreted as grade equivalents. Results would not necessarily correspond to placement in a basal reading series either, because there is such variability among reading series. Three sections assess a child's ability to read color words, number words, and common signs. Seventeen items tap the ability to match consonants with pictures, 17 for substituting initial consonants, 5 for knowledge of short vowel sounds, and 5 for long vowel sounds. For this section, the *APH Tactile Supplement* is required for children with little or no usable vision.

Manuscript Writing.

In this section, the ability to print personal data, uppercase and lowercase letters in sequence, uppercase and lowercase letters dictated, and simple sentences is assessed. The quality of a child's printing is considered also. The *APH Tactile Supplement* would be needed for children with little or no vision. For example, the criteria for evaluating handwriting would be inappropriate for evaluating Braille writing. Hence, criteria appropriate for Braille writing are suggested instead in the *APH Tactile Supplement*.

Basic Math.

Subtests include rote counting, number concepts, reading numbers, matching numbers with quantities, and ordinal numbers. Also included are writing numbers in sequence, dictated, and preceding and following numbers. Beginning addition and subtraction facts are tested also. The ability to recognize money and tell time make up the final subtests. Items dealing with recognizing and writing numbers could be assessed in Braille. Items for telling time could be assessed using a Braille clock or watch for children with little or no vision.

It is important to consider that when Braille letters or numbers are used, the type of discriminations required are different and sometimes more difficult than those required for printed letters and numbers. The *APH Tactile Supplement* would provide materials needed for this section for children with little or no vision.

TECHNICAL ADEQUACY

Field testing.

The inventory was extensively field-tested in numerous states, resulting in revisions, addition of items, deletion of items, addition of reference material, and evaluation of the material to ensure that it was not prejudicial or stereotypic.

Reliability.

No information is provided in this area. Each skill should be observed at least three times to ensure that an adequate sample of skills is obtained.

Validity.

The items were selected based on an extensive review of the developmental literature and other tests. Sources are cited. The inventory was reviewed by over 100 professionals in different types of programs. Many improvements were made in this revision, including better organization of the material.

CONCLUSIONS

This inventory is comprehensive and well thought out. The revision is a considerable improvement over the prior version. The Speech and Language section should be supplemented as suggested for children who are not yet talking. Information should be interpreted in light of delays that often occur for children who are visually impaired or blind. Skills usually learned by children age 3 through 6 require more adaptations for children with a severe visual loss. The *APH Tactile Supplement* should be used for these children.

· ·

• The Carolina Curriculum for Infants and Toddlers with Special Needs– Second Edition

Authors: Nancy M. Johnson-Martin, Kenneth G. Jens, Susan M. Attermeier, & Bonnie J. Hacker

Publisher: Paul H. Brookes Publishing Company
P.O. Box 10624
Baltimore, MD 21285

Copyright: 1991

GENERAL DESCRIPTION

The Carolina Curriculum for Infants and Toddlers with Special Needs includes a curriculum-based measure to assess skills typically learned by children without disabilities from birth to 2 years of age. The *Carolina Curriculum* also includes an extensive curriculum for five areas of development that can be adapted for children with visual, motor, and hearing disabilities.

The *Carolina Curriculum* assesses five domains: Cognition, Communication, Social Adaptation, Fine Motor Skills, and Gross Motor Skills.

Scoring is based on observation of the caregiver playing with the child for a 15- to 20-minute period. Items that cannot be scored from this observation are scored by direct testing and from information obtained from the parent.

Results are in terms of skills demonstrated and those to be taught next. Each item is scored as *pass, fail,* or *emerging.*

Materials consist of the examiner's manual and a record book. Toys and materials are needed to test various skills; these items do not come with the *Carolina Curriculum.*

A preschool version of the *Carolina Curriculum* is available also, *The Carolina Curriculum for Preschoolers with Spe-*

cial Needs (Johnson-Martin, Attermeier, & Hacker, 1990). This version of the *Carolina Curriculum* covers skills usually learned by children between the ages of 24 and 36 months.

DESCRIPTION OF THE DOMAINS

The items are described in the manual as being arranged in "a logical teaching sequence" (p. 31). Emphasis is placed on teaching a child to have some control over the physical and social environment and to communicate. Adaptive functioning is emphasized, and adaptations are suggested for skills tested on children with physical disabilities.

The five domains are made up of 26 sequences of skills. Each item in a domain is to be tested five times, and all 26 sequences are to be used in an assessment.

Cognition.

This domain consists of eight sequences: Visual Pursuit and Object Permanence; Object Permanence: Motor and Visual; Auditory Localization and Object Permanence; Attention and Memory; Concept Development; Understanding Space; Functional Use of Objects and Symbolic Play; Problem Solving; and Visual Perception. This domain assesses Piagetian tasks, attention, and memory.

Communication.

Four sequences are assessed for this domain: Prevocabulary/Vocabulary; Imitation: Sound and Gestures; Responses to Communication from Others; and Conversation Skills. This domain covers expressive and receptive skills, including those used in conversation.

Social/adaptation.

The five sequences in this domain are: Self-Direction, Social Skills, Eating, Dressing, and Grooming. This domain addresses self-concept, responsibility, and interpersonal skills.

Fine motor skills.

The five sequences in this domain are: Tactile Integration; Reaching, Grasping, and Releasing; Manipulation; Bilateral Skills; and Pencil Control and Copying. Addressed are skills in using the hands, manipulating objects, and using tools.

Gross motor skills.

The three sequences in this domain are: Prone, Supine, and Upright (posture, locomotion, stairs, jumping, and balance).

TECHNICAL ADEQUACY

Field testing.

The *Carolina Curriculum* was field-tested in 22 programs in North Carolina and 10 additional programs around the country, including Alaska and Maryland. Feedback included information on the usefulness of the material and the effectiveness of the curriculum. Statistically significant differences were found for skills taught and those not considered a priority for children with mild and moderate disabilities. No difference was found for children with severe and profound disabilities. The authors suggested that the 3-month period of intervention for these children may have been insufficient.

Reliability.

This area is not addressed in the manual.

Validity.

Items were selected and age levels determined from various norm-referenced tests and the *Ordinal Scales of Psychological Development* (Uzgiris & Hunt, 1975), the *Callier-Azusa Scale* (Stillman, 1977), The Communicative Intention Inventory (Coggins & Carpenter, 1981), and skills the authors felt were important for children with special needs.

CONCLUSIONS

As a curriculum-based measure for infants and toddlers with special needs, the *Carolina Curriculum* could be very useful in planning intervention programs and monitoring children's progress. Adaptations are presented in the manual for children with little or no vision. As both an assessment measure and a curriculum, this measure is extensive. Assessment with the *Carolina Curriculum* could be quite time consuming. Examiners must be careful to recognize that the age levels for items are estimated based on information from other measures and that they do not represent norm-referenced information.

. . . .

• Informal Assessment of Developmental Skills for Visually Handicapped Students. Part Two: Informal Assessment of Developmental Skills for Younger Visually Handicapped and Multihandicapped Children

Authors: Rose-Marie Swallow, Sally Mangold, & Philip Mangold

Publisher: American Foundation for the Blind
15 West 16th Street
New York, NY 10011

Copyright: 1978

GENERAL DESCRIPTION

This series of checklists was developed to aid in assessing the special needs of infants and preschoolers who have little or no vision. Checklists were developed by teachers of children who are visually impaired or blind.

It is suggested that teaching objectives can be determined by noting the first behavior in each section that is not in a child's repertoire. There are five checklists: Self-Help, Psychomotor, Social-Emotional, Language, and Cognition.

Permission is given in the manual to duplicate the checklists for "educational use with visually handicapped children" (p. 2).

DESCRIPTION OF CHECKLISTS

Self-help.

The self-help areas tested are: feeding, dressing, undressing, washing hands, grooming, and toileting, with 4 to 12 items per area. Examiners or informants check the statement that best describes a child's performance, choosing from four to nine descriptions for each item. These descriptions are sequenced from beginning to advanced performance (e.g., "bottle feed" to "accepts and chews bite-sized pieces of solid food").

Psychomotor.

This checklist examines 28 gross motor skills and 18 fine motor skills. Locomotion and manipulation are emphasized because they are highly important for children who are visually impaired or blind. Gross motor skills range from the ability to make head movements to aquatic activities. Included are items particularly important for children with little or no vision, such as the ability to open and close doors. Such items do not appear on most other scales. The fine motor skills tested range from reflexive grasping to the use of scissors.

Social-emotional.

This area is of particular concern for children who are visually impaired or blind. Items assess a child's response to adults, to objects, and to other children. Self-confidence when playing and decision making are considered also. There are 14 items on the checklist, with three to nine descriptions of behaviors. Each item is designated as *developed, in transition,* or *not present*.

Language.

This checklist, which includes 19 items, covers nonverbal communication, imitation, receptive and expressive use of gestures or signs, fingerspelling, and verbal language. Pictures to facilitate communication and some reading and writing items are included as well. The *Ordinal Scales of Psychological Development* (Uzgiris & Hunt, 1989) (reviewed later in this section) would provide a more comprehensive and detailed assessment of children who are not yet talking. For preschoolers, however, this checklist could be combined with the more comprehensive *Revised Brigance Diagnostic Inventory of Early Development* (reviewed previously) to assess unique aspects of communication such as the use of signs or pictures.

Cognition.

This checklist is based on the *Ordinal Scales of Psychological Development* (Uzgiris & Hunt, 1975). It would be preferable to use the *Ordinal Scales* themselves, along with the supplementary manual by Dunst (1980). The *Ordinal Scales* is reviewed in detail later in this section. The manual by

Uzgiris and Hunt and the supplementary manual by Dunst provide more detailed and comprehensive information.

TECHNICAL ADEQUACY

No data are provided on field-testing, reliability, or validity of the checklists. The examiner must take the informal nature of the checklists into consideration when interpreting the results.

CONCLUSIONS

These checklists could provide useful information for planning programs for infants and toddlers who are visually impaired or blind. Results from the *Ordinal Scales* would be more helpful in the language area. The Social-Emotional checklist should be of benefit during instructional planning.

. . . .

• Ordinal Scales of Psychological Development

Authors: Ina Uzgiris & J. McVicor Hunt

Publisher: University of Illinois Press
Box 5081, Station A
54 Gregory Drive
Urbana, IL 61820

Copyright: 1989

Supplementary Manual:

Author: Carl Dunst

Publisher: PRO-ED
8700 Shoal Creek Boulevard
Austin, TX 78757-6897

Copyright: 1980

GENERAL DESCRIPTION

The *Ordinal Scales of Psychological Development* are based on Piaget's description of cognitive development from birth to 2 years of age, described as the sensorimotor period. Seven scales make up the test: Object Permanence, Means-Ends, Vocal Imitation, Gestural Imitation, Operational Causality, Construction of Objects in Space, and Schemes for Relating to Objects.

A good understanding of Piagetian theory is needed to correctly administer and interpret the *Ordinal Scales*. This is particularly important when adaptations of items are made for children who are visually impaired or blind so that the intended skills are tested. Dunst (1980) has written a manual to accompany the *Ordinal Scales.* In this manual, many items were added where gaps seemed to exist in the *Ordinal Scales,* the administration procedures are more fully described, and a few items were changed. The protocol in the Dunst manual is especially useful. This manual also describes results of studies using the *Ordinal Scales* with at-risk infants with disabilities.

Any or all of the *Ordinal Scales* can be used, but administration of the entire test would take about 2 hours.

The materials needed are the book for the *Ordinal Scales,* a record book, and easily obtained toys listed in the book. It is useful to have the manual by Dunst as well.

Items in each scale are organized in a hierarchy of development so that the item following a child's highest success would be the next skill to teach a child. Thus, the *Ordinal Scales* provide detailed information for instructional planning and for monitoring progress.

DESCRIPTION OF THE SCALES

It should be noted that Filler (1973) found that performance on the *Ordinal Scales* could be enhanced for a child with an impairment when objects for which the child previously had shown a preference were used for testing.

Object Permanence.

While there are 14 items on the original scale, Dunst added 7 items in his supplementary manual. This scale assesses a range of skills leading to the understanding that objects continue to exist even though they are no longer visually available. Skills progress from visual tracking to finding an object hidden under one of three screens. This scale requires vision, but some of the early items could be adapted by observing a child's tactile rather than visual search behavior.

Means-Ends.

With 13 items from the original scale and 12 items from the Dunst manual, this scale taps a child's problem-solving behavior. Items progress from hand watching to demonstrating foresight by not trying to stack a solid circle on a post. Vision is required on many items, but approximately one third of the items could be adapted easily. For example, one item assesses locomotion used to obtain an object that is out of reach; in this case, a musical toy could be used to facilitate locating the toy.

Vocal Imitation.

This is one of the most useful and important scales for children with disabilities. The nine items on the original scale are supplemented with six from Dunst. This scale does not require vision. Items progress from "responds to voice" up to "imitation of novel words." This seems to be the most comprehensive and useful published scale to assess vocal behavior for children under 2 years old.

Gestural Imitation.

The original scale contains nine items, and Dunst added eight items. The progression of skills on this scale is similar to that of Vocal Imitation except that gestures are involved. Nearly all of the items require vision. Much of the scale could be adapted by use of physical prompts such as banging the table with a child's hand to see if the child repeats the behavior.

Operational Causality.

The recognition of cause-and-effect relationships is assessed on this scale by seven items on the original scale and an additional four items added by Dunst. The recognition of cause and effect is important for sighted children and is particularly beneficial for children with a visual impairment or who are blind. All but the hand-watching item could be adapted for children with little or no vision. A clear understanding of Piagetian theory would be necessary to make the adaptations and ensure that the appropriate skills are tested.

Skills range from "vocalizes/smiles in response to adult talking" and "searches for causal mechanism" to "activates a wind-up toy."

Construction of Objects in Space.

This scale studies a child's use of skills for relating objects in meaningful ways. There are 11 items on the original scale and 10 items from Dunst. Items range from searching for sound with eyes to indicating the absence of familiar persons. Eleven items require vision; eight of these could be adapted. Play skills such as using a container and objects, building with blocks, and banging toys are involved.

Schemes for Relating Objects.

Composed of 10 items from the original scale and 6 items from the Dunst manual, this scale assesses a child's use of various sensorimotor skills with particular types of objects. Skills progress from mouthing to naming objects, with only one item requiring vision. Useful play skills are assessed, particularly for children under 12 months of age. Information from this scale could be used to determine appropriate toys, given the behaviors a child uses with objects.

TECHNICAL ADEQUACY

Field testing.

The original scale was field-tested three times, and items were revised based on the results obtained. Dunst reported results from use of the *Ordinal Scales* with 36 infants who were disabled or considered at risk.

Reliability.

Dunst (1980) reported interrater reliability data from four studies with correlations ranging from .85 to .99. He also reported test-retest correlations of .88 to .96 from several studies using "short-term intervals."

Validity.

Items were selected based on Piaget's description of cognitive development; thus there is a theoretical basis for the *Ordinal Scales*. Items were sequenced on the basis of a logical analysis of how skills develop and which skills are prerequisites to others. Dunst (1980) obtained correlations ranging from .70 to .92 when examining the intercorrelations of the subtests.

Using his procedure for determining an "estimated developmental age," Dunst found correlations ranging from .76 to .93 for subtests of the *Ordinal Scales* and results from the Griffiths subtests (Griffiths, 1954). Estimated Mental Age from the *Ordinal Scales* correlated .97 with the Griffiths' Mental Age.

Data do not support long-term stability of performance (Dunst, 1982).

Numerous studies have examined Piaget's contention of the hierarchical progression of sensorimotor development, and there is considerable evidence to support this progression (Dunst, 1982). Patterns of development during the sensorimotor period have been found to be similar for sighted infants and infants who are blind (Dunst, 1980).

CONCLUSIONS

The *Ordinal Scales* can provide useful information for planning educational programs for infants and toddlers who are visually impaired or blind. Skills that are assessed appear to be of significance in the development of cognition, language, and play. The Object Permanence, Means-Ends, and Gestural Imitation scales will be the least useful because of the visual requirements. Vocal Imitation requires no adaptation and provides detailed and comprehensive information for planning prespeech intervention. Operational Causality will require adaptations made by someone with a good understanding of Piaget's theory to ensure that appropriate skills are tested. Recognizing how to have an effect on objects in the environment is an essential skill for children who are visually impaired or blind. Construction of Objects in Space and Schemes for Relating Objects provide useful information on the development of cognition and play skills. Adaptation is needed for several items on the Construction of Objects in Space section and for one item on the Schemes section. This is a difficult test to learn to use but well worth the effort required.

• The Oregon Project for Visually Impaired and Blind Preschool Children–Fifth Edition

Authors: Sharon Anderson, Sue Boigon, & Kris Davis

Publisher: Jackson Education Service District
101 North Grape Street
Medford, OR 97501

Copyright: 1986

GENERAL DESCRIPTION

This curriculum-based inventory was written for children from birth to 6 years of age. Its purpose is to provide information for planning and monitoring instruction for young children who are visually impaired or blind.

Results are measured in terms of skills that were demonstrated and in percent of skills mastered for each area tested.

Eight areas are assessed: Cognitive, Language, Social, Vision, Compensatory, Self-Help, Fine Motor, and Gross Motor.

Items on this unique inventory have been assigned 1-year age levels appropriate for sighted children. Skills that often take a longer time for children who are visually impaired or blind to learn are coded as such.

There is an extensive recommendation section with the *Oregon Project* for teaching each skill tested. The recommendations are useful and clearly written, and several alternatives are provided for each skill.

Scoring can be based on interview, direct observation, or direct administration of the items. No specific procedures are described for administering items. Any toys or materials used in assessing skills have to be obtained by the examiner; the toys needed are those usually available to children, such as blocks and puzzles. For older children, some Braille letters and numbers may be necessary. Other than toys and Braille materials, the only materials needed are the manual and a record book.

Because the *Oregon Project* was designed for children who are visually impaired or blind, any adaptations needed for testing are indicated in the manual.

DESCRIPTION OF DEVELOPMENTAL AREAS

Cognitive.

There are 105 items in this section, testing skills ranging from "Alerts to daily tactual/visual/auditory/movement stimulation" to "Writes letters from dictation (upper or lower case)."

Language.

This section consists of 97 items that assess both receptive and expressive skills. Items range from "Has separate cry for different discomforts" to "Explains rules of simple board or card games to others."

Socialization.

This area consists of 63 items ranging from "Cuddles or snuggles when held by familiar person" to "Remains silent at appropriate times (when someone is talking)."

Vision.

This 70-item section includes skills that would not be relevant to young children who are Braille readers because they require vision. Skills range from "Stares at source of light" to "Cuts out a simply drawn picture." This section is new to this version of the *Oregon Project*.

Compensatory.

This section consists of 61 items considered important for young children likely to be Braille readers. This section also was added to this latest version of the *Oregon Project*. Skills tested range from "Explores textured surfaces by moving own hands and/or feet over them" to "Plays simple computer game using space bar, return, and escape keys."

Self-Help.

Consisting of 90 items, this section evaluates skills ranging from "Sucks and swallows liquid" to "Walks to a familiar location within a block of home independently."

Fine Motor.

This section, comprised of 69 items, assesses skills ranging from "Holds rattle with palmar grasp" to "Hits nail with real hammer into soft wood."

Gross Motor.

There are 85 items on this section. Items range from "Moves head side to side, thrusts arms about, kicks vigorously while on back" to "Coordinates several motor skills in one activity (jumping jacks, relay races, circle games)."

The examiner can use the *Oregon Project* repeatedly with a child to monitor progress, noting when a skill is finally mastered.

TECHNICAL ADEQUACY

Field testing.

The inventory was field-tested with children from Oregon and Arizona. Based on results of field testing and feedback on prior versions of the inventory, items were clarified, added, or deleted, and the hierarchy of some items was changed. A child's profile is used to summarize performance across each area.

Reliability.

No data are provided on reliability.

Validity.

Items were developed based on a review of the literature, records of children in the Southern Oregon Program for Visually Impaired, and input from preschool teachers of children who are blind. Input from professionals in the field was obtained also.

CONCLUSIONS

This inventory is a useful tool for planning instruction for children who are visually impaired or blind. The fact that the inventory was designed with the special needs of these children in mind is certainly an asset. Several areas are not as comprehensive as the *Revised Brigance Diagnostic Inventory of Early Development* (Brigance, 1991) and the *APH Tactile*

Supplement (Duckworth & Stratton, 1992). Hence, a combination of the two inventories would provide detailed and comprehensive information for planning instruction, while at the same time circumventing vision problems and taking into consideration the special needs of these children. The inventory is not as thorough as the *Ordinal Scales* (Uzgiris & Hunt, 1989) for children from birth to 12 months of age. The curriculum sections, however, are very useful for children from birth to age 6. The fact that this is a curriculum-based inventory should be considered to avoid overinterpretation of age levels for items.

Chapter 5

Assessment of Preschoolers

THE FIRST SECTION OF THIS CHAPTER ADDRESSES THE GENERAL issues related to planning an assessment of a preschool child who is visually impaired or blind, while the second section covers more specific issues regarding a comprehensive assessment. The final sections of this chapter offer detailed reviews of norm-referenced tests as well as criterion-referenced, curriculum-based, and informal measures.

THE ASSESSMENT PROCESS

For the purposes of this text, "preschoolers" will refer to children who are 3 and 4 years old. Many of the issues covered in Chapter 4 on infants and toddlers under the section titled The Assessment Process for Young Children apply to some preschoolers as well.

Under Public Law 99–457 (P.L. 99–457) (Education of the Handicapped Act Amendments, 1986), an Individualized Family Service Plan (IFSP) should be developed for families of preschoolers when it is appropriate and desired by the parents. A detailed discussion of family assessment appears in Chapter 4.

Several issues require consideration in planning an assessment of a preschooler who is visually impaired or blind. First, in order to obtain valid and useful information, several sessions will be needed to complete the assessment. Using several sessions will result in a more adequate sample of a child's behavior than a single session. Also, several sessions are required to comprehensively assess all important areas and maintain a child's interest and motivation.

To obtain sufficient background information for planning the assessment process, the examiner should complete as much of the Information-Organizing Checklist for Infants and Preschoolers Who Are Visually Impaired or Blind (see Figure 1.1) as possible through an interview with the parents. If a child attends a preschool or daycare program, information for this checklist should be obtained from the teacher's perspective as well. Upon completion of interviews with the parents and teacher, the examiner should give them any rating scales that they will need to complete. The parents and teacher may need to complete several of the rating scales that are described later in this chapter.

Prior to direct testing of a child, examine the medical records to ensure that vision and hearing examinations are up-to-date. A review of the functional vision assessment report completed by the consultant for students who are visually impaired should provide considerable guidance in selecting appropriate procedures and environments for testing.

Delays in development, especially in the areas of language, social skills, motor skills, and adaptive behavior may be evident for some children with severe visual losses, even through age 4. When norm-referenced tests standardized on sighted children are used to test children with severe visual losses, the examiner must take into consideration delays common to children with visual losses when interpreting results. These delays are discussed in Chapter 4. Understanding development patterns in these areas should help to prevent underestimating the ability of these children.

Given that delays are rather common in some areas for preschoolers who are visually impaired or blind, the limited number of appropriate tests for these children, and the rapid growth typical of preschoolers, it is wise to base conclusions on the results of periodic assessments rather than a single assessment. Examination of trends in data over time is more reliable and useful than data obtained from one assessment, even when that assessment consisted of several sessions.

Areas that are important to consider when planning an assessment of a preschooler who is visually impaired or blind include: social skills and play, language, cognitive development, early academic skills, motor skills, and adaptive behavior. Suggestions of appropriate measures for each area follow.

AREAS FOR ASSESSMENT

Social Skills and Play

Social and play skills are closely intertwined during the preschool years. Unfortunately, preschoolers who are visually impaired or blind often display problems in both of these areas. Because of their visual loss, these children miss nonverbal cues important for social interaction, such as the use of gestures and facial expressions by peers and adults. Furthermore, some of the behaviors they display frequently interfere with effective interaction with their peers. Skellenger, Hill, and Hill (1992) noted that interaction with peers was infrequent for these children and that they rarely initiated interaction. They noted that when these children do interact, the interaction often is obstructed by a lack of response to their peers. Imamura (1965) described the initiations to peers by preschoolers who were visually impaired as "monotonous and repetitious" (p. 236).

Because of their visual losses, these children have fewer opportunities to explore the environment. Some preschoolers lack motivation to explore and move about as well. As noted by O'Donnell and Livingston (1991), it is becoming increasingly clear that limited exploration and movement, rather than visual loss, can be the cause of many of the problems associated with visual impairments. Preisler and Palmer (1988) observed 2- and 3-year-old children with visual impairments while they were being mainstreamed into a regular nursery school in Sweden. They noted that the children sat without moving while noisy activities went on around them. In addition, the children frequently physically rejected interactions with their peers.

Using the appropriate toys can encourage preschoolers who are visually impaired or blind to interact with the environment. Toys that are large in size, provide auditory feedback, or are responsive to the child's behavior (i.e., move or make noise when touched) are appropriate (see Figure 5.1).

Hence, assessment and intervention for social and play skills are necessary to ensure adequate development not only in social and play skills but also in the development of other areas that require these skills, including language, cognition, early academic skills, and motor skills.

To define and measure problem behaviors, systematic direct observation is the most useful. Alessi and Kaye (1983) described methods of using local micronorms to compare a particular child's

Figure 5.1. Large lighted puzzle board. (Photo courtesy of American Printing House for the Blind).

performance with that of his or her peers when using systematic direct observation. Such data are critical in setting goals, planning remedial programs, and monitoring progress in the development of social skills.

There are several norm-referenced measures that, in addition to providing scores to describe performance, provide information useful in planning instructional programs. The *Social Skills Rating System* (SSRS) (Gresham & Elliott, 1990) is designed for children from preschool (beginning at age 3) through high school. Though standardized on a sighted population, the measure does not require vision. Administration at the preschool level requires one scale, covering 30 social skills and 10 problem behaviors, to be completed by parents and one scale, consisting of 39 social skills and 10 problem behaviors, to be completed by the teacher. The two forms allow an ecological assessment of social skills by providing information on the child's use of social skills at home and at school. To aid in planning intervention programs for social skills, each item on this comprehensive scale is rated on the frequency of occurrence as well as the importance to the rater.

Another norm-referenced measure is the 20-item Classroom Behavior subtest from the *Basic School Skills Inventory–Diagnostic* (BSSI–D) (Hammill & Leigh, 1983). The BSSI–D is completed by a teacher who has observed the child for a period of time in a preschool or day-care program, and is designed for children age 4 through 6-11. Though standardized on sighted children, the subtest requires little modification for a child with a visual loss. Because the items were developed based on skills teachers thought to be important for classroom functioning, results can be of some use in planning programs as well.

A third norm-referenced measure for this area is the Personal-Social domain of the *Battelle Developmental Inventory* (Newborg, Stock, Wnek, Guidubaldi, & Svinicki, 1984). Though standardized on sighted children from birth through age 8, this domain also does not require visual skills for preschool children. Items are scored by direct administration, observation, or from information obtained through interviews. There are 23 items at the 3- and 4-year-old level.

Measures useful in obtaining information for planning instruction in the area of play and social skills are listed in Table 5.1.

Language

Assessment of receptive and expressive language skills is particularly important for preschoolers who are visually impaired or blind. Problems with language development can negatively affect the development of skills in cognition, early academics, social development, motor development, and adaptive behavior. Young children with visual losses often display delays in the development of language skills, yet language is even more important for these children than for their sighted peers. For example, a child with a visual loss relies heavily on language skills for communication and language concepts (especially position words) for orientation and mobility.

Two concerns exist during the assessment of language skills for preschoolers who are visually impaired or blind. First, their language development may be overestimated because they have learned to use certain words or phrases by rote but lack an adequate understanding of their meaning. Certain concepts, such as *cow* or *castle,* are particularly difficult to learn with little or no vision. Trying to

TABLE 5.1. *Measures for Instructional Planning for Social Skills and Play for Preschoolers Who Are Visually Impaired or Blind*

Tests	Sections	Type of Assessment	Adaptations
Revised Brigance Diagnostic Inventory of Early Development (Brigance, 1991)	General Social & Emotional Development; Play Skills; Work-Related Skills	Criterion-referenced	None required
Informal Assessment of Developmental Skills (Swallow et al., 1978)	Social– Emotional	Informal checklist	None required
Oregon Project for Visually Impaired and Blind Preschool Children (Anderson et al., 1986)	Socialization	Curriculum-based	None required

teach these concepts using small replicas may convey incorrect information, and trying to teach the concept *cow* by having a child with little or no vision touch a cow provides the child information in only a piecemeal fashion. Hence, the examiner should probe verbal responses that are questionable in order to ascertain the degree of the child's understanding of a concept.

A second concern is that language skills may be underestimated for children who are visually impaired or blind because some items on the measures used may involve concepts that are particularly difficult for these children to learn. To address this concern, examine items missed and determine whether they were those that are usually difficult for these children. If this is the case and there are several of these items on the test that was used, it may be appropriate to consider the results to be an underestimate of the child's language skills.

For direct assessment of language skills, there are three norm-referenced options for preschoolers who are visually impaired or blind. All were standardized on sighted children, but few items require vision. The most comprehensive measure is the *Test of Language Development–Primary–Second Edition* (Newcomer & Hammill, 1988). This test can be administered beginning at age 4. Though a number of subtests require vision, four subtests do not: Oral Vocabulary (30 items), Sentence Imitation (30 items), Grammatic Completion (30 items), and Word Discrimination (20 items).

The Communication domain of the *Battelle Developmental Inventory* (Newborg et al., 1984), covering birth through age 8, is a second option. This measure includes 7 receptive items and 10 expressive items at the 3- and 4-year levels.

The *Basic School Skills Inventory–Diagnostic* (Hammill & Leigh, 1983) has a 20-item Spoken Language subtest. This test begins at age 4 and is completed by a teacher based on his or her observations of the child in the classroom. Only 1 item involving a picture requires vision.

Measures that can provide information useful for instructional planning for language development are listed in Table 5.2. It is particularly important to include a measure that will provide information on a child's understanding of directional and position words, such as the *Revised Brigance Diagnostic Inventory of Early Development* (Brigance, 1991).

Cognitive

As discussed in Chapter 4, no test of cognitive development has been standardized on children under age 6 who are visually impaired or blind. Furthermore, there is no test of cognitive development for children under 4 years old that does not require vision on a number of items. Thus, for 3-year-olds, the use of tests with age-referenced items as described in Chapter 4 is the primary option. Because the tests for assessing the cognitive development of these children are so limited, results from measures of cognitive development must be interpreted in light of test results from other areas (such as language and social skills), information obtained from interviews and school records, and, in particular, information from direct observation of the child in the classroom. Conclusions regarding cognitive development should be based on periodic assessments over time as well.

For norm-referenced assessment of cognitive development for 3-year-olds who are visually impaired or blind, the most appropriate option seems to be the Cognitive domain from the *Battelle Developmental Inventory*, supplemented with age-referenced items that do

TABLE 5.2. *Measures for Instructional Planning for Oral Language for Preschoolers Who Are Visually Impaired or Blind*

Tests	Sections	Type of Assessment	Adaptations
Revised Brigance Diagnostic Inventory of Early Development (Brigance, 1991)	Speech & Language; Directional/ Positional Concepts	Criterion-referenced	*APH Tactile Supplement* (Duckworth & Stratton, 1992)
Informal Assessment of Developmental Skills (Swallow et al., 1978)	Language	Informal checklist	None required
Oregon Project for Visually Impaired and Blind Preschool Children (Anderson et al., 1986)	Language	Curriculum-based	None required

not require vision from the *Cognitive Abilities Scale* (CAS) (Bradley-Johnson, 1987). The CAS is appropriate only for 2- and 3-year-old children. On the *Battelle,* the Cognitive domain has only 4 items at the 3-year-old level, one of which requires vision (though the examiner probably would test above and below these levels). There are 45 items on the CAS that do not require vision. When items that require vision are omitted, no overall score can be obtained from this measure, but items are age-referenced.

For 4-year-olds who are visually impaired or blind, the Verbal Scale of the *Wechsler Preschool and Primary Scale of Intelligence* (WPPSI) (Wechsler, 1967) can be administered. Unfortunately, this test is dated, and the Verbal Scale of the newer *Wechsler Preschool and Primary Scale of Intelligence–Revised* (Wechsler, 1989) cannot be used because many items requiring vision were added at the beginning of verbal subtests. Results from the WPPSI should be supplemented with results from the Cognitive section of the *Battelle Developmental Inventory,* which includes 8 items at the 4-year-old level. Two of these require vision.

TABLE 5.3. *Measures for Instructional Planning for Cognitive Development for Preschoolers Who Are Visually Impaired or Blind*

Tests	Sections	Type of Assessment	Adaptations
Revised Brigance Diagnostic Inventory of Early Development (Brigance, 1991)	General Knowledge & Comprehension	Criterion-referenced	*APH Tactile Supplement* (Duckworth & Stratton, 1992)
Oregon Project for Visually Impaired and Blind Preschool Children (Anderson et al., 1986)	Cognitive	Curriculum-based	None required

Given the tests currently available, results of the assessment for cognitive development of 3- and 4-year-olds who are visually impaired or blind will be based primarily on verbal skills. Because verbal skills often take longer to develop for young children with serious losses in vision, these results may underestimate a child's ability. Hence, the examiner should demonstrate caution when interpreting results from these measures.

A controversy continues to exist regarding the definition of intelligence. Furthermore, it is unclear what skills should be taught to improve performance in this area. At this time it seems more practical to focus instead on skills needed for success in educational tasks such as reading, writing, arithmetic, and oral language. Measures for obtaining information on cognitive development for instructional planning are listed in Table 5.3. The educational importance of each item in a test should be considered before using a particular measure, because both of the measures contain some items of questionable relevance.

Early Academics

The primary academic skills include reading, arithmetic, writing, and oral language. Assessment of oral language skills was addressed earlier in this chapter under Language. Early reading, mathematics, and writing skills for children who will be print readers can be assessed in much the same way as these skills are tested for sighted children. The development of these skills may, however, take longer than it would for sighted preschoolers.

There are no norm-referenced tests of early academic skills for 3- and 4-year-olds who will be Braille readers. Instruction in Braille usually does not begin in the preschool years, though readiness skills may be taught. Several informal measures, however, can provide useful information for planning early academic instruction for these children.

For assessing readiness skills for Braille reading, the *Revised Brigance Diagnostic Inventory of Early Development* (Brigance, 1991), used in conjunction with the *APH Tactile Supplement for the Revised Brigance Inventory of Early Development* (Duckworth & Stratton, 1992), can yield helpful information for planning instructional programs. For example, the *APH Tactile Supplement* has many items assessing tactile discrimination of symbols in the Readiness section.

The Oregon Project for Visually Impaired and Blind Preschool Children (Anderson, Boigon, & Davis, 1986) Compensatory Skills section contains several tactile discrimination tasks also. These tasks typically are demonstrated by children between 4 and 5 years old.

One of the most important areas for development of early arithmetic involves the skills needed for counting in a meaningful way. These skills are important for all young children but may require special instruction for some preschoolers who are visually impaired or blind. Englemann (1969) described the skills that form the basis for beginning addition. The four skills for counting in a meaningful way are being able to

(a) count 10 objects that are placed in a row, starting at either end, and answer the question "How many are there";

(b) count to a given number, and count out a specified number of objects from a group of ten objects;

(c) indicate the number that comes after any number in the 1–10 series;

(d) predict the number of objects that will be in a group when one is added (p. 253).

To demonstrate any of these skills, a child must first be able to rote count and to synchronize touch and count. This list of skills, in conjunction with up to 10 objects for counting, can be used to test if these skills have been learned. The list also can serve as a guide for determining what skills to teach. Hence, this list contains objectives for teaching and functions as an informal test for early arithmetic skills. For some children, it is more effective to practice counting quantities of 1 through 5 (rather than 1 through 10) first, and then to add quantities of 6 through 10 when the skills for 1 through 5 are mastered.

If the *Revised Brigance Diagnostic Inventory of Early Development* General Knowledge and Comprehension section is used along with the *APH Tactile Supplement,* useful information on a child's understanding of math concepts can be obtained from the Quantitative Concepts subtest.

Motor

As noted in Chapter 4, motor development skills may vary in sequence and take longer to develop for a child with a serious visual loss, especially in terms of fine motor development. Opportunities for play, encouragement for exploring the environment, and the level of the parents' protectiveness are factors important in the development of motor skills for children who are visually impaired or blind. As noted by Benner (1992),

> A blind child might be viewed as motorically delayed when compared with a sighted population, but when compared with other blind children the motor delay is not apparent. Proper interpretation of the child's performance is that he is delayed in motor development as typically seen in visually impaired children; this does not indicate a significant motor impairment in addition to the visual impairment. While we should provide intervention to reduce the motor delay, it would be a misdiagnosis to indicate that the child had a motor impairment separate from the visual problem (p. 51).

The Motor domain of the *Battelle Developmental Inventory* (Newborg et al., 1984) can yield a norm-referenced score. Of the 20 items specifically for 3- and 4-year-olds, 9 require vision.

A list of measures that can provide useful information for instructional planning for motor development is presented in Table 5.4.

Adaptive Behavior

As with motor development, the development of a number of adaptive behaviors may be delayed for children with little or no usable

TABLE 5.4. *Measures for Instructional Planning for Motor Development for Preschoolers Who Are Visually Impaired or Blind*

Tests	Sections	Type of Assessment	Adaptations
Revised Brigance Diagnostic Inventory of Early Development (Brigance, 1991)	Gross Motor Skills; Fine Motor Skills	Criterion-referenced	*APH Tactile Supplement* (Duckworth & Stratton, 1992)
Informal Assessment of Developmental Skills (Swallow et al., 1978)	Psychomotor	Informal checklist	None required
Oregon Project for Visually Impaired and Blind Preschool Children (Anderson et al., 1986)	Fine Motor; Gross Motor	Curriculum-based	None required

vision. Many variables such as overprotection, the age at which orientation and mobility training is begun, and the amount of environmental stimulation affect the rate of development of these behaviors. Examiners must keep this in mind when interpreting test results, especially from tests standardized on sighted children.

One norm-referenced measure of adaptive behavior for 4-year-olds who are in a classroom program is the Daily Living Skills subtest from the *Basic School Skills Inventory–Diagnostic* (BSSI–D) (Hammill & Leigh, 1983). This 20-item subtest is completed by a classroom teacher. Three items require adaptation for children who have little or no usable vision, and results provide information that can be somewhat useful for instructional programming.

Another norm-referenced measure is the Adaptive domain from the *Battelle Developmental Inventory,* which includes 16 items at the 3- and 4-year levels, 2 of which may not be appropriate for children with little or no usable vision.

The *Vineland Adaptive Behavior Scales–Expanded or Survey Version* (Sparrow, Balla, & Cicchetti, 1984) is a rating scale completed by a caregiver. It was standardized on sighted children and

TABLE 5.5. *Measures for Instructional Planning for Adaptive Behavior for Preschoolers Who Are Visually Impaired or Blind*

Tests	Sections	Type of Assessment	Adaptations
Revised Brigance Diagnostic Inventory of Early Development (Brigance, 1991)	Self-Help Skills	Criterion-referenced	None required
Informal Assessment of Developmental Skills (Swallow et al., 1978)	Self-Help Skills	Informal checklist	None required
Oregon Project for Visually Impaired and Blind Preschool Children (Anderson et al., 1986)	Self-Help Skills	Curriculum-based	None required

contains numerous items requiring vision. Hence, results from this scale are likely to underestimate the performance of a child who is visually impaired or blind. The supplemental norms for children who are visually impaired were collected only on residential samples.

Measures that can be used to obtain information useful in planning instruction for adaptive behavior are listed in Table 5.5.

NORM-REFERENCED TESTS

Tests were selected for review if they were (a) designed to be individually administered (to meet the legal requirements for special education eligibility decisions), (b) published within the last 15 years (so that the content and the norms were reasonably current), and (c) able to circumvent a visual disability (to ensure that a child who is visually impaired or blind would be capable of making the required responses). Some tests frequently mentioned in the literature (e.g., *A Social Maturity Scale for Blind Preschool Children,* Maxfield & Bucholz, 1957) are out-of-date. Such tests are pre-Sputnik and unlikely to be applicable today. One exception to tests that met the above-mentioned criteria is the *Wechsler Preschool and Primary Scale of Intelligence* Verbal Scale (Wechsler, 1967). Although dated, this test is included for review because the test options for assessing cognitive development are so limited for preschoolers with a visual loss that this test must be considered.

Many children with visual impairments can be tested with other instruments designed for sighted children. In some cases magnification or enlargement of test materials, special lighting, and other special procedures may be required.

The following norm-referenced tests were reviewed in detail using the criteria presented in Chapter 1 to evaluate technical adequacy of the tests. Descriptions of administration procedures, responses required, materials used, and number of items are presented also.

. . . .

• Basic School Skills Inventory– Diagnostic

Authors: Donald D. Hammill & James E. Leigh

Publisher: PRO-ED
8700 Shoal Creek Boulevard
Austin, TX 78757-6897

Copyright: 1983

GENERAL DESCRIPTION

The *Basic School Skills Inventory–Diagnostic* (BSSI–D) was planned for use with children between the ages of 4-0 and 6-11.

This test is made up of six subtests: Daily Living Skills, Spoken Language, Reading, Writing, Mathematics, and Classroom Behavior. Three of these subtests do not require vision (or require minor modifications for children with little or no usable vision): Daily Living Skills, Spoken Language, and Classroom Behavior. Hence, only these three subtests will be reviewed.

The test is designed to be scored by someone who has observed a child in a classroom setting over a period of time, such as a classroom teacher. Scores from the BSSI–D can be interpreted as percentiles, standard scores (mean = 10, standard deviation = 3) for subtests, and as a quotient for the total score (mean = 100, standard deviation = 15).

If the entire inventory were used, the administration time would be approximately 30 minutes. About half this time would be needed for the three subtests that do not require vision. Many items can be scored based on prior knowledge of the child and observation in the classroom.

Materials needed for the three subtests are: the manual, a recording form, primary scissors, paper, a pencil, a penny, a nickel, a dime, a Braille clock or watch, and a picture made of raised lines.

DESCRIPTION OF SUBTESTS

Daily Living Skills.

This 20-item subtest assesses a child's ability to participate in daily classroom activities. The manual suggests that "children who do well on these items are likely to be those who are considered independent and responsible" (p. 21). Examples of items include "Does the child wash hands and face properly?" and "Does the child use a handkerchief or tissue properly?"

Three items would be problematic for children with little or no vision unless adaptations were made. Regarding the item "Is the child able to fold paper and cut with scissors?", the examiner should consider when scoring that it may be difficult for the child to make an exact fold. Cutting with scissors could be adapted by drawing the square to be cut with a black crayon, making a heavy line that a child who is visually impaired could feel with his or her fingers. A child who is blind, however, would need a raised line square. The item "Can the child follow directions to underline, draw a circle and draw an X?" taps skills that are not relevant for a child who is blind. Underlining in Braille is done by the use of an italic sign before a word. For this item, the ability to follow directions should be tested using different tasks. The third troublesome item is "Can the child tell time by looking at a clock?" This would require use of a Braille clock or watch or one with raised numbers.

Spoken Language.

To assess the type of spoken language a child uses in the classroom, this subtest contains 20 items. Examples include

"Can the child articulate speech sounds correctly?" and "Can the child use possessive forms correctly?" Two items need special consideration when interpreting results for children with little or no vision. "Does the child use the pronoun *I* correctly?" is a skill likely to be delayed for these children. Also, "Can the child describe the contents of a picture?" would be an impossible task for a child without vision unless the picture were adapted. A simple raised line drawing could be used in this case.

Classroom Behavior.

All 20 items on this subtest could be used without modification for children with little or no vision. Examples of items include "Can the child wait his turn?" and "Does the child follow classroom rules?" Some items would need to be scored in light of the fact that the child has a visual problem. For example, "Can the child go through the normal school day without becoming overly tired and listless?" may be a particularly difficult task for a child who is visually impaired because extended use of usable vision can be very tiring. The examiner should consider this issue when planning a child's classroom program but should not penalize a child who is visually impaired for this physical limitation when scoring the item.

TECHNICAL ADEQUACY

Standardization.

The 376 children on whom this test was standardized were selected to correspond to data in the 1980 *Statistical Abstract of the United States*. The demographic characteristics of the sample approximate these data for gender and urban/rural residence. For occupation of parents, however, there were too few white-collar parents (28% compared to 51%) and too many blue-collar parents (61% compared to 36%). For race, black students were underrepresented (6% compared to 12%), and in terms of geographic distribution, the South was overrepresented (53% compared to 33%), and the West was underrepresented (1% compared to 19%).

Reliability.

No test-retest data are provided.

Internal consistency correlation ranges were .85 to .90 for Daily Living Skills, .81 to .93 for Spoken Language, and .93 to .97 for Classroom Behavior.

Standard errors of measurement are provided for all subtests by age level.

Validity.

Content validity is supported by the use of teacher input used to develop the items, and the items were field-tested four times to eliminate those items teachers thought were vague or unimportant. Further, according to item analysis, the items are adequate in terms of discriminating power and difficulty.

For criterion-related validity, teacher rankings were correlated with BSSI–D results. Correlations were .35 for Daily Living Skills, .38 for Spoken Language, and .37 for Classroom Behavior.

In terms of construct validity, the scores were found to increase with age, and correlations for interrelationship of the subtests ranged from .34 to .83. The BSSI–D was found to discriminate between a group of 12 "learning disabled" and 12 "normal" students for all subtests except Classroom Behavior.

CONCLUSIONS

The BSSI–D could provide some useful information about a child's behavior and language skills in a classroom setting. Because information is obtained from the teacher or someone who has observed the child for some time in the classroom, it is particularly relevant. The scores, however, would need to be interpreted in light of information from other measures because of limitations in the standardization sample and in the reliability data. More information with larger samples is needed for diagnostic and criterion-related validity. Besides the score, the BSSI–D would provide some beneficial information for planning classroom activities. Several special considerations were noted that are important when scoring and interpreting the subtests for children who are visually impaired or blind.

· ·

• Battelle Developmental Inventory

See review in Chapter 4.

. . . .

• Cognitive Abilities Scale

See review in Chapter 4.

. . . .

• Social Skills Rating System

Authors: Frank M. Gresham & Stephen N. Elliott

Publisher: American Guidance Service
Circle Pines, MN 55014

Copyright: 1990

GENERAL DESCRIPTION

This system of scales is designed to assess the social skills of students from preschool through high school. The *Social Skills Rating System* (SSRS) consists of three rating scales that can be used separately or in combination. Teachers, parents, and students each complete a different scale. The student scale, however, is only appropriate for students in grades 3 through 12.

Though the primary emphasis of the SSRS is on positive social behaviors (the Social Skills domain), there is a Problem Behavior domain and an Academic Competence domain as well. The Social Skills domain consists of subscales for cooperation, assertion, responsibility, empathy, and self-control. Problem Behaviors appears only on the teacher and parent scales and consists of externalizing problems, internalizing problems, and hyperactivity. The Academic Competence domain appears only on the teacher form for elementary and secondary levels and does not have subscales. This system of scales requires no adaptation when used with a child or adolescent who is visually impaired or blind.

Results are described in terms of a standard score or percentile rank for each of the domains. Behavior levels for subscales indicate normative ratings in terms of *fewer, average,* or *more than average.* In addition, each item is rated in terms of both frequency of occurrence and importance of the behavior from the rater's perspective. Such results help to plan instructional programs.

Completing the ratings on a scale for the SSRS takes approximately 15 to 25 minutes.

Materials consist of the examiner's manual and the record books for each rater.

DESCRIPTION OF THE DOMAINS

The number of items per scale varies with the level of the scale used (e.g., preschool or high school). For the Social Skills domain the number of items ranges from 30 to 40, and for the Problem Behaviors domain the number ranges from 10 to 18. The Academic Competence domain includes 9 items.

The frequency scale for each item ranges from 0 (never) to 2 (very often); the importance scale ranges from 0 (not important) to 2 (critical).

For the student scale (appropriate only for students in grades 3 through 12), items may be read to students with reading difficulties.

Social Skills Domain.

The Cooperation subscale taps behaviors that include helping, sharing, and complying with rules and directions. The Assertion subscale addresses behaviors such as asking for information and responding to the behavior of others, while the Responsibility subscale covers skills in communicating with adults and showing "regard for property or work." The Empathy subscale addresses showing "concern and respect for others' feelings and viewpoints," and the Self-control subscale covers "behaviors that emerge in conflict situations, such as responding appropriately to teasing, and in nonconflict situations that require taking turns and compromising" (examiner's manual, p. 3).

Problem Behaviors Domain.

Behaviors such as verbal and physical aggression, loss of temper, and arguing are assessed through the Externalizing Problems subscale, while the Internalizing Problems subscale includes sadness and anxiety. Examples from the Hyperactivity subscale include impulsive behavior and excessive movement.

Academic Competence Domain.

In this relatively brief domain the teacher rates, for example, a student's motivation, performance in reading, or performance in math.

TECHNICAL ADEQUACY

Standardization.

The sample population for this measure consisted of 4,170 students, 1,027 parents, and 259 teachers. Students in special education classes and those who were mainstreamed were included. Of the special education students that constituted 17% of the sample, 10.2% were learning disabled, 2.2% were behaviorally disordered, 3.5% were mentally handicapped, and 3.6% were labeled as "other." The "other" category included students who were visually impaired and hearing impaired, for example. There were at least 341 students per grade level, except at grades 11 (44 students) and 12 (80 students). The demographic characteristics of the sample were similar to census data in terms of gender, race, and urban/rural residence. Parental education was somewhat low for the group with less than a high school education (9.5% compared to 16.8%), and the percentage of Hispanic children, at only 6.1%, was also low.

Reliability.

Test-retest reliability was examined with a 4-week interval. Correlations were: (teacher form) Social Skills .85, Problem Behaviors .84, and Academic Competence .93; (parent form) Social Skills .87 and Problem Behaviors .65 and; (student form) Social Skills .68. When domain scores are used, results appear to be reasonably reliable for all domains on the teacher form and for the Social Skills domain of the parent form. The low reliability for the student form is similar to correlations obtained with other rating scales in which students rate their own behavior.

Internal consistency for the teacher form ranged from .86 to .94 for Social Skills, .74 to .89 for Problem Behaviors, and .95 for Academic Competence. For the parent form, correlations ranged from .65 to .90 for Social Skills and from .51 to .87 for Problem Behaviors. For the student form, correlations ranged from .51 to .83 for Social Skills.

Standard errors of measurement are provided for standard scores.

Validity.

Content validity was addressed through an extensive survey of literature conducted during item development, and the scale was revised as a result of information generated from a national tryout. Importance ratings address the issue of social validity.

For criterion-related validity, the system was compared with the *Social Behavior Assessment* (Stephens, 1978) for teachers, the *Child Behavior Checklist* (Achenbach & Edelbrock, 1983, 1986) teacher and parent forms, the *Harter Teacher Rating Scale* (Harter, 1985), and the *Piers-Harris Children's Self-Concept Scale* (Piers, 1984). The correlations generally were acceptable. The student form correlated the least well with other measures.

Extensive information is provided on construct validity in the manual. All subscales of the Social Skills domain correlated satisfactorily with each other; the Problem Behaviors domain did not always correlate well with the Social Skills domain; and the Academic Competence domain correlated satisfactorily with other subscales.

Hyperactivity items were not included at the secondary level because factor loadings showed that these items were not sufficiently strong at this level. No developmental trend was found with Social Skills or Academic Competence. Girls were rated higher on the Social Skills and Academic Competence domains, whereas boys were rated higher on the Problem Behaviors domain.

Factor analysis provided general support for the structure of the system. Convergent validity information is provided for the various forms. The domain scores indicated convergent validity, as did a number of the subscales. Discriminate validity was addressed as well. The SSRS seemed to reliably discriminate children with disabilities from children without in several studies, indicating that children with disabilities have less well-developed social skills than their peers without disabilities.

CONCLUSIONS

The standardization sample for the SSRS is quite representative, except that more students are needed at grades 11 and 12 and more Hispanic students are needed. Only the teacher and parent forms are sufficiently reliable for use in eligibility decisions. The validity work is extensive and impressive. Useful norm-referenced results can be obtained from this assessment system if its limitations are kept in mind. Also, considerable information for planning instructional programs and for measuring the social validity of the interventions can be obtained from the SSRS. Results can be used to help define behaviors to observe directly in the classroom also. No adaptations are necessary for children and adolescents who are visually impaired or blind. Considering that social skills often are a concern for these children, results from this system can make an important contribution to the assessment process.

· ·

• Test of Language Development–Primary–Second Edition

Authors: Phyllis L. Newcomer & Donald D. Hammill

Publisher: PRO-ED
8700 Shoal Creek Boulevard
Austin, TX 78757-6897

Copyright: 1988

GENERAL DESCRIPTION

The *Test of Language Development–Primary–Second Edition* (TOLD–P:2) was designed to assess receptive and expressive language for children age 4-0 through 8-11.

Seven subtests make up the TOLD–P:2: Picture Vocabulary, Oral Vocabulary, Grammatic Understanding, Sentence Imitation, Grammatic Completion, Word Discrimination, and Word Articulation. Subtests that do not require vision are: Oral Vocabulary, Sentence Imitation, Grammatic Completion, and Word Discrimination. These four subtests will be the focus of this review.

Results are provided in terms of quotients (mean = 100, standard deviation = 15) for the Overall Spoken Language score and for the composites of Listening, Speaking, Semantics, Syntax, and Phonology. Neither the Overall Spoken Language result nor the composites can be obtained for a child with limited vision. Scores for the subtests that do not require vision can be obtained, however, in terms of a standard score (mean = 10, standard deviation = 3) or a percentile.

Time for administration of the subtests that do not require vision varies from approximately 20 to 30 minutes.

Materials needed for these subtests include the examiner's manual and a record book.

DESCRIPTION OF SUBTESTS

Oral Vocabulary.

This 30-item subtest studies a child's ability to use correct vocabulary when speaking (i.e., expressive semantics). The examiner gives the child a word orally, and the child is asked to define the word. Words range in difficulty from "bird" and "apple" to "bamboo" and "kayak." The word "castle," which appears on this subtest, is an example of a word that is particularly difficult for children with little or no usable vision to understand.

Sentence Imitation.

This 30-item subtest assesses a child's ability to use correct grammar and word order when speaking (i.e., expressive syntax). The examiner presents sentences of increasing difficulty to a child who is asked to repeat exactly what the examiner has said.

Grammatic Completion.

Consisting of 30 items, this subtest evaluates a child's ability to use correct grammar when speaking (i.e., expressive syntax). The examiner orally presents sentences that have a word missing. The child's task is to supply a grammatically correct word to complete the sentence.

Word Discrimination.

This 20-item subtest assesses a child's ability to recognize differences in speech sounds (i.e., receptive phonology). The examiner presents word pairs, and the child indicates whether the words sound the same or different.

TECHNICAL ADEQUACY

Standardization.

The number of subjects per age level in the sample ranged from 315 to 622, for a total of 2,436 children. Only a sighted sample was used in the standardization. The demographic characteristics of the sample correspond closely to the 1985 U.S. census data in terms of gender, geographic distribution, socioeconomic level, race, ethnicity, and urban/rural residence.

Reliability.

Test-retest reliability was examined in two studies. One study used a 5-day retest interval and reported correlations collapsed across age levels as follows: Oral Vocabulary .93, Sentence Imitation .98, Grammatic Completion .96, and Word Discrimination .94. McNeilly (1987) examined the test-retest reliability of the TOLD–P:2 for ages 4, 6, and 8 with a 2-week retest interval. Ranges for the correlations were as follows (correlations corrected for restricted range): Oral Vocabulary .75 to .90, Sentence Imitation .93 to .97, Grammatic Completion .86, and Word Discrimination .42 to .86.

Internal consistency coefficients ranged from .86 to .91 for Oral Vocabulary, .91 to .95 for Sentence Imitation, .88 to .92 for Grammatic Completion, and .82 to .94 for Word Discrimination.

Standard errors of measurement are presented by age level.

Validity.

In terms of content validity, 100 professionals rated the subtests as being consistent with the model on which the test is based, assessing listening and speaking skills as well as semantics and syntax.

For criterion-related validity, results of the TOLD–P:2 were compared with nine criterion tests. Correlation ranges and criterion tests for subtests that do not require vision were as follows: Oral Vocabulary and the *Wechsler Intelligence Scale for Children–Revised*–Vocabulary (Wechsler, 1974) .67 to .76; Sentence Imitation and the *Northwestern Syntax Screening Test*–Expressive (Lee, 1971) .55 to .66 and the *Detroit Test of Learning Aptitude–Second Edition*–Related Syllables (Hammill, 1985) .68 to .78; Grammatic Completion and the *Illinois Test of Psycholinguistic Abilities*–Grammatic Closure (Kirk, McCarthy, & Kirk, 1968) .49 to .78; Word Discrimination and the *Auditory Discrimination Test* (Wepman, 1968) .57 to .70. Additional studies are reported in the manual with similar results.

Numerous studies on construct validity are presented in the manual. The TOLD–P:2 results were shown to: (a) increase with age, (b) correlate adequately with measures of intelligence for various groups of children, and (c) correlate adequately with measures of achievement for various groups of children. The subtests also correlated adequately with each other, and it was possible to distinguish between groups of children with different types of disabling conditions using test results. Several factor analyses found only two factors. The authors suggested, however, that linguistic abilities are highly interrelated and tend to load on a common factor. They suggested that results of the factor analytic studies, therefore, should not be interpreted necessarily to mean that the TOLD–P:2 measures only two aspects of language.

CONCLUSIONS

The data on the technical adequacy of the TOLD–P:2 show that the test is well standardized, reliable, and, generally speaking, valid. The Word Discrimination subtest, however, is not reliable for 6- or 8-year-olds. Three of the four subtests that do not require vision seem to provide useful norm-referenced information on the oral language skills of young children with a visual loss. Three of the subtests tap expressive skills for vocabulary and grammar, and the fourth assesses auditory discrimination abilities. To avoid underestimating the ability of a child, the content of missed items should be examined to determine whether concepts were involved that are particularly difficult for children who are visually impaired or blind.

. . . .

• Vineland Social Maturity Scale

Because this instrument is designed primarily for students older than 4 years of age, the review for the *Vineland Scale* appears in Chapter 6.

• Wechsler Preschool and Primary Scale of Intelligence

Author: David Wechsler

Publisher: The Psychological Corporation
555 Academic Court
San Antonio, TX 78204

Copyright: 1967

GENERAL DESCRIPTION

Though a revision of this test has been published, vision is required on the more recent version, making it inappropriate for many children who are visually impaired or blind. Hence, the older version, which does not require vision on the verbal section, will be reviewed. This individually administered intelligence test is designed for children 4 to 6½ years old.

The *Wechsler Preschool and Primary Scale of Intelligence* (WPPSI) is made up of 11 subtests, 6 of which make up the Verbal Scale and 5 of which make up the Performance Scale. Only the Verbal Scale will be reviewed because the Performance Scale requires vision and cannot be adapted to circumvent a visual problem. Subtests for the Verbal Scale are: Information, Vocabulary, Arithmetic, Similarities, Comprehension, and Sentences (a supplementary subtest). Though Sentences can be used as an additional subtest, it is not used in calculating an IQ score.

Results are calculated in terms of quotients for the overall results and the Verbal and Performance scales (mean = 100, standard deviation = 15) and scaled scores for the subtests (mean = 10, standard deviation = 3).

Administration time is approximately 50 to 75 minutes. Using only the Verbal Scale would require approximately half this time.

The materials for the Verbal Scale include the manual, record forms, and a set of blocks. No adaptations are presented for children who are visually impaired or blind. If the Verbal Scale is used with a child with little or no vision, however, the examiner will need four special cards with raised drawings for the first four items on the Arithmetic subtest.

DESCRIPTION OF SUBTESTS

Information.

During this subtest, consisting of 23 items, the examiner asks the child questions such as "How many ears do you have?" Other than the first item, which requires that a child touch his or her nose, only verbal responses are required.

Vocabulary.

This subtest, consisting of 22 items, requires the child to define words for the examiner. Examples include "shoe," "donkey," and "nuisance."

Arithmetic.

Of the 20 items on this subtest, 12 require a verbal response. Four of the items have pictures (raised figures are needed for children with little or no vision) requiring a child to point. The remaining 3 items ask a child to count a given number of blocks, and, in one case, to give the examiner some blocks.

Similarities.

This subtest includes 16 items. The format for the first 10 items requires that a child complete a sentence such as "Milk and water are both good to _____." For the remaining 6 items a child must explain how two objects are alike (e.g., piano/violin).

Comprehension.

For the 15 items on this subtest, children must answer questions given verbally by the examiner. An example is "Why should children who are sick stay home?"

Sentences.

This supplementary test involves 10 sentences that the examiner gives orally and asks the child to repeat. This subtest provides an estimate of a child's verbal memory, which may be helpful to consider in planning instruction for children who are visually impaired or blind and who must rely on auditory input for learning.

TECHNICAL ADEQUACY

Standardization.

The sample for the WPPSI contained 100 boys and 100 girls per age level, for a total of 1,200 children. The demographic data for these children correspond very closely to the 1960 census data in terms of geographic distribution, father's education, and urban/rural residence. Furthermore, there is a close correspondence for race (white and nonwhite) by geographic distribution and by urban/rural residence. The sample seems to be a good representation of the U.S. population for the 1960s.

Reliability.

Test-retest data are given only for 50 children between 5½ and 5¾ years of age. The retest interval was 48 to 117 days. Correlations for the Verbal subtests ranged from .60 to .89, and the correlation for the Verbal IQ was .86. More data are needed by age level.

Internal consistency data on Verbal subtests ranged from .77 to .88. Verbal IQ correlations ranged from .93 to .95.

Standard errors of measurement are given for each subtest and the Verbal Scale. These data are presented by age level.

Validity.

The average intercorrelation of the subtests on the Verbal Scale ranged from .46 to .60. Average intercorrelations of the Verbal IQ and the Verbal subtests ranged from .62 to .73.

The WPPSI has been compared in many research studies with other tests for concurrent validity. The manual reports correlations with two other intelligence tests: *Stanford-Binet Intelligence Scale* (Terman & Merrill, 1960) and *Pictorial Test of Intelligence* (PTI) (French, 1964). Correlations with the *Binet* for the Verbal subtests ranged from .39 to .63, and with the PTI from .22 to .56. WPPSI Verbal IQ correlated .76 with the *Binet* IQ and .53 with the PTI.

CONCLUSIONS

This is a well-standardized test, though normative data are not available for children who are visually impaired or blind, and the norms are dated. Validity data are good, but test-retest data are needed by age level. Except for several of the first items on the Arithmetic subtest, no visual skills are needed to respond to the items on the Verbal Scale. Due to the emphasis on verbal skills, results of this scale must be interpreted carefully because verbal skills seem to take longer to develop for young children who are visually impaired or blind. Results of the WPPSI may underestimate the abilities of some of these children for this reason. Compared with using the entire scale, using only the Verbal section of the WPPSI reduces the sample of a child's behavior that is obtained. Hence, it is important to consider WPPSI results in light of a child's adaptive behaviors and language skills as well.

· ·

CRITERION-REFERENCED TESTS AND INFORMAL MEASURES

· ·

• Revised Brigance Diagnostic Inventory of Early Development

See review in Chapter 4.

(List continues on next page.)

· ·

- **Informal Assessment of Developmental Skills for Visually Handicapped Students.
  Part Two: Informal Assessment of Developmental Skills for Younger Visually Handicapped and Multihandicapped Children**

  See review in Chapter 4.

· ·

- **The Oregon Project for Visually Impaired and Blind Preschool Children–Fifth Edition**

  See review in Chapter 4.

Chapter 6

Assessment of School-Age Students

ASSESSMENT OF A SCHOOL-AGE STUDENT WHO IS VISUALLY impaired or blind cannot be carried out satisfactorily with simply the administration of an intelligence test and one or two achievement tests. The issues involved in the assessment of a student's academic performance are very complex and require a thorough and well-planned approach in order to be useful in problem solving. The emphasis in this chapter is on obtaining information that aids in instruction. Issues that deserve consideration in the various areas of assessment are discussed, and detailed reviews of norm-referenced tests as well as criterion-referenced and curriculum-based measures and informal procedures are presented.

AREAS FOR ASSESSMENT

Achievement

To be helpful in solving problems, results of an assessment need to be related to instructional practices in the classroom. For several reasons, results from criterion-referenced tests and curriculum-based assessment are more relevant to instructional planning than results from norm-referenced tests. Criterion-referenced tests and curriculum-based assessment are developed from curricular materials and, therefore, provide results related to classroom instruction. Furthermore, these measures allow ongoing assessment, whereas norm-referenced testing is carried out only every few months or once a year. Frequent monitoring of student progress with criterion-referenced tests or curriculum-based assessment provides a much more extensive data base to describe a student's progress over time. Hence, information from criterion-referenced tests or curriculum-based assessment can be used to formulate decisions regarding instructional programs. In addition, these measures allow greater flexibility in administration than norm-referenced tests, an important advantage when working with students with a disability.

One goal for assessing achievement is to determine a student's strengths and areas of difficulty. In order to do this for a student who is visually impaired or blind, any adaptive devices or materials used in the classroom should be used during testing. Examples include Braille rulers, clocks, watches, and graphs. Students who know how to use an abacus could use this device on arithmetic tests that allow sighted students to write out their computations. If a student who is adventitiously blind knows how to write, then he or she could use paper with embossed lines during spelling tests. This paper, or paper with heavy black lines, also could be helpful for students who are visually impaired when written expression is assessed. Computers, low-vision aids, or closed-circuit television systems also may aid a student in responding to test items.

No individually administered achievement tests have been standardized on students who are visually impaired or blind. Some group-administered, norm-referenced tests have been transcribed into Braille or printed in large type, but individually administered tests are needed for decisions regarding eligibility for special education services. However, one group-administered test, the *Stanford Achievement Test*–Form J (SAT) (Psychological Corporation, 1989) deserves special consideration. When this test was transcribed into Braille at the American Printing House for the Blind (APH), some items had to be eliminated because they could not be transcribed adequately into Braille. Using the original normative data, the Psychological Corporation renormed the test, eliminating these items. Thus, the performance of students who are visually impaired or blind now can be compared to that of their sighted peers using either the fall or spring norms for the test. The SAT in Braille or large type begins with spring norms for grade 2 and goes through grade 12.

There are many subtests for the SAT that vary depending on the level of the test used. Generally, each level covers reading, written language, and mathematics, although science and social studies are included for many levels. The supplementary subtest, Study Skills, covers a range of library and research skills as well. Braille takes about 2½ times as long to read as print (Duckworth & Caton, 1986). Thus, the entire test given in Braille will take approximately 7½ hours to complete. The Braille transcription of the SAT (Duckworth, undated) and a large-type edition (Psychological Corporation, 1989) are available through the American Printing House for the Blind.

Reading

To assess Braille reading skills, an examiner must have a thorough knowledge of Braille. For students who are able to read large type, normal-size reading material can be enlarged or large-type versions of tests can be used. If material is enlarged, a sharp contrast between the print and the paper must be maintained.

To obtain a norm-referenced score for reading, the examiner can use the reading sections of the Braille transcription or large-type edition of the *Stanford Achievement Test*. Though typically group administered, the Braille and large-type versions can be given individually.

To obtain more detailed information on a student's reading decoding and comprehension skills with a norm-referenced test, the examiner could choose the Braille transcription (Duckworth, 1992) or large-type edition of the *Diagnostic Reading Scales* (DRS) (Spache, 1981). This technically adequate measure provides information on oral and silent reading levels and types of decoding errors. Comprehension and decoding are assessed using passages (i.e., "real" reading material rather than word lists). The DRS assesses comprehension requiring memory, and a supplementary section assesses knowledge of phonics skills using a criterion-referenced format. Besides norm-referenced results, the DRS provides information that can be very helpful in planning instruction.

Fortunately there are a number of useful measures for obtaining detailed information for planning instructional programs for reading. These measures include criterion-referenced tests, curriculum-based measurement, and informal measures.

For beginning Braille readers, the Braille Reading Readiness Skills section of the *Informal Assessment of Developmental Skills for Visually Handicapped Students* (Swallow, Mangold, & Mangold, 1978) can be useful. This informal 29-item checklist completed by the teacher can provide information regarding readiness skills for Braille, such as the ability to identify two geometric shapes as being the same or different.

For young children (up to about age 7), the *Revised Brigance Diagnostic Inventory of Early Development* (Brigance, 1991) Readiness and Basic Reading Skills sections can provide information on readiness skills, word recognition, and phonics. The Auditory Discrimination and Matches Initial Consonants with Pictures subtests can be skipped because they do not assess reading skills. For children who are or will be Braille readers, the *APH Tactile Supplement for the Brigance Diagnostic Inventory of Early Development* (Duckworth & Stratton, 1992) will be needed.

For Braille readers, the *Braille Unit Recognition Battery* (Caton, Duckworth, & Rankin, 1985) can comprehensively assess students' ability to recognize and identify Braille units. Information from this battery can be used to determine specifically which Braille units have been learned and which need to be taught. The Braille Mechanics section also addresses behaviors a student uses when reading Braille.

Though more general than the *Braille Unit Recognition Battery,* the Diagnostic Assessment of Braille Reading Skills section from the *Informal Assessment of Developmental Skills* (Swallow et al., 1978) could provide some additional information on Braille reading that would be relevant to instruction. This informal checklist covers many behaviors involved in Braille reading including book position, hand position, page turning, Braille errors, and word-analysis skills.

Because Braille takes more time to read, reading rate may be a concern. The *Basic Reading Rate Scale–Braille Edition* (Duckworth & Caton, 1986) measures the rate at which a student reads Braille material. Material on the scale is written in Grade 2 Literary Braille.

To monitor progress in Braille reading over time, curriculum-based measurement (CBM) can be used repeatedly without practice effects. This procedure involves having a student orally read Braille passages selected from material used for reading instruction. As the student reads, the examiner follows along with a copy of the passages and codes errors made by the student. When this procedure is used with sighted students, they are asked to read from each passage for 1 minute, and three 1-min. samples of a student's reading abilities are obtained. Because Braille requires more time to read, a sample of 2 minutes, with 6 seconds (rather than 3) for error correction, seems to correlate best with results from norm-referenced tests (Morgan, 1993). The result obtained from the use of CBM is the number of words read correctly. Because variability among the three passages is likely, the median of the three scores typically is used as the measure of performance. Passages for reading are randomly selected from the instructional material for the year. The use of different passages to measure performance allows this procedure to be used repeatedly (several times a week, if desired) to monitor performance over time. Graphing results helps to determine whether a student is making adequate progress in reading. A lack of improvement in the number of words read indicates that the student needs a change in reading instruction. Performance also can be compared to other average peers to help decide whether a student's progress is adequate. In a study by Morgan (1993) with elementary-age Braille readers, results from CBM were found to correlate well (r = .80) with results from the *Diagnostic Reading Scales* (Spache, 1981). In terms of test-retest reliability, Morgan found the correlation over a 2-week retest interval to be .98 for this procedure. Shinn (1989) offered a detailed presentation of the procedures for using CBM and the issues involved. CBM can be used with large-type material. Whether samples longer than the 1-min. samples used with sighted students are needed for large type remains to be investigated. It does, however, take longer to read large type.

To comprehensively assess word-analysis skills for the purpose of planning instruction, the *APH Tactile Supplement for the Brigance Diagnostic Comprehensive Inventory of Basic Skills* (Duckworth & Abbot, undated) is available from the American Printing House for the Blind. The *Brigance Diagnostic Comprehensive Inventory of Basic Skills,* in combination with the *APH Tactile Supplement,* allows a detailed assessment of skills for phonics, structural analysis, and functional word recognition (e.g., warning and safety signs and directional words). Each skill is tested at least three times.

To comprehensively assess a student's knowledge of sight words, the Dolch word list (Dolch, 1955) is available on cards in a Braille and large-type edition from the American Printing House for the Blind. This list consists of 220 sight words and 95 picture words and can be supplemented with words from the Fry (1980) list of instant words (described in the review of the Dolch cards in this chapter).

Thus, many options are available for obtaining information to plan instruction for students reading Braille or large type. Information about a student's knowledge of sight words, word-analysis skills, Braille units, and reading rate is needed for effective instruction. Information for Braille and large-type readers on oral and silent reading achievement levels from the DRS also helps in program planning. Monitoring progress in reading through curriculum-based measurement procedures is important to ensure efficient instruction. Though time consuming, such a comprehensive assessment will provide valuable information for instructional planning. Table 6.1 summarizes the options for assessing reading skills.

Mathematics

The best option for obtaining a norm-referenced score for mathematics seems to be the SAT (1989) for students in elementary and secondary grades. Braille or large-type editions are available from APH.

To obtain information for program planning for young children or older students having difficulty with addition, the steps for meaningful counting (described in Chapter 5) would be appropriate. Understanding of quantitative and shape concepts, numeral comprehension, ability to read Braille numbers, and knowledge of ordinal position can be assessed for these children with the *Revised Brigance Diagnostic Inventory of Early Development* (Brigance, 1991) in conjunction with the *APH Tactile Supplement* (Duckworth & Stratton, 1992) for this inventory.

A student's ability to recognize the numbers in Braille can be tested with the *Braille Unit Recognition Battery* (Caton et al., 1985). This battery provides detailed information on the Braille numbers a student can recognize and those that need to be taught.

To determine a student's strengths and difficulties with beginning number concepts, math facts, operations, fractions, decimals, measurement, and mathematics vocabulary, the *Brigance Diagnostic Comprehensive Inventory of Basic Skills* (Brigance, 1983) can be used. For Braille readers, the *APH Tactile Supplement* (Duckworth & Abbot, undated) will be needed. Each skill is assessed at least three times to ensure reliable results. This measure covers skills taught in the elementary and middle grades.

Unfortunately, no studies have been carried out to investigate the use of curriculum-based measurement of mathematics skills for Braille readers or those who need large type. For a discussion of the use of curriculum-based measurement with sighted readers, see Shinn (1989).

Measures for obtaining information on a student's math performance are listed in Table 6.2.

Written language

The best option for obtaining a norm-referenced score for written language for students in the elementary or secondary grades

TABLE 6.1. *Measures for Assessing Skills in Reading for Students Who Are Visually Impaired or Blind*

Tests	Skills Assessed	Type of Assessment	Adaptations
Basic Reading Rate Scale: Braille Edition or Large Type (Duckworth & Caton, 1986) (Beginning Braille readers through adults)	Reading rate	Norm-referenced	None required
Braille Unit Recognition Battery (Caton, Duckworth, & Rankin, 1985) (Grades 3 through 12)	Identification of Braille units	Criterion-referenced	None required
Brigance Diagnostic Comprehensive Inventory of Basic Skills (Brigance, 1983) (Skills taught in kindergarten through grade 9	Detailed word analysis; word recognition	Criterion-referenced	*APH Tactile Supplement* (Duckworth & Abbot, undated)
Revised Brigance Diagnostic Inventory of Early Development (Brigance, 1991) (Birth through age 7)	Readiness; phonics; word recognition	Criterion-referenced	*APH Tactile Supplement* (Duckworth & Stratton, 1992)

(continued)

TABLE 6.1. *Continued*

Curriculum-Based Measurement (Shinn, 1989; Morgan, 1993) (Any grade level)	Progress in reading	Curriculum-based	None required with Morgan's (1993) procedure
Diagnostic Reading Scales (Spache, 1981) (Mid-1st through mid-7th grade)	Word analysis; comprehension; oral & silent reading levels	Norm-referenced; Criterion-referenced	*APH Braille transcription* (Duckworth, 1992) or large-type edition
Dolch Word List (Dolch, 1955) (About age 6 through 9 or older)	Sight vocabulary	Informal checklist	APH Braille and large-type cards
Informal Assessment of Developmental Skills (Swallow et al., 1978) (Preschool through school-age)	Readiness for Braille; reading behaviors; Braille unit recognition; word analysis	Informal checklist	None required
Stanford Achievement Test (Psychological Corporation, 1989) (Grades 2 through 12)	Word study skills; vocabulary; comprehension	Norm-referenced	APH Braille transcription (Duckworth, undated) or large-type edition

seems to be the SAT (1989). A Braille or large-type edition is available from APH.

The *Informal Assessment of Developmental Skills* (Swallow et al., 1978) contains several informal checklists that measure skills involved in Braille writing, script writing for students who are visually impaired or blind, and typing. These checklists are completed by the teacher, and the information obtained is relevant to instruction.

TABLE 6.2. *Measures for Assessing Skills in Mathematics for Students Who Are Visually Impaired or Blind*

Tests	Skills Assessed	Type of Assessment	Adaptations
Braille Unit Recognition Battery (Caton et al., 1985) (Grades 3 through 12)	Recognition of Braille numbers	Criterion-referenced	None required
Brigance Diagnostic Comprehensive Inventory of Basic Skills (Brigance, 1983) (Kindergarten through grade 9)	Number concepts; facts; operations; measurement; vocabulary	Criterion-referenced	*APH Tactile Supplement* (Duckworth & Abbot, undated)
Revised Brigance Diagnostic Inventory of Early Development (Brigance, 1991) (Birth through age 7)	Math concepts; reading Braille numbers; numeral comprehension	Criterion-referenced	*APH Tactile Supplement* (Duckworth & Stratton, 1992)
Stanford Achievement Test (Psychological Corporation, 1989) (Mid-2nd through grade 12)	Math concepts; computation; application	Norm-referenced	APH Braille transcription (Duckworth, undated) or large-type edition
Steps for Meaningful Counting (Englemann, 1969) (Preaddition skills)	Meaningful counting	Informal measure	None required

The *Brigance Diagnostic Comprehensive Inventory of Basic Skills* (Brigance, 1983) and the *APH Tactile Supplement* for Braille readers (Duckworth & Abbot, undated) can be used to obtain detailed information on skills mastered and skills to be taught. Areas assessed include capitalization, punctuation, spelling, writing sentences, addressing envelopes, and writing letters.

When assessing spelling for students who are having difficulty, especially for students beyond the sixth grade, Bradley-Johnson and Lesiak (1989) recommended testing the words students use most frequently in their writing. Hillerich (1978) published a list of 100 words that account for 60% of words used by elementary school children (through sixth grade) in their writing, making them important words for students to be able to spell. Using these words for assessment can provide useful information about which words the students need to learn.

Measures that can be used to obtain information on a student's written language skills are listed in Table 6.3.

Oral language

When assessing the oral language skills of a young school-age student with little or no vision, several issues discussed for assessing oral language of preschool children are relevant. The use of personal pronouns may be delayed (Fewell, 1983; Goldman & Duda, 1978), and the use of possessive pronouns such as *her* and *their* also may take longer to learn (Brown, Simmons, & Methvin, 1979). Position concepts such as *up* and *right* are particularly important for these children. Hence, the examiner should be sure these concepts are understood clearly.

A number of alternatives exist for obtaining norm-referenced results for oral language skills of school-age students who are visually impaired or blind. For students through age 6, the Spoken Language subtest of the *Basic School Skills Inventory–Diagnostic* (Hammill & Leigh, 1983) could be completed by a teacher to describe a child's use of language in the classroom. No vision is needed for this measure. Also, for children through age 8, the Communication domain of the *Battelle Developmental Inventory* (Newborg et al., 1984) could be used. This measure can be completed by observation, interview, or direct testing. Both receptive and expressive items are included on the *Battelle*. Another measure for children through 8 years of age is the *Test of Language Development–Primary: Second Edition* (Newcomer & Hammill, 1988). The subtests that do not require vision are: Oral Vocabulary, Sentence Imitation, Grammatic

TABLE 6.3. *Measures for Assessing Skills in Written Language for Students Who Are Visually Impaired or Blind*

Tests	Skills Assessed	Type of Assessment	Adaptations
Brigance Diagnostic Comprehensive Inventory of Basic Skills (Brigance, 1983) (Kindergarten through grade 9)	Spelling; punctuation; capitalization; writing letters and envelopes	Criterion-referenced	*APH Tactile Supplement* (Duckworth & Abbot, undated)
Hillerich's (1978) High-Frequency Word List (Upper elementary grades and older)	Spelling	Informal word list	None required
Informal Assessment of Developmental Skills (Swallow et al., 1978) (All grades)	Braille writing; script writing; typing	Informal checklist	None required
Stanford Achievement Test (Psychological Corporation, 1989) (Mid-2nd through grade 12)	Varies with level	Norm-referenced	APH Braille transcription (Duckworth, undated) or large-type edition

Completion, and Word Discrimination. The first three subtests tap expressive skills and the fourth receptive. This test is administered directly to a child.

To assess oral language skills of students in the elementary and middle grades, the entire *Test of Language Development–Intermediate: Second Edition* (TOLD–I:2) (Hammill & Newcomer, 1988) can be given without adaptations to a student with a visual loss. The TOLD–I:2 assesses both expressive and receptive skills. The Speaking Vocabulary and Speaking Grammar subtests from the *Test of Adolescent Language–Second Edition* (Hammill, Brown, Larsen, & Wiederholt, 1987) can be used with students in the middle and upper grades because these subtests do not require vision. These two subtests, however, would assess only expressive language. Another alternative that does not require vision is to use the Story Comprehension, Characteristics, Synonyms, and Grammatic Completion subtests from the *Diagnostic Achievement Battery–Second Edition* (Newcomer, 1990). This test was designed for students through age 14-11, and these subtests address both expressive and receptive skills.

To obtain more detailed information related to instruction, the *Revised Brigance Diagnostic Inventory of Early Development* (Brigance, 1991) or the *Brigance Diagnostic Comprehensive Inventory of Basic Skills* (Brigance, 1983) can be administered along with the corresponding *APH Tactile Supplement* (Duckworth & Abbot, undated; Duckworth & Stratton, 1992) for students with little or no vision. Sections that are particularly important are those testing a student's ability to give personal data and follow verbal directions and his or her knowledge of directional/positional concepts. All of these skills are essential for students who are visually impaired or blind because they contribute to their safety and independence.

Though the information would be more general than that obtained from the Brigance tests, results from the *Informal Assessment of Developmental Skills* (Swallow et al., 1978) and the *Oregon Project* (Anderson et al., 1986) may be useful in planning instruction for children up to age 6 or 7.

Table 6.4 lists the measures that can be used to assess oral language for these students.

Cognitive Assessment

Interpreting results of intelligence tests for students who are visually impaired or blind requires considerable reflection and caution. This population of students is heterogeneous in terms of educational needs; hence, assessment must be designed to meet each student's unique needs.

Ashman (1982) suggested that to avoid overinterpreting test results for these students the standard error of measurement should be used to describe a range of performance rather than a single score. This approach is good practice when reporting results for any

TABLE 6.4. *Measures for Assessing Oral Language for Students Who Are Visually Impaired or Blind*

Tests	Sections	Type of Assessment	Adaptations
Basic School Skills Inventory– Diagnostic (Hammill & Leigh, 1983) (Age 4 through 6)	Spoken Language	Norm-referenced	2 items require vision
Battelle Developmental Inventory (Newborg et al., 1984) (Birth through age 8)	Communication domain	Norm-referenced	3 items require vision
Brigance Diagnostic Comprehensive Inventory of Basic Skills (Brigance, 1983) (Kindergarten through grade 9)	Speaking; Listening	Criterion-referenced	*APH Tactile Supplement* (Duckworth & Abbott, undated)
Revised Brigance Diagnostic Inventory of Early Development (Brigance, 1991) (Birth through age 7)	Speech & Language Skills	Criterion-referenced	*APH Tactile Supplement* (Duckworth & Stratton, 1992)
Diagnostic Achievement Battery– Second Edition (Newcomer, 1990) (Age 6-0 to 14-11)	Listening; Speaking	Norm-referenced	None required

(continued)

TABLE 6.4. *Continued*

Informal Assessment of Developmental Skills (Swallow et al., 1978) (Early elementary)	Language	Informal checklist	None required
Oregon Project for Visually Impaired and Blind Preschool Children (Anderson et al., 1986) (Birth through age 6)	Language	Curriculum-based	None required
Test of Adolescent Language– Second Edition (Hammill et al., 1987) (Age 11-0 to 18-5)	Speaking Grammar; Speaking Vocabulary	Norm-referenced	None required
Test of Language Development– Intermediate: Second Edition (Hammill & Newcomer, 1988) (Age 8-6 to 12-11)	All receptive and expressive subtests	Norm-referenced	None required
Test of Language Development– Primary: Second Edition (Newcomer & Hammill, 1988) (Age 4 through 8)	Sentence Imitation; Oral Vocabulary; Grammatic Completion; Word Discrimination	Norm-referenced	None required

student but is especially important when assessing students with disabilities.

Numerous studies have been carried out to examine any differences that might exist in *Wechsler Intelligence Scale for Children* (WISC) (Wechsler, 1949) Verbal Scale profiles for students who are visually impaired or blind. Though the studies are dated, results indicated that students who are blind tend to score higher on Digit Span and lower on Similarities. This effect was consistent across age levels from 7 through 11 years (Tillman & Osborne, 1969). Several other studies (Gilbert & Rubin, 1965; Hopkins & McGuire, 1966) found significantly high means on Information and low means on Comprehension for students who were blind. These authors suggested that including Digit Span as a subtest and prorating scores based on results of all six subtests resulted in spuriously high IQ scores. Tillman (1967) found that using this approach did yield a higher mean IQ for a group of 38 subjects. Including the Digit Span subtest, however, raised the mean IQ about as much as the Comprehension and Similarities subtests lowered it.

In a review of studies on the reliability of the WISC, Tillman (1973) found that internal consistency and test-retest coefficients were about the same for students who were blind as for sighted students. He noted that few studies have been done with students who were blind on the validity of the WISC. Questions exist regarding the appropriateness of the content for these students, and predictive validity studies are lacking.

In order to avoid underestimating performance when interpreting results from intelligence tests, it is important to consider that abstract concepts tend to take longer to develop for some students who are visually impaired or blind than for sighted students (Ashman, 1982). An examination of missed items can help the examiner decide whether the presence of such concepts on the test influenced results.

If intelligence tests are to continue to be required for eligibility decisions for special education services, then there certainly is a need for a new test of intelligence for students who are visually impaired or blind. As Hopkins and McGuire (1966) noted, it would be desirable to have two sets of norms "so that a blind child might not only be compared with those of like handicap, but also with those with whom he must compete in the academic and vocational world" (p. 73).

No current tests of intelligence have been standardized on students who are visually impaired or blind. Hence, when assessing the intelligence of these students, the examiner has to use tests that have less-than-adequate technical adequacy or use sections that do not require vision from tests standardized on sighted students. Given the limitation of the measures that must be used, it is wise to administer at least three of the measures that follow in order to obtain as adequate a data base as possible for decision making.

One option is to use the Verbal Scale from one of the Wechsler scales. For children through age 6 who have little or no vision, the *Wechsler Preschool and Primary Scale of Intelligence* (WPPSI) (Wechsler, 1967) must be given because the Verbal Scale of the *Wechsler Preschool and Primary Scale of Intelligence–Revised* (WPPSI–R) (Wechsler, 1989) requires vision. To avoid underestimating the intellectual ability of young children with a severe visual loss, keep in mind that some concepts are difficult to learn without the aid of vision and that vocabulary is slower to develop for these children. For older students the Verbal Scale of the *Wechsler Intelligence Scale for Children–Third Edition* (Wechsler, 1991) can be given. The Digit Span subtest can be substituted for the Arithmetic subtest, which requires vision on many items. A Verbal Comprehension Index Score can be obtained. The examiner can avoid overestimating the intellectual ability of students who are visually impaired or blind by probing questionable responses to ensure adequate understanding of concepts. This will help to prevent the examiner from crediting rote responses that lack sufficient depth. For students age 16 and older, the Verbal Scale of the *Wechsler Adult Intelligence Scale– Revised* (1981) can be administered.

The only nonverbal intelligence test standardized on students who are visually impaired or blind is the *Blind Learning Aptitude Test* (BLAT) (Newland, 1971). This test, designed for students age 6 through 16, may provide some useful information on nonverbal problem solving, but its age and problems with technical adequacy must be considered. Observing a student's behavior on this test may help the examiner understand a student's problem-solving strategies. In this author's work with the BLAT, the results often are inflated, but this is not surprising, given the age of the test.

Four subtests from the *Detroit Test of Learning Aptitude–Third Edition* (DTLA–3) (Hammill, 1991) can provide useful supplemental information on intelligence. These subtests are: Word Opposites, Sentence Imitation, Basic Information, and Word Sequences. The technical adequacy for these subtests is good, and the DTLA–3 is a current measure.

Another alternative for supplemental information is to use the three subtests that do not require vision from the *Differential Ability Scales* (Elliott, 1990). The subtests are: Word Definitions, Similarities, and Recall of Digits. Unfortunately, the test-retest reliability of these subtests is not adequate.

A list of possible measures for assessing cognitive development is presented in Table 6.5.

Assessment of Social Skills

"Appropriate social interaction is the logical prerequisite to social acceptance" (Raver-Lampman, 1990, p. 70). Unfortunately, the development of adequate social skills is delayed for many students who are visually impaired or blind (Skellenger, Hill, & Hill, 1992).

Attempting to address this problem by simply including students who are visually impaired or blind in regular classroom environments is not sufficient to foster adequate social interaction between these students and their sighted peers. As Tuttle (1984) noted, "Physical integration does not necessarily result in social integration" (p. 11). Jones, Lavine, and Shell (1972) examined sociometric ratings of 20 children who were visually impaired and mainstreamed in fourth through sixth grades. Their classmates rated these children below the class medians for social acceptance in most areas.

It is likely that limitations in visual input account, at least in part, for the difficulty these students have in learning social skills (Skellenger et al., 1992; Van Hasselt, Hersen, Kazdin, Simon, & Mastantuono, 1983). Sighted persons depend a great deal on visual cues when learning social skills.

As noted by Skellenger et al. (1992), the ability of students who have severe visual impairments to receive and produce nonverbal behavior that supports or takes the place of verbal expression is limited. Several studies have shown that the use of nonverbal behavior by students who are visually impaired or blind is not comparable to that of their sighted peers (Parke, Shallcross, & Anderson, 1980; Van Hasselt, Simon, & Mastantuono, 1984). Other social skill problems that have been noted for students who are visually impaired or blind include lower frequencies of interactions with sighted peers (Hoben & Lindstrom, 1980), greater isolation (Eaglestein, 1975; MacFarland, 1966), and fewer initiations for social contact (Markovits & Strayer, 1982). Consistent with these observations, teachers also have reported that during noninstructional time these students spend more time alone and more time waiting for initiations than their sighted peers (Hoben & Lindstrom, 1980).

Hence, the assessment of social skills for students who are visually impaired or blind is an important aspect of educational planning for

TABLE 6.5. *Measures for Assessing Cognitive Development for Students Who Are Visually Impaired or Blind*

Tests	Age Level	Sections
Blind Learning Aptitude Test (Newland, 1971)	6 through 16	Entire test
Detroit Test of Learning Ability–Third Edition (Hammill, 1991)	6 through 17	Word Opposites; Sentence Imitation; Word Sequences
Differential Ability Scales (Elliott, 1990)	6 through 17	Word Definitions; Similarities; Recall of Digits
Wechsler Adult Intelligence Scale–Revised (Wechsler, 1981)	16 and older	Verbal Scale
Wechsler Intelligence Scale for Children–Third Edition (Wechsler, 1991)	6 through 16	Verbal Scale
Wechsler Preschool and Primary Scale of Intelligence (Wechsler, 1967)	4 through 6½	Verbal Scale

these students. The sooner intervention can be implemented for students with problems in social skills, the more likely it is to be effective.

A particularly important component to any assessment of social skills is the use of systematic direct observation in the natural environment. Data from such observation aids in assessment and program planning as well as in monitoring progress once intervention is begun.

For young children, there are several norm-referenced options for assessing social skills. The Classroom Behavior section of the *Basic School Skills Inventory–Diagnostic* (Hammill & Leigh, 1983) is completed by the classroom teacher and provides some general information for instructional planning as well as norm-referenced scores.

No visual skills are required on the section of the *Battelle Developmental Inventory* (Newborg et al., 1984) assessing social skills for children through age 8. In addition to norm-referenced results, this measure can provide some general information for program planning.

A recent contribution to the assessment of social skills is the *Social Skills Rating System* (SSRS) (Gresham & Elliott, 1990). Though the representation of students who are visually impaired or blind in the sample for the SSRS was small, these students were included when the test was standardized. In addition to providing norm-referenced results, this scale supplies specific information on both prosocial behavior and inappropriate behavior that is helpful in planning instruction. Each item is rated in terms of frequency and importance to the rater. Because there is a separate form for parents and for teachers, an ecological approach to assessing social skills is possible. There is also a student form for students in third grade and up, but student ratings tend to be quite unreliable.

The combination of systematic direct observation and results from the SSRS would provide a considerable amount of useful information on social skills. For young, elementary-age students (up to about age 7), some additional information for planning instruction can be obtained from the *Oregon Project* (Anderson et al., 1986), the *Revised Brigance Diagnostic Inventory of Early Development* (Brigance, 1991), and the *Informal Assessment of Developmental Skills* (Swallow et al., 1978).

Table 6.6 presents a list of measures that provide information on social skills.

Adaptive Behavior

Delays in the development of adaptive behavior may occur for students who are visually impaired or blind. Reasons for such delays include overprotection by adults, delays in the fine motor skills needed for some adaptive behaviors, or impairment of visual input.

If a student who is visually impaired or blind can successfully carry out tasks such as self-care and household chores using adaptive equipment, the student should be given credit for these skills on measures used to assess adaptive behavior. Examples of such adaptive equipment include knives with slicing guides, adaptive measuring devices, Braille clocks or watches, and tools that can be used by persons without vision.

Some critical adaptive behaviors for students who are visually impaired or blind are those related to orientation and mobility. As Ashman (1982, p. 11) noted, *(text continued on page 175)*

TABLE 6.6. *Measures for Assessing Social Skills for Students Who Are Visually Impaired or Blind*

Tests	Sections	Type of Assessment	Adaptations
Basic School Skills Inventory– Diagnostic (Hammill & Leigh, 1983) (Age 4 through 6)	Classroom Behavior	Norm-referenced	None required
Battelle Developmental Inventory (Newborg et al., 1984) (Birth through age 8)	Personal– Social domain	Norm-referenced	1 item requires vision
Revised Brigance Diagnostic Inventory of Early Development (Brigance, 1991) (Birth to age 7)	Social & Emotional Development	Criterion-referenced	None required
Informal Assessment of Developmental Skills (Swallow et al., 1978) (Early elementary age)	Socio- Emotional	Informal checklist	None required
Oregon Project for Visually Impaired and Blind Preschool Children (Anderson et al., 1986) (Birth through age 6)	Socialization	Curriculum-based	None required

(continued)

TABLE 6.6. *Continued*

Social Skills Rating Scale (Gresham & Elliott, 1990) (Preschool through high school)	Entire scale	Norm-referenced	None required

> Minimal ability to get around in a public school setting is often misinterpreted as amazingly good by public school staff unfamiliar with the performance of the well trained blind individual. Intensive individual instruction in this area contributes strikingly to the blind child's independent functioning and social acceptability, as well as to positive self-concept.

Thus, the input of an orientation and mobility instructor is very important in assessment and educational planning.

Students may function differently in their home environment than in the school setting because the home is more familiar. For this reason both the teacher and the parents should complete an adaptive behavior measure. Dissimilar results can occur due to differences in the perspectives and expectations of the teacher and parents, variations in the tests used, or real differences in performance. Follow-up on differences in measures of adaptive behavior can provide important information for planning instruction.

There are several norm-referenced options for assessing adaptive behavior for students who are visually impaired or blind. All of these measures provide some information for planning instruction as well.

When the teacher is the informant, the most technically adequate, norm-referenced measure for adaptive behavior is the *Adaptive Behavior Inventory* (ABI) (Brown & Leigh, 1986). This measure addresses adaptive behavior used in the classroom, including self-care skills, communication, social skills, academic skills, and occupational skills. The ABI has norms for students without impairments as well as norms for students who are mentally retarded.

The *Vineland Adaptive Behavior Scales–Expanded or Survey Version* (Sparrow, Balla, & Cicchetti, 1984) is designed with the caregiver as the informant. Though the test is very extensive, many items on the scales require vision. Hence, results may underestimate the performance of students who are visually impaired or blind.

For students through age 6, the Daily Living Skills section of the BSSI–D (Hammill & Leigh, 1983) can be completed by the classroom teacher for a norm-referenced score. For students through age 8, the Adaptive domain of the *Battelle Developmental Inventory* (Newborg et al., 1984) can be used. The ABI or *Vineland,* however, would provide more comprehensive information than results from these subtests.

For elementary-age students up to about age 7, additional information for planning instruction in this area can be obtained from the *Revised Brigance Diagnostic Inventory of Early Development* (Brigance, 1991), the *Informal Assessment of Developmental Skills* (Swallow et al., 1978), and the *Oregon Project* (Anderson et al., 1986).

Table 6.7 summarizes the various measures for assessing adaptive behavior.

NORM-REFERENCED TESTS

Tests were selected for review if they were (a) designed to be individually administered (to meet the legal requirements for special education eligibility decisions), (b) published within the last 15 years (so that the content and the norms were reasonably current), and (c) able to circumvent a visual disability (to ensure that students who were visually impaired or blind would be capable of making the required responses). Exceptions to these criteria were the *Blind Learning Aptitude Test* (Newland, 1971) and the *Wechsler Preschool and Primary Scale of Intelligence* (Wechsler, 1967). These tests were included because the options for assessing cognitive development are so limited that these tests must be given consideration.

Many school-age students who are visually impaired can be tested with measures for sighted students. In some cases magnification devices or enlargement of test materials, special lighting, and other special procedures may be required.

The *Perkins-Binet Test of Intelligence for the Blind* (Davis, 1980) is mentioned frequently in the literature for assessing cognitive development. It was not reviewed, however, because it has been withdrawn from the market (Perkins School for the Blind, personal communication, November, 1984).

Evaluation of the following norm-referenced measures is based on the criteria presented in Chapter 1. Descriptions of administration and scoring procedures, materials, and types of responses required are included. Adaptations of some items on tests designed for sighted students are suggested also.

TABLE 6.7. *Measures for Assessing Adaptive Behavior for Students Who Are Visually Impaired or Blind*

Tests	Sections	Type of Assessment	Adaptations
Adaptive Behavior Inventory (Brown & Leigh, 1986) (Age 5-0 to 18-11)	Entire inventory	Norm-referenced	Minimal adjustments required
Basic School Skills Inventory– Diagnostic (Hammill & Leigh, 1983) (Age 4 through 6)	Daily Living Skills	Norm-referenced	3 items require adaptation
Battelle Developmental Inventory (Newborg et al., 1984) (Birth through age 8)	Adaptive domain	Norm-referenced	Minimal adjustments for school-age students
Revised Brigance Diagnostic Inventory of Early Development (Brigance, 1991) (Birth through age 7)	Self-Help Skills	Criterion-referenced	None required
Informal Assessment of Developmental Skills (Swallow et al., 1978) (Early elementary grades)	Self-Help Skills	Informal checklist	None required
Oregon Project for Visually Impaired and Blind Preschool Children (Anderson et al., 1986) (Birth through age 6)	Self-Help Skills	Curriculum-based	None required

(continued)

TABLE 6.7. *Continued*

Vineland Adaptive Behavior Scales (Sparrow et al., 1984) (Birth through age 18)	Entire test	Norm-referenced	Numerous items require vision

. . . .

• **Adaptive Behavior Inventory**

Authors: Linda Brown & James Leigh

Publisher: PRO-ED
8700 Shoal Creek Boulevard
Austin, TX 78757-6897

Copyright: 1986

GENERAL DESCRIPTION

The *Adaptive Behavior Inventory* (ABI) is appropriate for students without disabilities from age 5-0 to 18-11 and for students who are mentally retarded from age 6-0 to 18-11.

The ABI is comprised of five scales: Self-Care, Communication, Social, Academic, and Occupational. An abbreviated short form consists of 50 items taken from each of the scales. Vision is not required for most items, and items requiring vision could be adapted easily.

Overall results are expressed as quotients (mean = 100, standard deviation = 15), and results for the individual scales are expressed as standard scores (mean = 10, standard deviation = 3) or percentiles.

The ABI is completed by a teacher to describe a student's adaptive behavior in the classroom, though some items pertain to behaviors used outside the classroom. About 20 to 25 minutes is required to complete the inventory.

Materials consist of an examiner's manual and a record book.

DESCRIPTION OF SCALES

Self-Care.

The 30 items on this scale range from "Moves independently from one area to another at school/work" to "Is aware of basic social service agencies (e.g., employment commission, community counseling services, planned parenthood clinic)."

Communication.

The 32 items on this scale range from "Communicates needs and desires to others using spoken language" to "Describes and explains abstract ideas in writing."

Social.

The 30 items on this scale range from "Knows and refers to others by name" to "Organizes and leads group activities."

Academic.

The 30 items on this scale range from "Identifies the letters of the alphabet when they are out of sequence" to "Performs advanced math tasks (e.g., geometry, algebra problems)."

Occupational.

The 28 items on this scale range from "Arrives at school or work on time" to "Supervises other people."

TECHNICAL ADEQUACY

Standardization.

The number of students per age level is not stated in the manual, though there were 1,296 students without disabilities and 1,076 who were mentally retarded. The demographic characteristics of the sample were very similar to the 1980 census data in terms of gender, geographic distribution, residence, occupational level, race, and ethnicity.

Reliability.

A 10- to 14-day interval was used to evaluate test-retest reliability. The data are not given by age level, but correlations were greater than .85 for all subtests and the overall results.

Correlations for internal consistency also were greater than .85 for all subtests and the overall results.

Standard errors of measurement are given for the scales and overall results by age level.

Validity.

Construct validity is addressed by showing that results of the ABI increase with age and are related to results from intelligence and achievement tests.

No data are given on factor analysis of the scales to provide evidence that the scales are measuring separate areas of adaptive behavior. Some of the scales correlate highly with each other.

Data are provided to demonstrate that the ABI discriminates among students of different intelligence and achievement levels.

CONCLUSIONS

The ABI provides a useful option for norm-referenced assessment of adaptive behavior of school-age students who are visually impaired or blind. In addition, results from the scales provide some general information to aid in planning instruction. Test-retest data by age level and factor analysis data would be desirable. This is the most technically adequate measure currently on the market for assessing adaptive behavior with the teacher as the informant.

· ·

• Basic School Skills Inventory– Diagnostic

See review in Chapter 5.

· ·

• Battelle Developmental Inventory

See review in Chapter 4.

· ·

• Blind Learning Aptitude Test

Author: T. Ernest Newland

Publisher: University of Illinois Press
P.O. Box 5081, Station A
Urbana, IL 61820

Copyright: 1971

GENERAL DESCRIPTION

The *Blind Learning Aptitude Test* (BLAT) was written for students 6 through 16 years old to measure learning potential. The manual suggests, however, that the test discriminates best for ages 6 through 12.

The 49 items assess six different types of nonverbal problems. There are two practice items at the beginning of each set of problems.

Results are expressed in terms of Learning Quotients (mean = 100, standard deviation = 15). Also, it is possible to report a Test Age.

The BLAT must be given individually and requires 10 to 45 minutes for administration.

Materials include an examiner's manual, a response sheet, and a set of plastic sheets containing raised figures (bas-relief).

DESCRIPTION OF ITEMS

No knowledge of Braille is required to interpret the raised (bas-relief) figures on the plastic sheets. The figures are relatively large; consequently no fine discriminations are required. A student may make a verbal response to answer a question, but pointing in response also is acceptable. Tactile discrimination is necessary to solve the problems.

The first set of 8 items requires finding the figure that differs from the others. Classification skills are required.

The second set of 7 items requires a student to choose a figure that matches a model figure. This set of items requires matching-to-sample.

The third set of 6 items requires choosing a figure to complete a progression (e.g., for a series of figures that increase in size). A student is given several figures from which to choose, and sequencing is required.

There are 16 items in the fourth set of problems. A student must select from several figures the one that goes with another figure, making a pair of figures that goes together in the same way as another pair of figures, thus assessing the ability to recognize analogous relationships.

Five items make up the fifth set. On these items a student selects from several figures the one that is needed to complete an incomplete figure, testing knowledge of part–whole relationships.

The last set of problems consists of 7 items. A student is presented with a matrix consisting of several figures with one missing. The task is to select the missing figure from several alternatives. Pattern completion (i.e., recognition of the relationship between the figures and the use of the relationship rule to determine what figure would come next) is required.

This test is not timed, a positive characteristic for a measure to be used with students who are visually impaired or blind.

TECHNICAL ADEQUACY

Standardization.

The sample included 961 students, 446 girls and 515 boys age 6 through 21. The norm tables, however, only go through age 16. The number of students for age 6 through 16 varies from 19 to 106. Only at ages 10 and 14 were the number of students close to 100 per level. Hence, the number of subjects per age level was too small to provide an adequate sample. The students were drawn from 12 states from the four regions of the country, but proportions do not correspond to census data. The sample closely approximated the 1966 census data in terms of white and nonwhite students and the 1960 census data in terms of occupational level for most of the occupational categories. No data are given for urban/rural residence. Seventy-nine percent of the students (760) were from residential schools, and 201 were from day school programs. This sample is not representative of today's population of students, who are enrolled primarily in public school programs. Hence, in addition to being dated, there are a number of problems with the representativeness of the sample.

Reliability.

A 7-month interval was used to evaluate test-retest reliability with 93 students 10 to 16 years old. A correlation of .87 was obtained. Also, correlations were obtained for 24 students 6 to 10 years old ($r = .87$) and for 53 students 12 to 16 years old ($r = .90$), and no difference was suggested between the age levels. Data were not presented by age level.

A correlation of .93 was obtained to describe internal consistency of the test.

Validity.

The construct validity of the BLAT might be questioned. The manual indicates that the test assesses processes or operations needed for learning. Whether the skills tested are, in fact, necessary for learning remains to be demonstrated. Ideas for the majority of items were drawn from "culture free" tests for sighted students to minimize the effects of acculturation.

Concurrent validity data were obtained with the *Hayes-Binet* (Hayes, 1942, 1943) and the WISC Verbal Scale (Wechsler, 1949). With the *Hayes-Binet* the correlation for 663 students was .74; with the WISC Verbal Scale the correlation for 552 students was .71.

CONCLUSIONS

An insufficient sample size was used for all but two age levels. Though the sample appeared to be representative in terms of gender, race, and occupational level in 1960, it was not geographically representative, and no data were given for urban/rural residence. Furthermore, 79% of the students came from residential schools, whereas today most students who are visually impaired or blind are in regular classrooms.

Though the test-retest correlations were satisfactory, no data were given by age level.

Again, whether the BLAT assesses skills important for learning remains to be investigated.

The BLAT could be used as one source of norm-referenced information on cognitive development, but results would have to be supplemented with data from other sources that require responses other than tactile discrimination. The limitations in the technical adequacy of this test necessitate caution when interpreting results. Given the age of the BLAT, results are likely to be inflated.

· ·

• Detroit Test of Learning Aptitude– Third Edition

Author: Donald D. Hammill

Publisher: PRO-ED
8700 Shoal Creek Boulevard
Austin, TX 78757-6897

Copyright: 1991

GENERAL DESCRIPTION

The *Detroit Test of Learning Aptitude–Third Edition* (DTLA–3) was developed to assess mental ability of students 6-0 through 17-11 years old.

There are 11 subtests on this measure: Word Opposites, Design Sequences, Sentence Imitation, Reversed Letters, Story Construction, Design Reproduction, Basic Information, Symbolic Relations, Word Sequences, Story Sequences, and Picture Fragments. Four of these subtests (Word Opposites, Sentence Imitation, Basic Information, and Word Sequences) are verbal tasks that do not require vision. These subtests will be the focus of this review.

Results are described in terms of standard scores (mean = 10, standard deviation = 3), percentiles, and age equivalents for subtest results, and quotients (mean = 100, standard deviation = 15), percentiles, and age equivalents for overall results.

The DTLA–3 is administered individually and requires 50 minutes to 2 hours for the entire test. The 4 subtests that do not require vision would require about one-third that amount of time.

Materials for the 4 subtests that do not require vision include an examiner's manual and a record book. The pictorial materials, cubes, and student booklet that come with the kit are not needed for these subtests.

DESCRIPTION OF SUBTESTS

Word Opposites.

This 50-item subtest tests expressive vocabulary. For each item the examiner gives the student a word orally, and the student is asked to give an antonym.

Sentence Imitation.

This 30-item subtest measures the ability to use correct syntax in speaking and memory. A student is asked to repeat sentences verbatim that are given orally by the examiner.

Basic Information.

This 40-item subtest assesses a student's general knowledge. The examiner presents questions orally for the student to answer.

Word Sequences.

This 30-item subtest covers auditory memory for unrelated words. The examiner presents word strings orally, and the student is asked to repeat them. The strings gradually increase in complexity.

TECHNICAL ADEQUACY

Standardization.

The sample consisted of 1,532 students tested in 1984 on 6 subtests of the DTLA–2 that also appear on the DTLA–3 and 1,055 tested in 1989–90 on the DTLA–3. The number of students per age level ranged from 151 to 337. The demographic characteristics of the sample were similar to the 1990 census data in terms of gender, race, ethnicity, residence, and geographic location. No information was presented on the socioeconomic status of the families.

Reliability.

A 2-week retest interval was used to examine test-retest reliability for children 6 through 16 years old. Correlations for the 4 subtests that do not require vision were .89 or greater. Data were not presented by age level.

Internal consistency correlations for these subtests were .85 or greater.

Standard errors of measurement were given by age level for subtests and overall results.

Validity.

In terms of content validity, item analysis was used in item selection, and a detailed rationale is presented for the items and the formats used. The relationship of subtests and composites to popular theories of intelligence is discussed.

Construct validity was addressed by showing that raw scores increase with age, the subtests correlate well with the overall results, results correlate as expected with tests of achievement, and factor analysis suggested that one factor underlies the overall test result.

For concurrent validity, moderate to high correlations were found between results of the DTLA–2 and the *Wechsler Intelligence Scale for Children–Revised* (Wechsler, 1974) and the *Peabody Picture Vocabulary Test–Revised* (Dunn & Dunn, 1981). High correlations were found for results from the DTLA–3 and the *Detroit Test of Learning Aptitude–Primary: Second Edition* (Hammill & Bryant, 1991), the *Kaufman Assessment Battery for Children* (Kaufman & Kaufman, 1983), the *Scholastic Aptitude Scale* (Bryant & Newcomer, 1991), and the *Woodcock-Johnson Psycho-Educational Battery* (cognitive component) (Woodcock & Johnson, 1989).

CONCLUSIONS

The 4 subtests of the DTLA–3 that do not require vision could provide useful supplemental information to results from other intelligence tests. Whenever only sections of a test instrument are used, cautious interpretation of results is warranted because results are based on a smaller sample of skills. Except for the lack of data on socioeconomic level, the standardization is excellent. The reliability data are good also, though additional test-retest data by age level would be helpful. Considerable thought went into the construction of this test, and the validity data are comprehensive and encouraging. It appears to be worth the relatively small amount of time needed to administer these 4 subtests to students who are visually impaired or blind in order to have the additional information the DTLA–3 provides. Given the problems noted for other measures of intelligence for these students, this additional information could be quite helpful.

. . . .

• Diagnostic Achievement Battery– Second Edition

Author: Phyllis L. Newcomer

Publisher: PRO-ED
8700 Shoal Creek Boulevard
Austin, TX 78757-6897

Copyright: 1990

GENERAL DESCRIPTION

The *Diagnostic Achievement Battery–Second Edition* (DAB–2) was designed for students age 6-0 to 14-11. Assessed are the areas of reading, mathematics, written expression, and oral language. Only the oral language sections do not require vision; hence, only these sections will be addressed in this review. Oral language skills are assessed in a Listening section and a Speaking section.

The DAB–2 is individually administered. If the entire test were given, it would require about 1 to 2 hours.

Results can be reported in terms of percentiles and standard scores (mean = 100, standard deviation = 15 for composites; mean = 10, standard deviation = 3 for subtests).

Materials consist of an examiner's manual, a student booklet, a student work sheet (not required for the oral language sections), and a profile sheet.

DESCRIPTION OF SUBTESTS

Listening.

Two subtests make up this section. In the Story Comprehension subtest, consisting of 35 items, students are asked questions about stories read to them. The length of the stories increases, and the number of questions asked per story increases from one to five. The second subtest, Characteristics, has 35 items that test understanding of vocabulary. Students are asked if statements such as "All trees are oaks" are true or false.

Speaking.

Two subtests make up this section also. The Synonyms subtest consists of 25 items assessing expressive vocabulary. A student is given a word and asked to give another word with the same meaning. The Grammatic Completion subtest has 27 items assessing how well a student uses grammar when speaking. A student is asked to complete incomplete sentences requiring different forms of grammar.

TECHNICAL ADEQUACY

Standardization.

There were 2,623 students in the sample, with more than 100 students per age level, except at age 14 where there were 86. Their demographic characteristics were similar to the 1985 census data in terms of urban/rural residence, gender, geographic distribution, race, and socioeconomic status. No data were presented in the manual on ethnicity.

Reliability.

Test-retest reliability for the DAB–2 was carried out with 52 students in first through seventh grades with a 1-week interval. Correlations were reported, however, only for the written language sections. A test-retest study of the earlier version of the test, the DAB, involved a 2-week interval and 34 students age 9-11 to 13-3. Correlations for the oral language sections were: Story Comprehension .89, Characteristics .93, Synonyms .90, and Grammatic Completion .94. The correlation for the Listening Composite was .94 and Speaking Composite .95. Though these correlations are encouraging, test-retest data are needed on the DAB–2 by age level.

Of the 18 internal consistency correlations for the listening subtests, 16 were .85 or higher; of the 18 coefficients for the speaking subtests, 12 were .85 or higher. All correlations for the Listening Composite and the Speaking Composite were above .85.

Standard error of measurement data are presented for the subtests and composites by age.

Validity.

Data on concurrent validity for the oral language section show moderate correlations with the *Test of Language Devel-*

opment–Primary (Newcomer & Hammill, 1982) and the *Test of Language Development–Intermediate* (Hammill & Newcomer, 1982).

In terms of construct validity, results were shown to increase with age and grade, subtest intercorrelations were low to moderate, moderate correlations were found with the *Detroit Test of Learning Aptitude–Primary* (Hammill & Bryant, 1986) and the *Wechsler Intelligence Scale for Children–Revised* (Wechsler, 1974), and results were found to discriminate students who were learning disabled from students who were not learning disabled in two studies.

For content validity, several of the questions for Listening Comprehension are not passage dependent. Because of the true/false format of the Characteristics subtest, guessing may affect results. The DAB–2 addresses both listening and speaking skills in addition to considering both vocabulary and grammar.

CONCLUSIONS

Though the standardization looks quite good for the DAB–2, only sighted students were included. No adaptations are needed, however, on the oral language sections for students who are visually impaired or blind. More test-retest data with a 2-week interval on the current version of the test by age level would be desirable. In general, the DAB–2 is a useful option for assessing oral language (speaking and listening).

. . . .

• **Diagnostic Reading Scales**

Author: George D. Spache

Publisher: CTB/McGraw-Hill
Del Monte Research Park
Monterey, CA 93940

Copyright: 1981

GENERAL DESCRIPTION

The *Diagnostic Reading Scales* (DRS) tests oral and silent reading skills, listening comprehension, word analysis skills, and behaviors related to reading. Material on the DRS ranges from midfirst through midseventh grade level.

The administration time is approximately 45 minutes but varies depending on how much of the test is administered. The test is given individually.

A Braille transcription (Duckworth, undated) and a large-type edition are available from the American Printing House for the Blind.

Grade levels are used to describe results from the oral, silent, and listening sections. Word analysis skills are tested with a criterion-referenced format. Behaviors related to reading are to be noted on two checklists that appear at the end of the record book.

Materials include the examiner's manual, a record book, a book from which a student reads, and a cassette tape. The purpose of the cassette tape is to help examiners learn to score the oral reading sections and to provide practice in scoring difficult cases.

DESCRIPTION OF SECTIONS

Word lists.

Performance on three graded word lists at the beginning of the test determines where to begin testing a student on the passages. Though the manual suggests that these lists provide information on a student's sight vocabulary, these lists would not provide a comprehensive assessment of sight vocabulary. A comparison of the three lists with Fry's list of instant words (Fry, 1980) indicated that list 1 contains 30 high-frequency words, list 2 contains 3 high-frequency words, and list 3 does not have any words of high frequency. For students who have many reading problems, it is helpful to begin testing in the passages one level below that indicated by the word lists. Doing so would ensure some success and avoid too much frustration in the beginning of testing (Lesiak & Bradley-Johnson, 1983).

Passages.

The DRS consists of two sets of passages labeled *r* and *s*. The reading level of the passages gradually increases. A student begins reading orally in one set of passages while the examiner codes errors in word recognition in the record book. Examiners with limited experience in coding errors for oral reading can tape-record a student's oral reading to allow rechecking of scoring. When a student completes a passage, the examiner asks seven or eight comprehension questions. The oral reading level is determined by both the number of errors in word recognition and the number of comprehension questions answered correctly. Most of the questions require the recall of facts from the passage, but several require the ability to draw an inference.

Reading levels for the passages were determined by several factors shown to correlate highly with each other. Initially, readability formulas were used to estimate levels. The final levels were based on the following data from the standardization sample: students' mean grade level, mean level of reader used in instruction, mean estimate of students' reading levels by teachers, and students' performance on standardized tests.

In an attempt to make the comprehension questions passage dependent, students at the grade level of a passage were given the comprehension questions without the passage. Questions that many students were able to answer without the passage were eliminated. Despite this procedure, a few questions appear to be passage independent. Attempts were made to eliminate sexual bias in the material as well.

Though comprehension questions are answered from memory, it may be useful after scoring the test to give a student the passages and ask if he or she can locate the answer to questions that were missed. Though this information cannot be used in scoring, knowledge of a student's level of comprehension with locating versus comprehension with memory can help the examiner plan instruction. Spache considers the oral reading level the instructional level. Because the level of basal readers varies considerably, it seems more appropriate to refer to this level as the "oral reading achievement level" (Lesiak & Bradley-Johnson, 1983). Because of the way in which the grade levels were determined, the examiner should interpret grade levels from the DRS as being approximately at the beginning, middle, or end of a grade level. For example, a grade level of 1.4 could be interpreted as approximately midfirst-grade level.

Once the oral reading level is defined, a student's silent reading level is determined using the other set of passages.

Spache considers this level the independent level. If an independent level cannot be determined, the manual suggests that the examiner assume the independent level to be the same as the instructional level. The examiner could obtain more useful information if he or she begins testing for silent reading at the oral reading achievement level. Then, the examiner could test forward or backward, depending on the student's performance, to determine the actual level at which the student is able to comprehend when reading silently. Some students do not comprehend at the same level when reading silently as they do when reading orally. It seems more appropriate to refer to this level as the "silent reading achievement level" (Lesiak & Bradley-Johnson, 1983) instead of the independent level.

After this phase, the examiner is directed to read passages to a student and ask the student comprehension questions in order to determine a potential level. This information is of little use and can be omitted.

Word Analysis Skills.

Using a criterion-referenced format, 12 subtests assess a student's knowledge of consonant sounds, consonant digraphs, consonant blends, vowels, vowels with *r*, vowel diphthongs and digraphs, common syllables, blending, and auditory discrimination. Results indicate skills that have been learned and those that need to be taught. Long and short vowels are assessed within one subtest. The directions for this subtest are confusing to some students. To avoid this problem, the long and short vowel subtests on the *Brigance Diagnostic Comprehensive Inventory of Basic Skills* (Brigance, 1983) along with the *APH Tactile Supplement* (Duckworth & Abbot, undated) could be used.

Checklists.

At the end of the record book are two checklists covering behaviors relevant to reading that can be useful during instruction planning. Examiners should determine which behaviors on the checklist are relevant for a particular student.

TECHNICAL ADEQUACY

Standardization.

The sample consisted of 534 students in first through eighth grades. The number of students from each grade level was low, ranging from 63 to 77. The representativeness of the sample in terms of geographic distribution is unclear from the data presented. The students were from 31 states, but percentages by region were not presented. The characteristics of the sample were similar to the census data in terms of gender, ethnicity, and race. Urban/rural residence and socioeconomic level were not addressed.

Reliability.

Test-retest reliability was evaluated for the passages using a 2- to 8-week retest interval and alternate forms (r and s). The correlation was .89. Data were not given for each grade level.

Validity.

Grade levels for the DRS passages were highly correlated with students' mean grade in school, mean assigned reading level, mean teacher estimate of reading level, and mean grade equivalent on standardized group-achievement test results.

In terms of content validity, students are asked to read passages rather than word lists, which are used on many other norm-referenced tests for reading. Thus, the DRS uses "real" reading material for the assessment.

CONCLUSIONS

The DRS is the most technically adequate norm-referenced measure currently available for determining reading achievement levels. It has the advantage of assessing actual reading by using passages instead of word lists. Though no students who are visually impaired or blind were included in the sample, a Braille transcription and a large-type edition are available from the American Printing House for the Blind. The test is not without its limitations, however, because data are lacking on the urban/rural residence and socioeconomic level of the sample. The representativeness of the sample in terms of geographic distribution is unclear, and the sample was small. Though the test-retest data provided are encouraging, further data by grade level are needed. Comparing oral and silent reading levels and using the information obtained from observing a student reading orally and silently can be beneficial in planning instruction. Suggestions in this review for using the DRS should make its use more efficient and its results more useful.

· ·

• Differential Ability Scales

Author: Colin D. Elliott

Publisher: The Psychological Corporation
555 Academic Court
San Antonio, TX 78204

Copyright: 1990

GENERAL DESCRIPTION

The *Differential Ability Scales* (DAS) are designed for children and adolescents age 2-6 through 17-11. The battery covers both cognitive development and achievement. The entire achievement section requires vision, and only the three subtests of the cognitive section that do not require vision will be reviewed (Word Definitions, Similarities, and Recall of Digits).

The overall (General Conceptual Ability) and cluster or composite scores are described as standard scores (mean = 100, standard deviation = 15). Only subtest scores are possible when sections requiring vision are circumvented. Subtest results are described as *T* scores (mean = 50, standard deviation = 10).

The DAS is administered individually, and the entire test requires 45 to 60 minutes.

Materials include an examiner's manual, a technical handbook, a record form, and a kit containing the various toys and pictorial materials. The subtests that do not require vision are verbal and, hence, do not require the toys or pictures.

DESCRIPTION OF SUBTESTS

Word Definitions.

This 42-item subtest is appropriate for children and adolescents age 5-0 through 17-11. The examiner presents words orally, and the student is asked to define them. Words range in difficulty from "gift" and "tiny" to "alacrity" and "hirsute."

Similarities.

During this 34-item subtest, appropriate for children and adolescents age 5-0 through 17-11, the examiner presents a set of three words and asks the student to name the class to which the three words belong. Item sets range in difficulty from "banana," "apple," and "orange" to "democracy," "justice," and "equality."

Recall of Digits.

This 36-item subtest is appropriate for children and adolescents age 2-6 through 17-11. Students are asked to repeat strings of digits, ranging in length from two to nine digits.

TECHNICAL ADEQUACY

Standardization.

The sample consisted of 175 subjects at each 6-month age level from 2-6 through 4-11 and 200 subjects per 1-year level from 5-0 through 17-11. A total of 3,475 children and adolescents were included. The demographic characteristics of the sample corresponded closely to the 1986 census data in terms of gender, race, ethnicity, parental education, and geographic region. Communities with populations under 100,000 were somewhat underrepresented. The percentage of children enrolled in preschool programs and the percentage classified under special education categories (with the exception of severely mentally or emotionally impaired) were similar to percentages for the U.S. population as well.

Reliability.

Test-retest reliability was evaluated for only four age ranges (3-6 to 4-5, 5-0 to 6-3, 5-9 to 6-11, 12-0 to 13-11) with an interval ranging from 2 to 6 weeks. Correlations for the Similarities and Recall of Digits subtests were all below .85; for the Word Definitions subtest the correlations were .80 for 5-9 to 6-11 and .87 for 12-0 to 13-11. Thus, the reliability of these individual subtests is less than adequate.

Internal consistency reliabilities are given by age levels. For Word Definitions correlations ranged from .75 to .85, reaching .85 only for age 13. Reliabilities for the Similarities subtest ranged from .73 to .84, and the Recall of Digits subtest had correlations ranging from .85 to .90.

Standard errors of measurement are provided for all sections of the test by age level.

Validity.

Intercorrelations of subtests not requiring vision ranged from .13 to .64.

Results of the DAS were compared with other cognitive measures. Only results for subtests not requiring vision will be addressed. Comparison of results from the DAS preschool-level Recall of Digits with the *Wechsler Preschool and Primary Scale of Intelligence–Revised* (Wechsler, 1989) indicated correlations of .22 to .31; with the *Stanford-Binet Intelligence Scale–Fourth Edition (Binet IV)* (Thorndike, Hagen, & Sattler, 1986) .21 to .34; with the *McCarthy Scales of Children's Abilities* (McCarthy, 1972) .01 to .33; with the *Kaufman Assessment Battery for Children* (K-ABC) (Kaufman & Kaufman, 1983) .18 to .48; and with the *Woodcock-Johnson Psycho-Educational Battery–Preschool Cluster* (Woodcock & Johnson, 1977) .19.

Results for subtests not requiring vision for the school-age level and other cognitive measures were as follows. For Word Definitions correlations with the *Wechsler Intelligence Scale for Children–Revised* (WISC–R) (Wechsler, 1974) ranged from .44 to .87, with the *Binet IV* .45 to .80, and the K-ABC .13 to .72. Correlations for the Similarities subtest ranged from .36 to .83 with the WISC–R, .40 to .68 with the *Binet IV,* and .19 to .33 with the K-ABC. For Recall of Digits correlations ranged from .49 to .63 with the WISC–R, .17 to .48 with the *Binet IV,* and –.14 to .57 with the K-ABC.

Students who are educable mentally impaired and learning disabled were shown to score as expected on the DAS, given their classifications.

Items on the DAS were evaluated using both subjective and empirical procedures to change or eliminate items that may have been biased in terms of gender, race, ethnicity, or region.

CONCLUSIONS

Though no data are available on children and adolescents who are visually impaired or blind, the DAS was well standardized on sighted students. The three subtests that do not require vision, however, have less-than-adequate reliability.

The data on validity are weak for Recall of Digits but are acceptable, for the most part, for the subtests at the school-age level. Thus, for students who are visually impaired or blind, the DAS can provide some limited supplementary data on intelligence. Results must be interpreted cautiously, however, given the problems with the reliability of these subtests.

· ·

• Social Skills Rating System

See review in Chapter 5.

· ·

• Test of Language Development– Intermediate: Second Edition

Authors:　Donald D. Hammill & Phyllis L. Newcomer

Publisher:　PRO-ED
8700 Shoal Creek Boulevard
Austin, TX 78757-6897

Copyright:　1988

GENERAL DESCRIPTION

The *Test of Language Development–Intermediate: Second Edition* (TOLD–I:2) was designed to assess receptive and expressive language for students age 8-6 through 12-11.

Six subtests make up the TOLD–I:2: Sentence Combining, Vocabulary, Word Ordering, Generals, Grammatic Comprehension, and Malapropisms. No vision is required on the test.

Results are described in terms of quotients (mean = 100, standard deviation = 15) for the Overall Spoken Language score and for the composites of Listening, Speaking, Semantics, and Syntax. Subtest results are described in terms of a standard score (mean = 10, standard deviation = 3).

The test is administered individually and takes approximately 30 to 45 minutes.

Materials needed for the TOLD–I:2 include the examiner's manual and a record book.

DESCRIPTION OF SUBTESTS

Sentence Combining.

This 25-item subtest assesses a student's ability to use correct grammar and word order in speaking. For each item the examiner gives a student several sentences that the student is to combine into one sentence.

Vocabulary.

Consisting of 35 items, this subtest assesses a student's understanding of vocabulary. For each item the examiner gives a student two words, and the student is to indicate whether the words mean nearly the same, are opposites, or have nothing to do with each other.

Word Ordering.

This 25-item subtest measures a student's ability to use correct word order when speaking. The examiner gives the student several words for each item and asks the student to make the words into a sentence.

Generals.

This 25-item subtest determines how well a student is able to use vocabulary when speaking. The examiner gives a student three words for each item and directs the student to indicate how the words are alike.

Grammatic Comprehension.

This subtest, consisting of 40 items, assesses a student's ability to recognize correct grammar. The examiner presents a sentence, and the student determines whether the sentence is grammatically correct or incorrect.

Malapropisms.

This 30-item subtest tests a student's ability to understand vocabulary. For each item the examiner gives a student a sentence containing an incorrect word. The student is to correct the sentence.

TECHNICAL ADEQUACY

Standardization.

The number of subjects in the sample ranged from 214 to 375 per age level, except at age 8 where there were only 66 subjects. The norms for the Vocabulary, Malapropisms, and Word Ordering subtests, however, consisted of only 471 subjects across the five age levels. In terms of demographic characteristics, the sample corresponded closely to the 1985 census data for gender, geographic distribution, socioeconomic level, race, ethnicity, and urban/rural residence.

Reliability.

Test-retest reliability was examined in two studies. One study used a 1-week retest interval and a previous version of the test. Correlations collapsed across age levels were: Sentence Combining .83, Word Ordering .92, Generals .90, and Grammatic Comprehension .91. Fodness, McNeilly, and Bradley-Johnson (1991) examined the test-retest reliability of the TOLD–I:2 with a 2-week interval for ages 8, 10, and 12. The correlations for the four composites were .87 or higher at all age levels.

Internal consistency correlations for the composites were .91 or higher at all age levels. Subtest correlations ranged from .78 to .97.

Standard errors of measurement are provided by age level for subtest and composite results.

Validity.

In terms of content validity, 180 professionals rated the subtests as being consistent with the model on which the test was based, assessing listening and speaking skills as well as semantics and syntax.

For criterion-related validity, moderate to high correlations were found when results of the TOLD–I:2 were compared with results of the *Test of Adolescent Language* (Hammill, Brown, Larsen, & Wiederholt, 1980).

Numerous studies on construct validity are presented in the manual. The results indicated that scores increase with age, subtests correlate adequately with each other, and results correlate well with other aspects of achievement. A group of students receiving language therapy scored significantly below average on the test. Factor analysis found that the subtests of the TOLD–I:2 loaded on only one factor. The authors suggest, however, that the examiner should expect the different aspects of language to be highly related.

CONCLUSIONS

The standardization, reliability, and, generally speaking, the validity of the TOLD–I:2 are good. The fact that the 8-year-old level included only 66 subjects in the sample is reason to be cautious when interpreting results for this age level. No adaptations are required to administer the test because no vision is required. Hence, this measure should provide useful norm-referenced results when assessing the oral language of students.

· ·

• Test of Language Development– Primary: Second Edition

See review in Chapter 5.

· ·

• Test of Adolescent Language– Second Edition

Authors: Donald D. Hammill, Virginia L. Brown, Stephen C. Larsen, & J. Lee Wiederholt

Publisher: PRO-ED
8700 Shoal Creek Boulevard
Austin, TX 78757-6897

Copyright: 1987

GENERAL DESCRIPTION

The *Test of Adolescent Language–Second Edition* (TOAL–2) was developed for students age 12-0 through 18-5 to assess skills in reading, writing, listening, and speaking. Only the speaking section, composed of Speaking Vocabulary and Speaking Grammar, will be reviewed because it is the only section that does not require vision.

Results can be reported in terms of percentiles or standard scores (mean = 100, standard deviation = 15 for composites; mean = 10, standard deviation = 3 for subtests).

The TOAL–2 is administered individually. Administration time for Speaking Vocabulary ranges from 5 to 15 minutes and Speaking Grammar 5 to 20 minutes.

Materials consist of an examiner's manual, a record book, and a profile sheet. The student work sheet is not required for the speaking section.

DESCRIPTION OF SUBTESTS

Speaking Vocabulary.

This 25-item subtest measures how well a student is able to use vocabulary when speaking. For each item the examiner gives a student a word orally, and the student is asked to use the word in a sentence. Examples of items include "cheap" and "shirk."

Speaking Grammar.

Assessing a student's ability to use correct grammar when speaking, this subtest includes 30 items. For each item the examiner presents a sentence orally and asks the student to repeat the sentence verbatim.

TECHNICAL ADEQUACY

Standardization.

The standardization sample included 110 to 536 students per age level, with demographic characteristics similar to the 1985 census data in terms of gender, residence, geographic distribution, race, and ethnicity. No information is given in the manual on socioeconomic level.

Reliability.

A 2-week retest interval was used to evaluate test-retest reliability for students age 11 through 14. Correlation coefficients were: Speaking Vocabulary .85, Speaking Grammar

.79, and the Speaking Quotient .85. Data are not given by age level.

Internal consistency coefficients for the Speaking Quotient were .89 or higher. Ranges for the subtests were .83 to .90 for Speaking Vocabulary, and .80 to .87 for Speaking Grammar.

Interscorer reliability for Speaking Vocabulary was investigated with six examiners because of the somewhat subjective nature of the scoring. The correlation was .96.

Standard errors of measurement are provided for all sections of the TOAL–2 by age level.

Validity.

In terms of content validity, items were selected based on item analysis. Also, various theories of development and results from field testing were considered in selecting the formats and the items.

Moderate correlations were found between the TOAL–2 and other relevant measures of achievement: the *Peabody Picture Vocabulary Test–Revised* (Dunn & Dunn, 1981), the Memory for Related Syllables subtest from the *Detroit Tests of Learning Aptitude* (Baker & Leland, 1967), the Reading and Language sections of the *Comprehensive Test of Basic Skills* (California Test Bureau, 1968), and the *Test of Written Language* (Hammill & Larsen, 1983).

Construct validity was addressed by showing that scores tend to increase with age. Also, results of the TOAL–2 were shown to discriminate between students who are learning disabled (LD) and students who are mentally retarded, LD and students without disabilities, and LD and students who are emotionally disturbed. Moderate correlations were found among the subtests. Low to moderate correlations were found between TOAL–2 results and results from *California Short-Form Test of Academic Aptitude* (California Test Bureau, 1973).

CONCLUSIONS

The standardization for the TOAL–2 is good, except that data on socioeconomic status are not provided. The reliability for the Speaking Quotient and Speaking Vocabulary is satisfactory, though the reliability for Speaking Grammar is low.

Test-retest data by age level would be desirable. Validity for the speaking section of the test seems to be good as well.

The TOAL–2 can provide useful norm-referenced information on the speaking skills of adolescents who are visually impaired or blind. Because of the reliability, the examiner should use the Speaking Quotient, rather than subtest scores, when reporting results.

· ·

• Vineland Adaptive Behavior Scales– Expanded

Authors: Sara S. Sparrow, David A. Balla, & Domenic V. Cicchetti

Publisher: American Guidance Service Publishers Building Circle Pines, MN 55014

Copyright: 1984

GENERAL DESCRIPTION

The *Vineland Adaptive Behavior Scales* consists of three tests: the Survey Form, the Expanded Form, and the Classroom Edition. The *Vineland Scales* were designed to provide norm-referenced scores and detailed information for planning individual programs for adaptive behavior. The Expanded Form will be reviewed because it provides more extensive information, can be used for children and adolescents from birth to 18 years old, and provides a better sample of behavior than the Survey Form. The Classroom Edition is designed only for students from 3-0 to 12-11. The *Vineland Scales* are designed to measure "the performance of the daily activities required for personal and social sufficiency" (p. 6).

The Expanded Form is made up of five domains: Communication, Daily Living Skills, Socialization, Motor Skills, and Maladaptive Behavior. These can be broken down into subdomains and combined to obtain an Adaptive Behavior Composite.

Results for the domains and the Adaptive Behavior Composite are expressed as standard scores (mean = 100, standard deviation = 15), percentile ranks, stanines, adaptive levels (e.g., *high, moderately high*), and age equivalents. Adaptive levels and age equivalents may be determined for the subdomains.

Administration time for the Expanded Form ranges from 60 to 90 minutes. Information is obtained by interviewing the caregiver. Items are scored 2 (yes, usually), 1 (sometimes or partially), 0 (no, never), N (no opportunity), and DK (don't know).

Materials needed are an examiner's manual, an item booklet, a summary and profile booklet, and a program-planning report.

DESCRIPTION OF DOMAINS

Communication.

This domain contains 133 items: 23 for receptive skills, 76 for expressive skills, and 34 for written skills. The subdomains for receptive and expressive skills could be used for students with little or no vision. The Written subdomain contains items that students with little or no vision would not be able to perform unless the items were adapted (e.g., "copies at least 5 letters of the alphabet from a model," "addresses envelopes completely"). However, some of these items are not adaptable. An examiner could leave this domain out of an assessment and use results only from the other two subdomains, or the examiner could indicate that the score obtained should be interpreted in light of the fact that many of the items required vision.

Daily Living Skills.

This domain includes 201 items. The Personal subdomain contains 90 items, the Domestic subdomain 45 items, and the Community subdomain 66 items. Most of the Personal items could be used with students who are visually impaired or blind. Examples are "Eats solid food" and "Covers mouth and nose when coughing and sneezing." Some of the skills (e.g., using fasteners and caring for hair) may develop later for students who are visually impaired or blind than for sighted students. This should be considered when interpreting scores. One item that would need to be adapted or avoided is "Uses oral thermometer without assistance." Many items on the Domestic subdomain must be adapted, and some may not be appropriate for students with little or no vision. Examples include "Uses basic tools" and "Uses household cleaning products appropriately and correctly." (This last item requires that a student be able to read instructions on products.) Similar problems exist for items on the Communication subdomain. Examples of inappropriate items for students with little or no vision are "Obeys traffic lights and Walk and Don't Walk signs" and "Discriminates between bills of different denominations."

Socialization.

There are 134 items on this domain: 50 for Interpersonal Relationships, 48 for Play and Leisure Time, and 36 for Coping Skills. Numerous items at the lower level of Interpersonal Relationships require vision (e.g., "Follows with eyes a person moving at cribside or bedside"). Upper-level items are more appropriate (e.g., "Converses with others on topics of mutual interest"). For the Play and Leisure Time subdomain, most items can be used with students with little or no vision, although several items may require adaptive materials. Examples of items that may require special materials are the items on card or board games. Items for the Coping Skills subdomain do not require vision.

Motor Skills.

This domain includes 73 items: 42 in the Gross Motor subdomain and 31 in the Fine Motor subdomain. Many of the early skills on the Gross Motor subdomain involve skills likely to be delayed in development for children with little or no vision (e.g., sitting and walking). For the Fine Motor subdomain, tasks such as completing puzzles, drawing, and using scissors require vision.

Maladaptive Behavior.

This domain is appropriate for use only with students who are 5 years of age or older. There are two parts to the domain: Part 1 describes minor maladaptive behaviors, and Part 2 addresses more serious problem behaviors. Examples of the behaviors measured in Part 1, consisting of 21 items, are "Is overly active" and "Teases or bullies." For Part 2, only the supplementary norm groups can be used for comparison. Items are rated for frequency and intensity. Examples of the more serious behaviors are "Uses bizarre speech" and "Displays behaviors that are self-injurious."

TECHNICAL ADEQUACY

Standardization.

Only the Survey Form of the *Vineland Scales* was standardized. Norms for the Expanded Form were developed based on data from the standardization of the Survey Form using Rasch-Wright item-calibration estimates (an item-sampling procedure). The Survey Form and Maladaptive Behavior domain were standardized on 3,000 individuals, with 200 subjects per age level (birth to 18 years). The sample included 1,500 females, and the demographic characteristics of the sample closely resembled the 1980 census data in terms of geographic distribution, parents' educational attainment, race or ethnic group, and community size. The sample also corresponded to the census data in terms of educational placement (e.g., regular classroom, classroom for mentally retarded). The "other" category for educational placement included children who are visually impaired (as well as deaf, orthopedically impaired, etc.). The "other" category constitutes .7% of the U.S. population, while .4% of the *Vineland Scales* sample (i.e., 12 children) fit the "other" category. Twelve children is an insufficient number to adequately represent this heterogeneous subgroup of children.

Supplementary norms were developed for several disabling conditions. Included as one of these groups were 200 children with visual disabilities, 6 through 12-11 years old, attending residential facilities. These norms are not likely to be representative of most students who are visually impaired or blind today because most of these students attend public schools rather than residential facilities.

Reliability.

Test-retest reliability data are presented for the Survey Form for 484 subjects age 6 through 18-11. A 2- to 4-week retest interval was used. Correlation coefficients across the domains ranged from .80 to .98. For the Maladaptive Behavior section ($n = 340$, age 5-0 to 8-11), correlations ranged from .84 to .89.

Internal consistency correlation coefficients for the Expanded Form ranged from .83 to .97 for the domains, from .94 to .99 for the Adaptive Behavior Composite, and from .77 to .88 for the Maladaptive Behavior domain (Part 1). Internal consistency correlations for the supplementary norms ranged from .95 to .99 for the domains. Correlations for the Composite were all .99 across domains. For Part 1 of the Maladaptive Behavior domain, a coefficient of .74 was obtained.

Validity.

In terms of content validity, the items were developed from a review of other adaptive behavior measures and the child development literature. These items were field-tested and then subjected to a tryout on a national basis.

For concurrent validity, the test was compared to the original *Vineland Social Maturity Scale* (Doll, 1965), resulting in a correlation of .55. The test also was compared to the *Adaptive Behavior Inventory for Children* (Mercer & Lewis, 1978) and correlated .58 ($n = 9$), and the *AAMD Adaptive Behavior Scale–Revised Edition* (Nihira, Foster, Shellhaas, & Leland, 1974) and correlated .40 to .70 across domains. The *Vineland Scales* was examined in terms of its relationship to the *Kaufman Assessment Battery for Children* (Kaufman & Kaufman, 1983), and correlations ranged from .07 to .52. Correlation ranges with the *Peabody Picture Vocabulary Test–Revised* (Dunn & Dunn, 1981) were .12 to .37 for the domains. The relationship of the *Vineland Scales* (Survey Form) results for the supplementary norms and IQ test results were assessed, and the following correlation ranges were obtained for students with visual disabilities living in residential facilities: WISC–R (Wechsler, 1974) ($n = 23$) .48 to .77; *Hayes-Binet* (Hayes, 1942, 1943) ($n = 21$) .73 to .84; and *Perkins-Binet* (Davis, 1980) ($n = 23$) .45 to .83.

In terms of construct validity, mean scores tend to increase with age. Factor analyses seem to support the structure of the test.

The mean standard scores of students with visual disabilities showed the largest deficits in adaptive behavior in all areas, compared to students with hearing impairments and students with emotional impairments. This result is probably due, at least in part, to the fact that many items on the *Vineland Scales* require vision and, hence, are inappropriate for this group of students.

CONCLUSIONS

The standardization, reliability, and validity data for the *Vineland Scales* (Survey Form) are impressive. When the measure is used with students who are visually impaired or blind, however, two problems exist. First, many items require vision; thus, these students will be penalized on these items. This is a greater problem for some domains than others. If the supplementary norms for students who are visually impaired are used, these norms are representative of the performance only of students in residential programs. Whether performance of public school students differs remains to be investigated, but similar performance cannot be assumed.

Second, any measure that uses an interview format can yield results that may not accurately characterize a student's performance. The accuracy is largely a function of the objectivity and reliability of the informant. Questionable information is best followed up with direct observation of a student's performance in the natural environment.

This version of the *Vineland Scales* is a major improvement over the prior version. It could provide useful information for program planning and may or may not yield valid scores for students who are visually impaired or blind. Whether results are valid depends on the informant, the number of items that cannot be scored because of a visual problem, and the type of educational program a student attends.

. . . .

• Wechsler Adult Intelligence Scale– Revised

Author: David Wechsler

Publisher: The Psychological Corporation
555 Academic Court
San Antonio, TX 78204

Copyright: 1981

GENERAL DESCRIPTION

The *Wechsler Adult Intelligence Scale–Revised* (WAIS–R) was designed for adolescents and adults age 16 through 74.

The WAIS–R is made up of a Verbal Scale and a Performance Scale. Because the Performance Scale requires vision, only the Verbal Scale will be reviewed. The Verbal Scale contains six subtests: Information, Digit Span, Vocabulary, Arithmetic, Comprehension, and Similarities.

Results can be described in terms of scaled scores for subtests (mean = 10, standard deviation = 3) and quotients (mean = 100, standard deviation = 15) for the Verbal and Performance Scales and for the Full Scale.

The test must be individually administered and takes 60 to 90 minutes. Approximately half this time is needed for the Verbal Scale.

Materials for the Verbal Scale consist of an examiner's manual, a record book, and seven blocks. A list of words in Braille or large type for the Vocabulary subtest may be helpful but is not required.

DESCRIPTION OF SUBTESTS

Information.

On this subtest, which includes 29 items, the examiner asks a question and the student responds verbally. Examples include "What is the shape of a ball?" and "On what continent is the Sahara Desert?"

Digit Span.

This subtest has 14 items. For the first 7, the examiner reads a string of three to nine digits and asks the student to repeat the digits. For the remaining 7 items, the examiner reads a string of digits, and the student must repeat the digits backwards.

Vocabulary.

There are 35 items on this subtest. The examiner presents a copy of the word list to the student, reads each word and points to it, and asks the student to tell what each word means. A Braille or large-type list of the words would be helpful for students who are visually impaired or blind. Examples of words are "penny" and "tirade."

Arithmetic.

For this subtest, 14 arithmetic problems are presented orally, and the student is asked for a verbal response. Only the first item requires blocks. For this item, seven blocks are placed on the table, and the student is to answer the question

"How many blocks are there altogether?" A student with little or no vision would have to count the blocks by touch.

Comprehension.

For this subtest of 16 items, the examiner asks questions such as "Why are child labor laws needed?"

Similarities.

This subtest includes 14 items and requires the student to describe how two things are alike. Examples include "egg–seed" and "fly–tree."

TECHNICAL ADEQUACY

Standardization.

The 1970 census data were used to select the sample, which includes 160 to 300 subjects per age level and equal numbers of males and females. Race by geographic region closely approximated the census data. The proportion of white and nonwhite subjects for each occupational category also is very similar to census data, as is the educational level of the sample. Urban/rural residence is reasonably close to that of the U.S. population.

Reliability.

The WAIS–R is appropriate for school-age students age 16 through 25. There are no test-retest data, however, for these ages. For an age group of 25- to 34-year-old subjects, the correlations for the Verbal Scale (2- to 7-week retest interval) ranged from .79 to .93. The Verbal Scale total correlation was .94. Test-retest data are needed for the various age levels of the test.

Internal consistency correlations for the Verbal Scale for age levels 16, 17, and 18 to 19 ranged from .70 to .96. Verbal Scale total correlations were .95 and .96, respectively.

Standard errors of measurement were given by age for subtests, both scales, and the Full Scale IQ score.

Validity.

In terms of content validity, tests were selected based on ratings of experienced clinicians, correlations with other tests of intelligence, and studies of several groups with known levels of intellectual performance. Many studies have been carried out to show that persons with lower levels of education do less well on the WAIS–R than those with a more extensive educational background. Research has shown that results of this test correlate with school performance.

Results of factor-analytic studies tend to support the structure of the test.

Many studies have examined the relationship of the WAIS and WAIS–R with other tests of intelligence. One study reported in the manual showed a correlation of .85 with the WAIS–R and *Stanford-Binet Intelligence Scale* (Terman & Merrill, 1972) for 52 male prisoners.

CONCLUSIONS

The standardization is excellent in terms of being representative and having a sufficient number of subjects per level.

Reliability data are good also, except that test-retest data are needed by age level.

The validity data seem adequate.

The Verbal Scale requires modification on only one item for students with little or no vision and provides a norm-referenced score for comparing the performance of a student with little or no vision to that of sighted students. Because of the lack of sufficient test-retest data and the use of only half of the test, information from other measures would be necessary also in order to provide an adequate data base for educational decisions.

· ·

• Wechsler Intelligence Scale for Children–Third Edition

Author: David Wechsler

Publisher: The Psychological Corporation
555 Academic Court
San Antonio, TX 78204

Copyright: 1991

GENERAL DESCRIPTION

The *Wechsler Intelligence Scale for Children–Third Edition* (WISC–III) was developed for use with students age 6 through 16-11. Though the test is made up of both a Verbal and a Performance Scale, only the Verbal Scale will be reviewed because the Performance Scale requires vision.

The WISC–III consists of 13 subtests; six measure verbal skills, and seven measure performance. Subtests for the Verbal Scale are: Information, Similarities, Arithmetic, Vocabulary, Comprehension, and Digit Span (a supplementary subtest). The Arithmetic subtest requires vision for many items, hence, Digit Span could be substituted for this subtest.

Results are described in terms of quotients for the Full Scale as well as Verbal and Performance Scales (mean = 100, standard deviation = 15). Subtest results are in terms of scaled scores (mean = 10, standard deviation = 3). Age equivalents and percentiles can be used to describe results also.

The WISC–III must be administered individually and requires about 50 to 70 minutes for the entire scale. Use of only the Verbal Scale would require considerably less time.

Materials needed for the Verbal Scale (when the Arithmetic subtest is eliminated) are the examiner's manual and a record form.

DESCRIPTION OF SUBTESTS

Information.

For this 30-item subtest, students are asked a series of general-knowledge questions such as "How many hours are there in a day?"

Similarities.

This subtest consists of 19 items. For each item, the examiner orally presents a pair of words and asks the student to indicate how the words are alike. An example is "anger and joy."

Vocabulary.

Students are asked to define words in this 30-item subtest. Examples of items include "clock" and "aberration."

Comprehension.

This subtest, consisting of 18 items, requires students to answer questions such as "Why do cars have seat belts?"

Digit Span.

There are 15 items on this subtest. For the first 8 items, students are asked to repeat a string of digits given by the examiner. The length of the strings ranges from two to nine digits. For the last 7 items, students are asked to repeat strings of digits backward. Length of these strings ranges from two to eight digits.

TECHNICAL ADEQUACY

Standardization.

The sample for the WISC–III included 100 boys and 100 girls at each age level, making a total of 2,200 subjects. The demographic data for these students were very similar to the 1988 census data in terms of geographic distribution, parents' education, race/ethnicity, and residence (metropolitan/non-metropolitan).

Reliability.

Test-retest reliability was examined with 353 students and a retest interval ranging from 12 to 63 days. Three age groups were involved: 6 through 7, 10 through 11, and 14 through 15. Corrected correlation ranges for the subtests were: Information .80 to .88, Similarities less than .85, Vocabulary .82 to .89, Comprehension less than .85, and Digit Span less than .85. The correlations for the Verbal IQ ranged from .90 to .93. Thus, the Verbal IQ results appear stable over time, but this is not the case for some of the subtests. Furthermore, data are needed for each age level.

Standard errors of measurement are presented by age for subtests and the Verbal IQ.

Interscorer reliability was evaluated for subtests that require somewhat subjective scoring. All correlations were in the .90s. Thus, it appears that the scoring system for this test is quite objective.

Validity.

Extensive research is presented in the manual to provide support for the construct validity of the WISC–III based on factor-analytic studies and correlation of the results with many other tests of intelligence. Support is provided for the measurement of a global ability as well as for verbal and performance factors.

Results of many studies are presented showing the relationship of results of the WISC–R and results from various achievement tests. More than 40 studies have been carried out to demonstrate criterion validity.

Research is presented to show that the Wechsler scales discriminate among special groups of students as expected. In other words, children who are mentally retarded tend to score well below average and gifted children well above.

Evidence is provided to show that the subtests of the Verbal Scale correlate quite well and that lower correlations are found when comparing Verbal with Performance subtests.

CONCLUSIONS

The WISC–III is a well-standardized measure of intelligence, though no normative information is available for children who are visually impaired or blind. Results of some subtests do not appear to be stable over time and so must be interpreted with caution. Because the Verbal Score is based on a larger sample of behavior and is more reliable than the subtests, this result should be used to describe performance. More data on test-retest by age level would be desirable.

Many years of research have demonstrated the validity of the instrument. To circumvent a visual loss, only the Verbal Scale should be used, with Digit Span substituted for Arithmetic. Because the Verbal Scale is only half of the test, results should be interpreted in light of a student's performance in other areas as well, including achievement, social skills, and adaptive behavior.

· ·

• Wechsler Preschool and Primary Scale of Intelligence

See review in Chapter 5.

· ·

CRITERION-REFERENCED TESTS AND INFORMAL MEASURES

A discussion of the use of criterion-referenced tests and informal measures is presented in Chapter 1. Instruments were selected for review if they were developed specifically for students who are visually impaired or blind or if a Braille transcription of the instrument was available.

One of the most useful methods of obtaining data on student performance for planning instruction is curriculum-based measurement. This procedure was described earlier in this chapter under the Achievement heading in the Areas for Assessment section.

The reviews of criterion-referenced tests and informal measures include descriptions of the content, administration procedures, and materials for each test. When data on technical adequacy were available, these data were evaluated.

· ·

• Basic Reading Rate Scale– Braille Edition

Authors of the Adaptation: Bill Duckworth & Hilda Caton

Publisher: American Printing House for
the Blind
P.O. Box 6085
Louisville, KY 40206

Copyright: 1986

GENERAL DESCRIPTION

The *Basic Reading Rate Scale–Braille Edition* (BRRS) is an adaptation of the *Tinker Speed of Reading Test* (Tinker, 1955) and can be used with beginning Braille readers through accomplished adult readers. The BRRS provides a measure of Braille reading rate for Grade 2 Literary Braille. A large-type edition of this scale is available from APH as well.

Administration of the scale can be done individually or in groups. Administration must be carried out by someone who is familiar with students who are visually impaired or blind and who is knowledgeable in Grade 2 Literary Braille. Administration time is about 15 minutes.

Materials consist of the directions for administering the BRRS and either a Braille or large-type booklet for each student.

DESCRIPTION OF SCALE

Sample passages are used to provide practice for a student in marking items prior to the actual testing. Upon completion of the practice sections, a student is instructed to read the test passage silently, with a time limit of 5 minutes. The reading level of the material is described as "very easy material" (directions, p. 3). Students are told that there are some incorrect words in the material, and while reading they are to draw a line through the incorrect words as they encounter them. This requirement controls for comprehension.

TECHNICAL ADEQUACY

Field testing and validity.

There were 146 students in grades 2 through 12 who participated in the field testing of the BRRS. The students were from California, Connecticut, Florida, and Oklahoma and had a minimum of 2 years of instruction in Braille. These students did not have impairments in addition to their visual loss.

Results from the field testing indicated that words read per minute correlated .27 with number of years in school, .24 with age, .45 with number of years of instruction in Braille, and .46 with intelligence level. Results from the BRRS also correlated .71 with reading achievement levels. The measure used for achievement was not indicated. Thus, results from this scale correlated moderately with length of instruction and intelligence level as would be expected. Also, results were related to progress through grades in school. The high correlation obtained with a measure of reading achievement provides some evidence of the validity of the BRRS for assessing reading skills.

When data on words read per minute on the BRRS were compared with words read per minute for sighted students, it was clear that Braille requires considerably more time to read than print.

Limited data are given in the directions manual on words read per minute by grade level and in terms of years of Braille instruction. Because of the limited sample, these data should not be considered norms.

CONCLUSIONS

Because of the length of time required for Braille reading, speed of reading necessarily must be considered. The BRRS can provide one measure of reading speed. Unlike curriculum-based measurement, the BRRS cannot be used repeatedly because of practice effects. It can, however, provide a quick measure of reading rate for either Braille or large type, while controlling for comprehension. Examiners must be knowledgeable in Grade 2 Literary Braille.

· ·

• Braille Unit Recognition Battery: Diagnostic Test of Grade 2 Literary Braille

Authors: Hilda Caton, Bill Duckworth, & Earl Rankin

Publisher: American Printing House for the Blind
P.O. Box 6085
Louisville, KY 40206

Copyright: 1985

GENERAL DESCRIPTION

This battery is designed primarily for students in grades 3 through 12 but can be used with younger children and older adults. The primary purpose of the battery is to assess students' abilities to recognize and identify the different Braille units and, from this information, determine which units require additional instruction. The battery also can be used to determine whether a student's overall ability to read Braille reaches a level considered indicative of a competent Braille reader.

Item selection and organization of the battery were based on *Patterns: The Primary Braille Reading Program* (Caton, Pester, & Bradley, 1980). The three sections of the battery are: Letters, Grams, and Modulations.

Administration of the battery can be done individually or in groups and takes about one hour. There are, however, no time limits.

Items are presented orally by the examiner, and students mark their answers in the test booklet using a pencil or crayon. A student selects his or her answer from four or five alternatives for each item. Practice in marking answers is given prior to administering the items.

This battery should be given by a psychologist or teacher who is familiar with working with students who are visually impaired or blind. Knowledge of the educational needs of these students and a thorough knowledge of Grade 2 Literary Braille is required.

Materials consist of an examiner's manual, a booklet for the student, a record form for reporting scores, and a checklist used to assess physical aspects of Braille reading, such as posture and hand position.

DESCRIPTION OF SECTIONS

Letters.

Two tests make up this section: Alphabetic Letters and Nonalphabetic Letters (numbers). The first test assesses recognition of each of the 26 letters of the alphabet. The second test requires recognition of the one-digit numbers 0 through 9, two-digit numbers (10 items), and three-digit numbers (10 items).

Grams.

There are three tests for this section: Phonograms, Morphograms, and Letter Words and Wordlets. The Phonograms test is made up of 50 one-shape (e.g., *ch, gh*) and multishape (e.g., *ity, less*) phonograms. A phonogram is a unit of Braille written in print with more than one alphabetic symbol. The Morphograms test taps knowledge of the elements of Braille that have the value of a word element. These include prefixes, suffixes, and inflectional endings. There are 27 items on this test (e.g., *con, ed*). The Letter Words and Wordlets test has two parts. Letter words are words that also have letter values.

There are 23 such items (e.g., *very, can*). Wordlets involve one or more shapes with a word value but no letter value. The 129 wordlets tested are divided into four subtests: one-shape, two-shape, three-shape, and four- and five-shape wordlets.

Modulations.

This section measures recognition of Braille units for punctuation, register items, and some additional nonalphabetic letters not previously tested. There are 30 items in this section. Punctuation items include: those that look back, such as a period or question mark; those that enclose material, such as quotation marks or parentheses; and those that link material, such as a dash or hyphen. Register items include a variety of units, such as those for italics or capitals. Non-alphabetic letters assessed in this section are Braille units such as the decimal point and apostrophe.

Braille Mechanics.

This part of the battery can be completed before or after administration of the battery. The checklist has 16 items, and each item has three to five alternatives to describe a student's behavior when reading Braille. Items describe a variety of behaviors, such as position of fingers, amount of pressure on fingertips, use of remaining vision, and use of either hand or both hands. These behaviors are helpful to note because correction of inappropriate behaviors could help a student read Braille more accurately and efficiently.

TECHNICAL ADEQUACY

Field testing.

An initial pool of 945 items was generated, consisting of three items for every unit of Braille in each of the categories. This pool of items was field-tested in three residential schools with 67 students (grades 3 through 12) who had at least 1 year of instruction in reading Braille and had no impairments in addition to blindness. An experimental version of the battery, with 315 items, was developed after faulty items were eliminated and items that were likely to result in a large number of correct responses were selected. This version was field-tested also with 150 students (grades 3 through 12) from residential and day school programs. These students also had at least 1 year of instruction in reading Braille and had no impairments besides blindness. Item analysis indicated that these items were satisfactory and that nearly all students had 80% or more of the items correct. Based on this information and input from six Braille consultants, the mastery level was set at 90%. This criterion was considered minimum for proficient Braille reading.

Reliability.

Use of the Subkoviak Group Coefficient of Agreement suggested that students who met the criterion and those who did not would fall into similar categories if they were to retake the battery. Standard errors of measurement are provided for each part of the battery. Pearson correlations suggested that the various parts of the battery are moderately related. Because a multiple-choice format is used, some results may be affected by guessing.

Validity.

Items were selected based on a review of existing tests and using the Braille terms developed for teaching Braille reading (Caton et al., 1980). All units for Grade 2 Literary Braille were included, except for diacritical marks and units of Braille used in foreign languages.

To avoid confusion that occurs with other tests, the format of this battery requires that students read and mark only single units of Braille and that the examiner present only single units of Braille. Finally, the categories of Braille that are used do not group together Braille units that are easily confused. Thus, it is easier to determine the specific skills a student has learned and those that require additional work.

The difficulty level of the items was kept low so that the battery could be used to identify students whose basic Braille skills are so poor that special assistance is necessary.

CONCLUSIONS

Results of this battery could be very useful in determining which units of Braille need to be taught and which have been mastered. It is important that the battery is administered by someone thoroughly familiar with Grade 2 Literary Braille as well as the needs of students who are visually impaired or blind. The format of this battery was developed carefully, and the information from the tests and checklist of behaviors is comprehensive. This criterion-referenced test is an important contribution to educational planning for students who are visually impaired or blind.

. . . .

• Brigance Diagnostic Comprehensive Inventory of Basic Skills

Author: Albert Brigance

Publisher: Curriculum Associates
5 Esquire Road
North Billerica, MA 01862

Copyright: 1983

• APH Tactile Supplement

Authors: Bill Duckworth & Doris Abbot

Publisher: American Printing House for the Blind
P.O. Box 6085
Louisville, KY 40296

Copyright: Undated

GENERAL DESCRIPTION

The *Brigance Diagnostic Comprehensive Inventory of Basic Skills* is a criterion-referenced test designed to assess skills typically taught in kindergarten through ninth grade. Areas assessed are readiness skills, reading, mathematics, oral language, writing, and study skills.

The test is administered individually, though some sections can be administered to groups. The time required depends on how many sections of the test are given. Several hours would be required to administer the entire test to a student.

Because this is a criterion-referenced test, results are in terms of skills learned and those that need to be taught next.

At the beginning of the sections for reading, math, and spelling, results are in terms of grade levels. These levels are based on the levels at which skills are usually taught and are not the same as grade equivalents from norm-referenced tests. The most useful sections are the detailed assessments of mastery of skills.

For students who are Braille readers, the *APH Tactile Supplement* (Duckworth & Abbot, undated) would be necessary. The *APH Tactile Supplement* is to be used in conjunction with materials for the print edition from Curriculum Associates. The *APH Tactile Supplement* provides alternative procedures and tactile materials for items that involve visual stimuli. Additional directions and suggestions are provided where necessary.

Materials consist of an examiner's manual and a record book. The *APH Tactile Supplement* includes a booklet of instructions for examiners, tabs to be added to the print edition to help examiners locate sections that require adaptations, and a booklet of tactile stimuli (e.g., Braille pages and raised figures).

DESCRIPTION OF SECTIONS

Readiness.

Many different skills are tested in this section. Subtests assess the ability to: identify body parts; recite personal data; recognize and name colors; understand directional and positional concepts; draw a person; use gross motor skills; use self-help skills; copy forms; cut with scissors; discriminate among forms, letters, and words; employ visual memory; demonstrate rote counting; recite the alphabet; name letters; count objects; recognize numbers; identify sets; write numbers in sequence; match quantities and numbers; write personal data; and respond to books.

Speech.

Skills tested include response to questions and a picture, articulation of sounds, and syntax and fluency.

Reading.

Three sections provide grade levels for word recognition, oral reading, and comprehension. Because this is not a norm-referenced test, these grade levels cannot be interpreted as norm-referenced results. The remaining sections indicate the grade levels at which skills typically are taught. Hence, results are in terms of skills mastered and those that need to be taught. There are extensive sections assessing phonics skills, structural analysis, and recognition of functional words (e.g., 75 direction words, 16 warning labels).

Listening.

Skills tapped in this section are auditory discrimination, memory for sentences, ability to follow oral directions, listening vocabulary, listening behaviors as observed by the teacher, and a listening comprehension level.

Spelling.

The first subtest yields a grade level for spelling. This is not a grade equivalent. The more useful sections tap skills for spelling initial consonants, blends and digraphs, suffixes, prefixes, number words, days of the week, and months of the year.

Writing.

Assessed in this section are skills for writing in cursive, personal data, sentences, capitalization, punctuation, addressing an envelope, and writing a letter.

Reference Skills.

This section covers skills in alphabetizing, outlining, using an encyclopedia, and using a library card catalog, parts of a book, index of a book, and a dictionary.

Graphs and Maps.

Assessed are skills in interpreting bar graphs, line graphs, pictographs, circle graphs, maps, and globes.

Math.

The first section yields grade levels, not grade equivalents. The more useful sections comprehensively cover: recognizing and writing numbers, math facts, computation (addition, subtraction, multiplication, division), fractions and mixed numbers, decimals, percents, metrics, math vocabulary, and measurement (time, money, linear measurement, liquid and weight measurement, and reading meters and gauges).

TECHNICAL ADEQUACY

Field testing.

The *Brigance* was field-tested by 141 professionals from 27 states and one Canadian province. Feedback from the field testing identified which items should be added or eliminated, which were not in sequence, and other comments regarding the content validity of the test.

Reliability.

Nearly every skill is assessed at least three times. This should result in reliable information regarding a particular student's performance.

Validity.

This is a text-referenced measure. In other words, items were selected from a review of basal series in order to determine the skills usually taught in each area and the order in which the skills are usually taught. The texts reviewed for each section are listed in the manual, and the reviews were extensive. Therefore, this test has good content validity in terms of testing skills that are taught in the classroom. An examiner still must review the skills in the test to determine that the skills in fact have been taught to a particular student. It is especially important when working with students with little or no vision to ensure that what is tested is what has been taught. Curricula for these students may differ from that used with sighted peers, especially in reading. Only the relevant sections for a student should be used.

CONCLUSIONS

The *Brigance Diagnostic Comprehensive Inventory of Basic Skills* is an exceptionally comprehensive criterion-referenced measure. For students with little or no vision, the *APH Tactile Supplement* to the *Brigance* will be necessary. Because nearly every skill is assessed at least three times, results obtained should be quite reliable. This measure should provide very detailed and useful information for planning instruction, especially in reading, math, and writing. Because of the comprehensiveness of this measure, only the sections relevant for a particular student should be used to avoid overtesting. The record booklets can be used multiple times, allowing progress to be monitored over time.

. . . .

• Revised Brigance Diagnostic Inventory of Early Development

See review in Chapter 4.

. . . .

• Dolch Word List

Author: Edward Dolch

Publisher: Braille and large-type version available
from the
American Printing House for the Blind
P.O. Box 6085
Louisville, KY 40206

Copyright: 1955

GENERAL DESCRIPTION

This word list is most appropriate for students in the early grades, about age 6 to 9. The words were selected from words commonly taught in basal reading series for the early elementary grades.

The materials consist of 220 cards of words from the Dolch list, along with 95 picture words. Each 3½-by-2-in. card has one word printed in both Braille and large type. The additional 95 nouns were added so that the cards could be used to create sentences for teaching.

Though there have been many changes in basal series since the publication of this list, most writers agree that words on the list make up about 50% of the vocabulary found in elementary grade materials, that many words are taught consistently from one series to the next, and that most words are taught in grades 1 and 2 (Lesiak & Bradley-Johnson, 1983).

To assess sight vocabulary using this list, cards are presented one at a time to a student. The student's task is to read each word orally.

CONCLUSIONS

The Dolch list in Braille or large type would provide useful information on a student's word-recognition skills. It would, however, be worthwhile to supplement this list with words from the Fry (1980) list of instant words. Words on the Fry list frequently occur in materials a person might read throughout a lifetime. The list is based on a frequency count of more than 5 million running words that appeared in 500 word samples, 1,045 books in 12 subject areas, fiction and nonfiction books, and magazines (Carroll, Davies, & Richman, 1971). The first 10 words make up 24% of words found in written material, the first 100 make up 50%, and the 300 words on the list account for 65% of the words in written material. Most of the words on the Fry list are mastered by third grade, and it is clear that these are important words to be able to recognize quickly for efficient reading. The Dolch list is based on those words commonly *taught,* but the Fry list contains those frequently *encountered* in reading material. The words from the Fry list could be added to the Dolch cards by printing them in Braille or large type.

. . . .

• Informal Assessment of Developmental Skills for Visually Handicapped Students (School-Age Section)

Authors: Rose-Marie Swallow, Sally Mangold, & Phillip Mangold

Publisher: American Foundation for the Blind
15 West 16th Street
New York, NY 10011

Copyright: 1978

GENERAL DESCRIPTION

This material consists of a series of checklists designed to assess informally the special needs of students who are visually impaired or blind. The checklists were developed by teachers of students with visual impairments.

Some of the checklists can provide information on academic performance, whereas other checklists address more functional skills such as orientation and mobility. The checklists are not meant to take the place of a comprehensive evaluation by an orientation and mobility specialist or a functional vision assessment by a teacher certified to conduct such an assessment. Instead, they are intended to provide more general information that would be useful to a classroom teacher.

The authors gave permission to duplicate the checklists for "educational use with visually handicapped children" (p. 2).

DESCRIPTION OF CHECKLISTS

Visual Functioning.

Two checklists are included for this area. One checklist is used to describe a student's functional vision both indoors and outdoors and the optimal conditions for sight. Examples of items include conditions needed for optimal viewing of audiovisual materials, classroom modifications, and a student's ability to see traffic lights during the day and at night. This checklist is quite lengthy and involves observation of a student in numerous settings such as the classroom, auditorium, a building with escalators, and outdoors.

The other checklist primarily involves reading print. It covers information on eye condition, visual aids, type of print, and reading skills such as reading behaviors, interests, and word attack skills. The reading behaviors such as "Tilts head and/or book" and "Jumps lines on return sweep" are particularly helpful to note. Word attack skills, however, could be assessed more comprehensively with the *Brigance Diagnostic Comprehensive Inventory of Basic Skills* (Brigance, 1983).

Unique Academic Needs.

This measure presents 12 checklists that tap communication skills needed for academic success. Two checklists assess Braille reading skills, 2 tap listening abilities, 2 involve a task analysis of use of the Optacon, 1 tests skills needed to use a Braillewriter, 1 assesses abilities required to use a slate and stylus, 1 taps script writing for students who are blind, 1 measures script writing for students with low vision, and the last 2 test typing skills. The production checklists that involve the Braillewriter, slate and stylus, script writing, and typing skills are particularly helpful. On the typing skills checklists, however, it is not clear on all items what is being tested, and several of the skills do not seem to be critical to successful performance, such as "Elbow close to side of body" and "Machine Parts–Erasure Table." The checklists in this section are based on detailed analyses of these tasks and could provide useful, specific information for planning educational programs. Consideration of listening skills is very important for students who are visually impaired or blind because so much information must be obtained auditorily. The two listening abilities checklists seem to highlight important skills.

Orientation and Mobility.

The authors noted that these checklists are not designed for an orientation and mobility instructor or an adaptive physical education specialist. Five checklists are presented. One checklist can be used to test spatial reasoning and fine motor control using blocks, puzzles, paper and crayons, bead stringing, cutting, tying, and pouring. A second checklist assesses gross motor skills, including balance and coordination, strength, agility, rhythm, and endurance. The third checklist measures knowledge of body parts, movements, laterality, and directionality. A fourth checklist can be used to test left-right discrimination and spatial orientation, and the last checklist has 59 tasks that measure body concepts, relational concepts, and movement around objects.

Vocational Skills.

Two checklists are provided for this area. One assesses adaptive behaviors, including survival skills such as "Locates public restrooms," "Mails a letter," and "Knows what to do if lost," telephone use, and organizational skills. Many of these skills are especially important for students who are visually impaired or blind and are not included on other scales. Because some items are general, such as "Cares for skin," subjective judgment is involved in rating. The second checklist can be used to test a variety of prevocational skills such as personal development, daily living skills, and basic manipulative skills.

Behavioral Rating Scale.

This detailed checklist addresses skills important to successful functioning in the classroom. A wide range of behaviors is addressed, including skills in organization, listening, language, self-discipline, and attention.

TECHNICAL ADEQUACY

No data are presented on field testing, reliability, or validity. Hence, results must be interpreted in light of the informal nature of the checklists.

CONCLUSIONS

These checklists can provide information helpful in planning instructional programs for students who are visually impaired or blind. The checklists consider many unique needs of these students. Given the subjective and general nature of the checklists, results must be interpreted cautiously, but the checklists are worth considering during the assessment of any school-age student who is visually impaired or blind.

. . . .

• Oregon Project for Visually Impaired and Blind Infants and Preschoolers– Fifth Edition

See review in Chapter 4.

References

Achenbach, T., & Edelbrock, C. (1983). *Child Behavior Checklist and Revised Child Behavior Profile.* Burlington: University of Vermont, Department of Psychiatry.

Achenbach, T., & Edelbrock, C. (1986). *Teacher Version of the Child Behavior Profile.* Burlington: University of Vermont, Department of Psychiatry.

Aiken, L. R. (1991). *Psychological testing and assessment* (7th ed.). Boston: Allyn & Bacon.

Alessi, G., & Kaye, J. H. (1983). *Behavior assessment for school psychologists.* Silver Spring, MD: National Association of School Psychologists.

Allen, T., White, C., & Karchmer, M. (1983). Issues in the development of a special edition for hearing-impaired students of the 7th edition of the SAT. *American Annals of the Deaf, 128,* 34–39.

American Foundation for the Blind. (undated). *Facts about blindness.* New York: Author.

American Psychological Association. (1981). Ethical principles of psychologists (rev.). *American Psychologist, 36,* 633–638.

Anderson, D. W., & Olson, M. R. (1981). Word meaning among congenitally blind children. *Journal of Visual Impairment and Blindness, 75,* 165–168.

Anderson, S., Boigon, S., & Davis, K. (1986). *The Oregon Project for Visually Impaired and Blind Preschool Children* (5th ed.). Medford, OR: Jackson County Education Service District.

Ashman, S. (1982). *An introduction to psychological assessment of visually impaired children.* Indianapolis: Indiana State School for the Blind.

Bagnato, S. J., & Neisworth, J. T. (1991). *Assessment for early intervention: Best practices for professionals.* New York: Guilford Press.

Bailey, D. B., Simeonsson, R. J., Winton, P. J., Huntington, G. S., Comfort, M., Isbell, P., O'Donnell, K. J., & Helm, J. M. (1986). Family-focused intervention: A functional model for planning, implementing, and evaluating individualized family services in early intervention. *Journal of the Division for Early Childhood, 10,* 156–171.

Bailey, D. B., & Simeonsson, R. J. (1988). *Family assessment in early intervention.* Columbus, OH: Merrill.

Baker, H. J., & Leland, B. (1967). *Detroit Tests of Learning Aptitude.* Indianapolis, IN: Bobbs-Merrill.

Bauman, M. K. (1973). Psychological and educational assessment. In B. Lowenfeld (Ed.), *The visually handicapped child in school* (pp. 27–60). New York: John Day.

Bayley, N. (1969). *Bayley Scales of Infant Development.* San Antonio, TX: Psychological Corporation.

Benner, S. M. (1992). *Assessing young children with special needs: An ecological perspective.* White Plains, NY: Longman.

Boyle, P. (1977). Psychology. In B. F. Jaffe (Ed.), *Hearing loss in children: A comprehensive text* (pp. 266–282). Baltimore: University Park Press.

Brackett, D. (1981). Assessment: Adaptations, interpretations, and implications. In M. Ross & L. W. Nober (Eds.), *Special education in transition: Educating hard of hearing children* (pp. 47–66). Washington, DC: Alexander Graham Bell Association.

Bradley-Johnson, S. (1987). *Cognitive Abilities Scale.* Austin, TX: PRO-ED.

Bradley-Johnson, S., & Lesiak, J. (1989). *Problems in written expression: Assessment and remediation.* New York: Guilford Press.

Brambring, M., & Troster, H. (1992). On the stability of stereotyped behaviors in blind infants and preschoolers. *Journal of Visual Impairment and Blindness, 86,* 105–110.

Brigance, A. (1983). *Brigance Diagnostic Comprehensive Inventory of Basic Skills.* North Billerica, MA: Curriculum Associates.

Brigance, A. (1991). *Revised Brigance Diagnostic Inventory of Early Development.* North Billerica, MA: Curriculum Associates.

Brown, D., Simmons, V., & Methvin, J. (1979). *The Oregon Project for Visually Impaired and Blind Preschool Children.* Medford, OR: Jackson County Education Service District.

Brown, L., & Leigh, J. (1986). *Adaptive Behavior Inventory.* Austin, TX: PRO-ED.

Bryant, B. R., & Newcomer, P. L. (1991). *Scholastic Aptitude Scale.* Austin, TX: PRO-ED.

California Test Bureau. (1968). *Comprehensive Test of Basic Skills.* Monterey, CA: Author.

California Test Bureau. (1973). *California Short-Form Test of Academic Aptitude.* Monterey, CA: Author.

Carroll, J., Davies, P., & Richman, B. (1971). *The American Heritage word frequency book.* Boston: Houghton-Mifflin.

Caton, H., Duckworth, B. J., & Rankin, E. (1985). *Braille Unit Recognition Battery: Diagnostic Test of Grade 2 Literary Braille.* Louisville, KY: American Printing House for the Blind.

Clemmer, S. C., Klifman, T. J., & Bradley-Johnson, S. (1992). Long-term predictive validity of the Cognitive Abilities Scale. *Journal of Psychoeducational Assessment, 10,* 265–275.

Coggins, T. E., & Carpenter, R. L. (1981). The Communicative Intention Inventory: A system for observing and coding children's early intentional communication. *Applied Psycholinguistics, 2,* 235–251.

Corn, A., & Coatney, L. (1984). Characteristics of teachers of the visually handicapped: A survey of Texas teachers. *Spectrum: Journal of School Research and Information, 2*(4), 20–25.

Cruickshank, W. (Ed.). (1980). *Psychology of exceptional children and youth.* Englewood Cliffs, NJ: Prentice-Hall.

Davis, C. (1980). *Perkins-Binet Test of Intelligence for the Blind.* Watertown, MA: Perkins School for the Blind.

Dolch, E. (1955). *Methods in reading.* Champaign, IL: Garrard.

Doll, E. A. (1965). *Vineland Social Maturity Scale.* Circle Pines, MN: American Guidance Service.

DuBose, R. F., & Langley, M. B. (1977). *Developmental Activities Screening Inventory.* Hingham, MA: Teaching Resources.

Duckworth, B. J. (1992). *APH Tactile Supplement for the Diagnostic Reading Scales.* Louisville, KY: American Printing House for the Blind.

Duckworth, B. J. (undated). Braille edition of the *Stanford Achievement Test.* Louisville, KY: American Printing House for the Blind.

Duckworth, B. J. (undated). Braille transcription of the *Diagnostic Reading Scales*. Louisville, KY: American Printing House for the Blind.

Duckworth, B. J., & Abbot, D. (undated). *APH Tactile Supplement for the Brigance Diagnostic Comprehensive Inventory of Basic Skills*. Louisville, KY: American Printing House for the Blind.

Duckworth, B. J., & Caton, H. (1986). *Basic Reading Rate Scale: Braille Edition or Large Type*. Louisville, KY: American Printing House for the Blind.

Duckworth, B. J., & Stratton, J. M. (1992). *APH Tactile Supplement for the Revised Brigance Diagnostic Inventory of Early Development*. Louisville, KY: American Printing House for the Blind.

Dunn, L. M., & Dunn, L. M. (1981). *Peabody Picture Vocabulary Test* (rev.). Circle Pines, MN: American Guidance Service.

Dunst, C. J. (1980). *A clinical and educational manual for use with the Uzgiris and Hunt Scales of Infant Psychological Development*. Austin, TX: PRO-ED.

Dunst, C. J. (1982). The clinical utility of Piagetian-based scales of infant development. *Infant Mental Health Journal, 3,* 259–275.

Dunst, C. J., & Leet, H. E. (1987). Measuring the adequacy of resources in households with young children. *Child Care, Health, and Development, 13,* 111–125.

Eaglestein, A. S. (1975). The social acceptance of blind high school students in an integrated school. *New Outlook for the Blind, 69,* 447–451.

Elliott, C. D. (1990). *Differential Ability Scales*. San Antonio, TX: Psychological Corporation.

Englemann, S. (1969). *Preventing failure in the primary grades*. Chicago, IL: Science Research Associates.

Fagan, J. F. (1982). New evidence for the prediction of intelligence from infancy. *Infant Mental Health Journal, 3,* 219–228.

Federal Register, (1977, August 23). Part II, Education of Handicapped Children, Implementation of Part B of the Education of the Handicapped Act. Vol. 42, 42474-42518.

Ferrell, K. A., Trief, E., Dietz, S. J., Bonner, M. A., Cruz, D., Ford, E., & Stratton, J. M. (1990). Visually Impaired Infants Research Consortium (VIIRC): First-year results. *Journal of Visual Impairment and Blindness, 84,* 404–410.

Fewell, R. R. (1983). New directions in the assessment of young handicapped children. In C. E. Reynolds & J. H. Clark (Eds.),

Assessment and programming for young children with low-incidence handicaps (pp. 1–41). New York: Plenum Press.

Field, T. (1982). Interaction coaching for high-risk infants and their parents. In H. A. Moss, R. Hess, & C. Swift (Eds.), *Prevention in human services* (Vol. 1, pp. 5–23). New York: Hawthorn Press.

Filler, J. (1973). Sensorimotor assessment performance as a function of task materials. In D. Bricker & W. Bricker (Eds.), *Infant, toddler and preschool research and intervention project report: Year III* (IMRID Behavioral Science Monograph No. 23). Nashville: George Peabody College.

Finkelstein, S. (1989). *Blindness and disorders of the eye.* Baltimore: National Federation of the Blind.

Flynn, J. R. (1984). The mean IQ of Americans: Massive gains 1932 to 1978. *Psychological Bulletin, 95,* 29–51.

Fodness, R. W., McNeilly, J., & Bradley-Johnson, S. (1991). Test-retest reliability of the Test of Language Development–2: Primary and Test of Language Development–2:Intermediate. *Journal of School Psychology, 29,* 161–164.

Fraiberg, S. (1974). Blind infants and their mothers. In M. Lucas & L. Rosenblum (Eds.), *The effects of the infant on its caregiver.* New York: Wiley and Sons.

Fraiberg, S. (1977). *Insights from the blind: Comparative studies of blind and sighted infants.* New York: Basic Books.

French, J. L. (1964). *Pictorial Test of Intelligence.* Boston: Houghton-Mifflin.

Fry, E. (1980). The new instant word list. *The Reading Teacher, 34,* 284.

Gelfand, D., & Hartman, D. P. (1984). *Child behavior analysis and therapy* (2nd ed.). New York: Pergamon Press.

Gilbert, J., & Rubin, E. (1965). Evaluating the intellect of blind children. *The New Outlook for the Blind, 59,* 238–240.

Ginsburg, H. P., & Baroody, A. J. (1983). *Test of Early Mathematical Ability.* Austin, TX: PRO-ED.

Goldman, F. H., & Duda, D. (1978). Psychological assessment of the visually impaired child. In R. K. Mulliken & M. Evans (Eds.), *Assessment of children with low-incidence handicaps* (pp. 52–57). Silver Springs, MD: National Association of School Psychologists Publications Office.

Gresham, F. M., & Elliott, S. N. (1990). *Social Skills Rating System.* Circle Pines, MN: American Guidance Service.

Griffiths, R. (1954). *The abilities of babies.* London: University of London Press.

Guilford, J. P. (1978). *Fundamental statistics in psychology and education.* New York: McGraw-Hill.

Guilford, J. P., & Hoepfner, R. (1971). *The analysis of intelligence.* New York: McGraw-Hill.

Hammill, D. D. (1985). *Detroit Test of Learning Aptitude* (2nd ed.). Austin, TX: PRO-ED.

Hammill, D. D. (1987). An overview of assessment practices. In D. D. Hammill (Ed.), *Assessing the abilities and instructional needs of students* (pp. 2–37). Austin, TX: PRO-ED.

Hammill, D. D. (1991). *Detroit Test of Learning Aptitude* (3rd ed.). Austin, TX: PRO-ED.

Hammill, D. D., Brown, V. L., Larsen, S. C., & Wiederholt, J. L. (1980). *Test of Adolescent Language.* Austin, TX: PRO-ED.

Hammill, D. D., Brown, V. L., Larsen, S. C., & Wiederholt, J. L. (1987). *Test of Adolescent Language* (2nd ed.). Austin, TX: PRO-ED.

Hammill, D. D., & Bryant, B. (1986). *Detroit Test of Learning Aptitude–Primary.* Austin, TX: PRO-ED.

Hammill, D. D., & Bryant, B. (1991). *Detroit Test of Learning Aptitude–Primary* (2nd ed.). Austin, TX: PRO-ED.

Hammill, D. D., & Larsen, S. (1983). *Test of Written Language.* Austin, TX: PRO-ED.

Hammill, D. D., & Leigh, J. E. (1983). *Basic School Skills Inventory–Diagnostic.* Austin, TX: PRO-ED.

Hammill, D. D., & Newcomer, P. L. (1982). *Test of Language Development–Intermediate.* Austin, TX: PRO-ED.

Hammill, D. D., & Newcomer, P. L. (1988). *Test of Language Development–Intermediate* (2nd ed.). Austin, TX: PRO-ED.

Harter, S. (1985). *Self-Perception Profile for Children.* Denver, CO: University of Denver.

Hatfield, E. M. (1975). Why are they blind? *Sightsaving Review, 45,* 3–22.

Hayes, S. P. (1942). Alternative scales for the mental measurement of the visually handicapped. *Outlook for the Blind, 36,* 225–230.

Hayes, S. P. (1943). A second test scale for the mental measurement of the visually handicapped. *Outlook for the Blind, 37,* 37–41.

Higgins, L. C. (1973). *Classification in the congenitally blind.* New York: American Foundation for the Blind.

Hill, E., Dodson-Burk, E., & Smith, A. (1989). Orientation and mobility for infants who are visually impaired. *Review, 21,* 47–60.

Hillerich, R. (1978). *A writing vocabulary of elementary children.* Springfield, IL: Charles C. Thomas.

Hoben, M., & Lindstrom, V. (1980). Evidence of isolation in the mainstream. *Journal of Visual Impairment and Blindness, 74,* 289–292.

Hopkins, K. D., & McGuire, L. (1966). The validity of the Wechsler Intelligence Scale for Children. *The International Journal for the Education of the Blind, 15,* 65–73.

Imamura, S. (1965). *Mother and blind child* (Research Series No. 14). New York: American Foundation for the Blind.

Individuals with Disabilities Education Act, 20 U.S.C. (1990). Chapter 33.

Individuals with Disabilities Education Act as amended October 30, 1990, by *P.L. 101–476,* 20 U.S.C. 1400 et seq.

Jan, D. E., Freeman, R. D., McCormick, A. Q., Scott, E. P., Robertson, W. D., & Newman, D. E. (1983). Eye-pressing by visually impaired children. *Developmental Medicine and Child Neurology, 25,* 755–762.

Joffee, E. (1988). A home-based orientation and mobility program for infants and toddlers. *Journal of Visual Impairment and Blindness, 82,* 282–285.

Johnson-Martin, N. M., Attermeier, S. M., & Hacker, B. (1990). *The Carolina Curriculum for Preschoolers With Special Needs.* Baltimore: Paul H. Brookes.

Johnson-Martin, N. M., Jens, K. G., Attermeier, S. M., & Hacker, B. J. (1991). *The Carolina Curriculum for Infants and Toddlers With Special Needs.* Baltimore: Paul H. Brookes.

Jones, R. L., Lavine, K., & Shell, J. (1972). Blind children integrated in classrooms with sighted children: A sociometric study. *New Outlook for the Blind, 66,* 75–80.

Justice, B., & Justice, R. (1976). *The abusing family.* New York: Human Sciences Press.

Kaufman, A. S., & Kaufman, N. L. (1983). *Kaufman Assessment Battery for Children.* Circle Pines, MN: American Guidance Service.

Kaufman, A. S., & Kaufman, N. L. (1985). *Kaufman Test of Educational Achievement* (Comprehensive Form). Circle Pines, MN: American Guidance Service.

Kekelis, L. S., & Andersen, E. S. (1984). Family communication styles and language development. *Journal of Visual Impairment and Blindness, 78,* 54–65.

Kirchner, C. (1983). Special education for visually handicapped children: A critique of data on numbers served and costs. *Journal of Visual Impairment and Blindness, 77,* 219–223.

Kirk, S., McCarthy, J., & Kirk, W. (1968). *Illinois Test of Psycholinguistic Abilities.* Chicago: University of Illinois Press.

Lee, L. (1971). *Northwestern Syntax Screening Test.* Evanston, IL: Northwestern University Press.

Lesiak, J., & Bradley-Johnson, S. (1983). *Reading assessment for placement and programming.* Springfield, IL: Charles C. Thomas.

Levack, N. (1991). *Low vision: A resource guide with adaptations for students with visual impairments.* Austin, TX: Texas School for the Blind and Visually Impaired.

Lowenfeld, B. (1980). Psychological problems of children with severely impaired vision. In W. M. Cruickshank (Ed.), *Psychology of exceptional children and youth* (4th ed.) (pp. 255–341). Englewood Cliffs, NJ: Prentice-Hall.

MacFarland, D. (1966). Social isolation of the blind: An underrated aspect of disability and dependency. *New Outlook for the Blind, 60,* 318–319.

Markovits, H., & Strayer, F. (1982). Toward an applied social ethology: A case study of social skills among blind children. In K. H. Rubin & H. Ross (Eds.), *Peer relationships and social skills in childhood* (pp. 301–322). New York: Springer-Verlag.

Mash, E. J., & Terdal, L. G. (1988). Behavioral assessment of child and family disturbance. In E. J. Mash & L. G. Terdal (Eds.), *Behavioral assessment of childhood disorders* (2nd ed.) (pp. 3–65). New York: Guilford Press.

Maurer, D., & Maurer, C. (1988). *The world of the newborn.* New York: Basic Books.

Maxfield, K. E., & Bucholz, S. (1957). *A Social Maturity Scale for Blind Preschool Children.* New York: American Foundation for the Blind.

McCarthy, D. (1972). *McCarthy Scales of Children's Abilities.* New York: Psychological Corporation.

McNeilly, J. (1987). *Test/retest reliability of the Test of Language Development–Primary.* Unpublished master's thesis, Central Michigan University, Mt. Pleasant.

Mercer, J. R., & Lewis, J. F. (1978). *Adaptive Behavior Inventory for Children.* New York: Psychological Corporation.

Morgan, S. (1993). *Technical adequacy of a curriculum-based mea-*

sure for visually impaired Braille readers. Unpublished master's thesis, Central Michigan University, Mt. Pleasant.

National Advisory Eye Council (1981). *Low vision and rehabilitation* (Panel Report). Program Planning Subcommittee.

Newborg, J., Stock, J. R., Wnek, L., Guidubaldi, J., & Svinicki, J. (1984). *Battelle Developmental Inventory.* Allen, TX: DLM/ Teaching Resources.

Newcomer, P. L. (1990). *Diagnostic Achievement Battery* (2nd ed.). Austin, TX: PRO-ED.

Newcomer, P. L., & Hammill, D. D. (1982). *Test of Language Development–Primary.* Austin, TX: PRO-ED.

Newcomer, P. L., & Hammill, D. D. (1988). *Test of Language Development–Primary* (2nd ed.). Austin, TX: PRO-ED.

Newland, T. E. (1971). *Blind Learning Aptitude Test.* Urbana: University of Illinois Press.

Nihira, K., Foster, R., Shellhaas, M., & Leland, H. (1974). *AAMD Adaptive Behavior Scale* (rev.). Washington, DC: American Association on Mental Deficiency.

O'Donnell, L. M., & Livingston, R. L. (1991). Active exploration of the environment by young children with low vision: A review of the literature. *Journal of Visual Impairment and Blindness, 85,* 287–291.

Parke, D. L., Shallcross, R., & Anderson, R. J. (1980). Difference in coverbal behavior between blind and sighted persons during dyadic communication. *Journal of Visual Impairment and Blindness, 74,* 142–149.

Piaget, J. (1952). *The origins of intelligence in children* (M. Cook, Trans.). New York: International Universities Press.

Piers, E. V. (1984). *Piers-Harris Children's Self-Concept Scale* (rev.). Los Angeles: Western Psychological Services.

Preisler, B., & Palmer, C. (1988). The blind child goes to nursery school with sighted children. *Child Care, Health and Development, 476,* 45–52.

Preisler, G. G. (August, 1988). *The development of communication in blind infants.* Paper presented at the International Symposium on Visually Impaired Infants and Young Children: Birth to Seven, Edinburgh, Scotland.

Psychological Corporation. (1989). *Stanford Achievement Test.* New York: Author.

Public Law 94–142. (1975). *Federal Register,* 22676-22692 (121a.532).

Public Law 99–457. (1986). *Education of the Handicapped Act Amendments.*

Raver, S. A., & Drash, P. W. (1988). Increasing social skills training for visually impaired children. *Education of the Visually Handicapped, 19,* 147–155.

Raver-Lampman, S. A. (1990). Effect of gaze direction on evaluation of visually impaired children by informed respondents. *Journal of Visual Impairment and Blindness, 84,* 67–70.

Reid, D. K., Hresko, W. P., & Hammill, D. D. (1981a). *Test of Early Language Development.* Austin, TX: PRO-ED.

Reid, D. K., Hresko, W. P., & Hammill, D. D. (1981b). *Test of Early Reading Ability.* Austin, TX: PRO-ED.

Reid, D. K., Hresko, W. P., & Hammill, D. D. (1989). *Test of Early Reading Ability* (2nd ed.). Austin, TX: PRO-ED.

Rogers, S. J., & Puchalski, C. B. (1984). Social characteristics of visually impaired infants' play. *Topics in Early Childhood Special Education, 3,* 52–56.

Ross, D. B., & Koenig, A. J. (1991). A cognitive approach to reducing stereotypic head rocking. *Journal of Visual Impairment and Blindness, 85,* 17–19.

Salvia, J., & Ysseldyke, J. E. (1991). *Assessment* (5th ed.). Boston: Houghton-Mifflin.

Schneekloth, L. H. (1989). Play environments for visually impaired children. *Journal of Visual Impairment and Blindness, 83,* 196–201.

Scholl, G. T. (1985). Visual impairments. In G. T. Scholl (Ed.), *The school psychologist and the exceptional child* (pp. 203–218). Reston, VA: Council for Exceptional Children.

Scholl, G. T., & Schnur, R. (1975). Measures of psychological, vocational, and educational functioning in the blind and visually handicapped: Introductory remarks. *The New Outlook,* 365–370.

Scott, E. P., Jan, J. E., & Freeman, R. D. (1985). *Can't your child see?* Austin, TX: PRO-ED.

Shinn, M. (1989). *Curriculum-based measurement: Assessing special children.* New York: Guilford Press.

Short, R. J., Simeonsson, R. J., & Huntington, G. S. (1990). Early intervention: Implications of Public Law 99–457 for professional child psychology. *Professional Psychology: Research and Practice, 21,* 88–93.

Skellenger, A. C., Hill, M. M., & Hill, E. (1992). The social functioning of children with visual impairments. In S. L. Odom, S. R. McConnell, & M. A. McEvoy (Eds.), *Social competence of young children with disabilities* (pp. 165–188). Baltimore: Paul H. Brookes.

Spache, G. (1981). *Diagnostic Reading Scales.* Monterey, CA: CTB/McGraw-Hill.

Sparrow, S. S., Balla, D. A., & Cicchetti, D. V. (1984). *Vineland Adaptive Behavior Scales*–Expanded or Survey Version. Circle Pines, MN: American Guidance Service.

Statistical abstract of the United States. (1980). Washington, DC: U.S. Department of Commerce, Bureau of the Census.

Stephens, T. (1978). *Social skills in the classroom.* Columbus, OH: Cedars Press.

Stillman, R. (1977). *Callier-Azusa Scale.* Dallas: University of Texas, Callier Center for Communication Disorders.

Swallow, R., Mangold, S., & Mangold, P. (1978). *Informal Assessment of Developmental Skills for Visually Handicapped Students.* New York: American Foundation for the Blind.

Terman, L. M., & Merrill, M. A. (1960). *Stanford-Binet Intelligence Scale.* Chicago: Riverside.

Terman, L. M., & Merrill, M. A. (1972). *Stanford-Binet Intelligence Scale.* Boston: Houghton-Mifflin.

Thorndike, R. L., Hagen, E. P., & Sattler, J. M. (1986). *Stanford-Binet Intelligence Scale* (4th ed.). Chicago: Riverside.

Tillman, M. H. (1967). The performance of blind and sighted children on the Wechsler Intelligence Scale for Children: Study 1. *The International Journal for the Blind, 16,* 65–74.

Tillman, M. H. (1973). Intelligence scales for the blind: A review with implications for research. *Journal of School Psychology, 11,* 80–87.

Tillman, M. H., & Osborne, R. T. (1969). The performance of blind and sighted children on the Wechsler Intelligence Scale for Children: Interaction effects. *Education of the Visually Handicapped, 1,* 1–4.

Tinker, M. A. (1955). *Tinker Speed of Reading Test.* Minneapolis: University of Minnesota Press.

Tuttle, D. W. (1984). *Self-esteem and adjusting with blindness.* Springfield, IL: Charles C. Thomas.

U.S. Department of Education (1992). *Fourteenth annual report to Congress on the implementation of the Individuals with Disabilities Education Act.* Washington, DC: Author.

Uzgiris, I., & Hunt, J. McVicor. (1975). *Ordinal Scales of Psychological Development.* Urbana: University of Illinois Press.

Uzgiris, I., & Hunt, J. McVicor. (1989). *Ordinal Scales of Psychological Development.* Urbana: University of Illinois Press.

Van Hasselt, V. B., Hersen, M., Kazdin, A. E., Simon, J., & Mastantuono, A. (1983). Training blind adolescents in social skills. *Journal of Visual Impairment and Blindness, 77,* 199–203.

Van Hasselt, V. B., Simon, J., & Mastantuono, A. K. (1984). Social skills training for blind children and adolescents. *Education of the Visually Handicapped, 14,* 34–40.

Wechsler, D. (1949). *Wechsler Intelligence Scale for Children.* San Antonio, TX: Psychological Corporation.

Wechsler, D. (1967). *Wechsler Preschool and Primary Scale of Intelligence.* San Antonio, TX: Psychological Corporation.

Wechsler, D. (1974). *Wechsler Intelligence Scale for Children* (rev.). San Antonio, TX: Psychological Corporation.

Wechsler, D. (1981). *Wechsler Adult Intelligence Scale—Revised.* San Antonio, TX: Psychological Corporation.

Wechsler, D. (1989). *Wechsler Preschool and Primary Scale of Intelligence* (rev.). San Antonio, TX: Psychological Corporation.

Wechsler, D. (1991). *Wechsler Intelligence Scale for Children* (3rd ed.). San Antonio, TX: Psychological Corporation.

Wepman, J. (1968). *Auditory Discrimination Test.* Chicago: Language Research Associates.

Woodcock, R. W., & Johnson, M. B. (1977). *Woodcock-Johnson Psycho-Educational Battery.* Allen, TX: DLM/Teaching Resources.

Woodcock, R. W., & Johnson, M. B. (1989). *Woodcock-Johnson Psycho-Educational Battery.* Allen, TX: DLM/Teaching Resources.

Subject Index